SUPERNATURAL PENNINES

Jenny Randles has been a professional researcher in the field of strange phenomena for twenty-five years. During that time she has published fifty books and sold well over a million copies. Her previous titles include *Beyond Explanation?*, *Abduction*, *Sixth Sense*, *Phantoms of the Soap Operas*, *Crop Circles: A Mystery Solved* (with Paul Fuller), *The Paranormal Year*, *Spontaneous Human Combustion* (with Peter Hough), *Aliens: The Real Story*, *Star Children*, and *Something in the Air* – all published by Hale. She has made hundreds of appearances on radio and television all over the world and wrote and presented her own highly popular BBC Television documentary on UFOs. She was also the story consultant to the hit ITV series *Strange but True?* Jenny Randles was born in the Rossendale Valley of Lancashire at the centre of the mysterious events reported in this book. She now lives in Buxton.

by Jenny Randles

Beyond Explanation?
Abduction
Sixth Sense
Phantoms of the Soap Operas
The Paranormal Year: 1993 Edition
Aliens: The Real Story
Star Children
Something in the Air

With Paul Fuller

Crop Circles: A Mystery Solved

With Peter Hough

Spontaneous Human Combustion

SUPERNATURAL PENNINES

JENNY RANDLES

ROBERT HALE · LONDON

© *Jenny Randles 2002*
First published in Great Britain 2002

ISBN 0 7090 6826 3 (hardback)
ISBN 0 7090 7144 2 (paperback)

Robert Hale Limited
Clerkenwell House
Clerkenwell Green
London EC1R 0HT

A catalogue record for this book is available from the British Library

2 4 6 8 10 9 7 5 3 1

Typeset in Palatino by
Derek Doyle & Associates, Liverpool.
Printed in Great Britain by
St Edmundsbury Press Limited, Bury St Edmunds
and bound by
Woolnough Bookbinding Limited, Irthlingborough

Contents

Illustrations

Between pages 144 and 145

Credits

Jenny Randles: 1–12, 15–18, 21.
Roy Sandbach: 13, 14, 19, 20, 22.

Introduction
The Haunted Hills

A glance at any topographical map of the United Kingdom will soon reveal why the Pennine Hills are called the backbone of England. Like a spine of millstone grit running from the northern parts of Lancashire and Yorkshire down through the limestone quarries of the Derbyshire's High Peak and into Staffordshire they dominate the central part of the British mainland in any atlas or satellite photograph.

As they wend their way southwards they divide ancient lands and ageless rivalries that remain as strong as ever. If you are born in a town or village close to the borders of the counties of the White Rose (Yorkshire) and the Red Rose (Lancashire), much will depend upon claiming the correct heritage. Indeed in Yorkshire being born only a mile across the border might recently have affected your chances of representing a 'foreign' sports team! And the newly invented local authority appellations such as Greater Manchester – born in the bureaucratic 'reforms' of the early 1970s – whilst loved by administrators have hardly dented the pride of the populace in towns such as Oldham and Rochdale. People here still call themselves Lancastrians and are not residents of some big city remotely located to their south and west.

However, what maps and geographical boundaries cannot tell you is the hidden secret of the Pennines. For these hills are haunted – and always have been. They form what researchers into the strange and mysterious call a

9

'window area' – and one of the most important, if not *the* most important, in Europe.

For centuries the level of extraordinary phenomena reported from these bleak moors, valley hamlets and cotton-bred townships has been far beyond the level experienced elsewhere. This area has generated more tales of boggarts and monsters, ghosts and UFOs than virtually anywhere else in the northern hemisphere. And the trend shows no sign of abating, as the facts and figures in part 4 of this book and the catalogue of weird tales in the following pages should more than demonstrate.

The Pennines *are* special – I know because I was born there in the Rossendale Valley and I now live near their southern edge amidst the Peak District. I have often seen their power in action.

Window Cleaning

The concept of a window area dates back to the 1960s when idiosyncratic New York journalist John Keel suggested that there might be pockets of bizarre activity scattered around the globe that act almost like portals into another reality. People from our universe can disappear – perhaps for ever – by 'popping' through these zones and all sorts of weird phenomena can enter our world whenever the window opens.

Keel wrote many books about areas across the USA where strange lights, aliens, monsters and other paranormal phenomena were prevalent on a scale unseen in more 'normal' locations. However, Keel's sense of humour and irony can at times leave one wondering just how much of his theorizing was really intended seriously. This was a feeling I got when I first met him at a conference in Nebraska where we were lecturing. The touch of cynicism behind his adventurous grin was infectious but odd.

You can get a flavour of some of this mix of absurdity and extreme reality from the movie *The Mothman Prophecies*

(2002). It was based on Keel's investigations into a wide range of curiosities in one Mid-Western American window during 1966. The rules in such places have virtually been rewritten – and like Alice visiting Wonderland, the laws of the universe no longer seem to apply.

The idea of 'windows' as tunnels between alternative universes also owed something to the concept of the Bermuda Triangle which developed in the swinging sixties. This is a supposedly mysterious region where ships and aircraft disappear in unprecedented numbers. This concept invoked a bad press for the window area, because this so-called region (which is rarely a triangle and varies in size up to half the Atlantic Ocean according to which source one consults!) seems to be of dubious provenance. Many of the vessels lost here went astray in perfectly ordinary circumstances (such as during violent storms or whilst carrying unstable cargo like TNT). There may be a basis for unusual atmospheric anomalies here but it is mostly a myth, and it is improbable that the Bermuda Triangle forms a bona fide window area.

So it has been necessary to do something of a 'window cleaning' exercise to see whether the theory of such 'terror zones' can survive. The evidence that emerges is that there are genuine window areas, even if we do not know precisely what causes them. In fact theories about their origin these days tend to be rather more terrestrial than interdimensional, settling on geophysical and sociological causes and rarely seeing them as openings into another realm.

About a hundred regions around the world seem to qualify as window areas (see p. 235–9). But quite a few that feature in popular lore barely rate that description. These are locations – such as Bonnybridge in Scotland or Gulf Breeze in Florida – where during the 1980s and 1990s intense bursts of activity (usually sightings of UFOs) received massive publicity. Once the location was singled out global hype ensured that the tourists and TV cameras flocked there and the idea that this was a 'special place' inevitably grew.

I have no doubt that there were genuine and intriguing sightings reported at these places, but they were having historically short spells of weird activity and their status may thus arise more by unconscious manufacture than by evolution. They will add something to our knowledge, but should not be considered as keys to the discovery of any hypothetical energy force or secret doorway that might lie at the heart of this mystery. They are just places where people report strange things a bit more often than elsewhere.

So how do we define a 'real' window? And are the Pennine Hills such a place? They certainly are in my view, they are as real as a window gets. This is because we can trace historically visible records in such locations – a track through the centuries regardless of hype. All real windows around the world have this long-term pedigree. For ages, an assortment of weird phenomena has been reported in their proximity by local people. In fact all that has changed is the way in which we interpret these events.

A strange glow above a hill in 1601 would be considered a 'ghost light' of demonic origin. In 2001 it would instead be reported as a UFO. An apparition seen wandering about a moor might once have been described as a demon or a ghoul, whereas these days most witnesses would regard it as an alien.

What changes is the social context. What remains constant is that extremely high levels of strange phenomena dominate any area we might properly define as a window.

That is undoubtedly true in the Pennines. And, whilst the whole area bounded roughly by the population centres of Bradford, Leeds, Sheffield and Manchester – and the mostly hilly terrain in between – forms the heart of the window there are also regions of intense activity of a more localized nature, as this book will prove. Rossendale/Todmorden, Wharfedale, the High Peak region between Glossop and Sheffield and the Staffordshire Moorlands are the most noticeably active within the Pennine zone.

Of course, there is no way that I could begin to cover all

the hundreds of oddities that have happened within this window, but I can reasonably attempt to give a general impression of what goes on.

Many of the experiences that seem to occur daily tend to fall into 'traditional' lines of familiar – if remarkable – phenomena. But the story that I report now to introduce this carnival of oddities is anything but. It might well be at home on the set of a Steven Spielberg movie – but on the windswept moor tops of West Yorkshire it seems almost ridiculous.

For *Jurassic Park* transcended fiction. It became real when a dinosaur flew over Bradford!

✴ Jurassic Lark

That any kind of dinosaur could live on over 60 million years after their supposed extinction is – to say the least – scientifically debatable. But if they do, the places you would look for them would be hidden swamps in the African hinterland, or deep lakes that have sat unchanged through geological epochs. You would be hard pressed to convince a zoologist that a pterodactyl – the winged monster that ruled the air for millions of years – could have survived, like an escapee from Noah's Ark, anywhere else. Especially only a few miles from some of the most densely populated areas of the northern hemisphere.

However, according to the evidence that is just what happened. Nor is this a single-witness event. The stories interweave – as they often do in the Pennines – to create a truly fascinating mystery.

The biggest 'flap' (so to speak) of sightings took place in the period 1982–3 in the area to the north of Bradford. Even this location is significant, being just 5 miles south of Ilkley Moor and Wharfedale – one of those hyperactive parts of the window long alive with monster stories (see p.163–71).

On 12 September 1982 the first report came from Shipley Glen near an area known as the Devil's Punchbowl.

Throughout the Pennines – indeed around the world – you will see sightings congregate near places with spooky names. Another example is the Devil's Elbow, near Glossop, Derbyshire, where strange lights and weird energies have often plagued motorists just as they once scared passing stagecoaches. This is usually no coincidence. In fact 'evil' names were often applied in the distant past *because* the area was linked with strange activity. If we were naming these same places today we would no doubt call them 'Alien's Lair' or some romantic space-age name. Back then the devil was typically made into the scapegoat for all things supernatural. You can also often find ring marks on stones at such spots dating back to early civilization and denoting how these places were regarded as 'special' even millennia ago.

Back to September 1982 and sleepy Shipley Glen. William Green told the West Yorkshire researcher Paul Bennett what he saw there. He said that the huge 'bird' – with a wing span at least 6 feet, perhaps more – appeared in mid-afternoon, 'flying in a rather haphazard manner' and 'keeping fairly low'. He likened the wings to the leathery appearance of a bat and said that it resembled nothing more than a pterodactyl as he had seen in the movies. It was grey in colour and was 'eerie' to look at.[1]

Three days later another sighting occurred at nearby Yeadon, where Jean Schofield even saw the huge 'monster bird' surrounded by a flock of rooks, allowing comparison (the rooks were much smaller, although they are pretty large by British standards). From her account the 'pterodactyl' must have had a wingspan in the order of 10 feet. She saw it head off towards the Leeds/Bradford airport – something that was disconcerting as this thing was an undoubted threat to civil aviation.

At this point the local media picked up on the story and the *Bradford Telegraph and Argus* tried to solve the mystery. They consulted ornithologists, looking for a giant bird that might be mistaken for a monster. But the most likely candidate, a heron, was firmly eliminated given the by now mounting witness testimony. The possibility that some large bird of prey had somehow escaped was considered – but witnesses were fairly adamant as to what they were seeing. It looked like a flying dinosaur!

An earlier sighting now turned up in the research carried out by those who study strange phenomena. It was from the first few days of September in Pudsey. In this case a man walking his dog claimed that the big bird had uttered 'a horrifying scream'. Richard Pollock then suggested that the pterodactyl had actually swooped down on him and his dog like a scene out of a horror movie.

The thing had rested on a nearby rooftop and seemed so heavy when it took off that it sank almost to the ground before regaining horizontal momentum. He also said the wing span was 8–10 feet and reported the leathery bat-like nature of its skin as a main feature of the appearance. As it 'dive-bombed' the man the frantic and laboured beating of its wings – in a manner not like normal birds – could be heard. Unsurprisingly Mr Pollock threw himself to the ground in shock as the thing swooped just over him and headed away. He noted at this proximity how the creature had the look of a reptile – especially in its face. It was a sort of cross between a bat, a bird and a crocodile!

Constance Hird also called it a 'reptile-looking bird' when she saw it at Eldwick in early October. This was a daylight sighting offering excellent views at close range.

One theory doing the rounds in 1982 was that the bird was an American condor that had got hopelessly lost during its migration south. Although no evidence was ever found for the cute idea it might have made sense – vaguely – if this was an isolated burst of sightings. But it did not prove to be so.

On 6 May 1983 the 'giant bird' was back. Various sightings occurred that summer in the same general area, such as at Thackley. A witness here interestingly observed how the creature did not fly gracefully like a bird but had 'very laborious' and short wing strokes. Presumably these caused the beatings heard by Richard Pollock.[2]

Intrigued by all these sightings investigator Mike Priestley actually scoured the skies that summer in the hope of seeing the thing for himself. He succeeded, and took a photo of it. Unfortunately his was a distant view and a huge telephoto lens was used. The grainy film and low light level at great magnification created little more than a silhouette image, but from it one can at least understand why people would describe this thing as a pterodactyl.

There were scattered sightings during the next two years, but in the main the story vanished from the perception of the locals. My enquiries led to the theory that it might have been a model aircraft built in the design of a flying dinosaur as part of a science research project into how they flew. But I was unable to confirm this interesting possibility. Certainly it is surprising – if this *was* the answer – that nobody came forward to set the minds of the locals straight. And in any case, if it was a model then it was extremely well designed to have behaved in the animated fashion reported. One would have expected the originator of such a wonder to have displayed this fine achievement proudly.

If this was all there was to the matter it would simply remain a curiosity. But in fact the reports of a similar creature date back even before the events north of Bradford and have continued since.

Mr Harris* told me about the series of odd events that happened to him 30 miles south of the above focus of activity – and also a decade earlier. This was in the vicinity of Totley, on the edge of the Derbyshire Peaks and west of the city of Sheffield.

His first odd experience was in 1972. Returning from school, he saw a strange effect coming out of the ground. It was shaped like a trident pointing vertically and 'rising slowly upwards'. It was blue, 'similar to the flame of a bunsen burner', and the three prongs and handle of this glowing fork were 'composed of square-shaped particles

---

* An asterisk throughout the text indicates that I have provided a pseudonym at the request of a witness.

with regular gaps between them'. The force 'glistened' but was 'more solid than a flame'. In fact it was a sort of glowing energy that was 'bleeding' upwards into the air.

One thing Mr Harris noted during these events was how his mind became oddly calm and subdued. Everything around him slowed to a crawl. Time itself almost seemed to stop. This peculiar effect on the consciousness of a witness is very common in such weird experiences. I call it the 'Oz Factor', because the percipient enters a magical state of awareness and seems to visit temporarily an alternative reality like the fictional land of Oz. This idea is, of course, quite consistent with Keel's window theories.

We can only speculate why this altered state happens, but an energy leaking from the ground in the hills – almost like slow lightning in reverse – well fits one theory about how windows activate. This suggests that they are conduits through which electrical energy stored within the earth itself passes into the atmosphere. If it charges the surrounding air and ionizes the molecules this effect can create glowing UFOs and has a physical power that can produce real symptoms in a witness – such as a tingling sensation, hair standing on end or other effects that might define proximity to a charged energy field.

More contentiously, brain specialist Dr Michael Persinger has tested in the laboratory claims that such energy fields (which he calls 'transients') can trigger hormonal changes in the brain's bioelectric circuitry, resulting in altered states of perception (perhaps experienced as the symptoms of the Oz Factor) and maybe even resultant hallucinations of fantastic phenomena.

But this is getting ahead of ourselves. Theories best come later. For now we can just note that this witness story fits a pattern recognized by researchers into this sort of phenomenon.

More important to our current discussion is what Mr Harris saw in November 1977 at Totley. He was in his garden when he heard a 'growling' noise and looked up to be confronted by a pterodactyl.

He says it was large and dark with reptile-like scales – not feathers – and vivid red eyes. As it glided over him he saw that its face was dog-like – long and blunt – and had teeth that were razor sharp. This was five years before the 'lost Condor' supposedly flew by or the 'model aviator' allegedly got busy in Bradford, implying that we may need a deeper answer to resolve all these matters.[3]

Moving forward quite a few years, to 13 March 1999, we have yet another case that could be relevant. This also occurred near Sheffield, at Mexborough, on a sunny afternoon when a man and his wife saw a dark object moving across their field of view whilst they stood on the balcony of their flat. The husband, was able to go inside, get his camcorder and film eight minutes of footage at sixteen times zoom as the object moved away on a very slow, straight course. It seemed to be gliding, as if on thermals, just below cloud.

Dave Baker and Jonathan Slater of the Yorkshire UFO Society (YUFOS) have gone to a lot of trouble chasing up this case and I went to Sheffield in November 2000, not long after the witness had belatedly come forward, to look at his video footage and discuss further action.

The case is still unexplained. Many ideas have been explored, such as airships (none was airborne), hang-gliders or microlites (again none was flying that day according to relevant records obtained by YUFOS). The object (and a possible second) is too distant to see a definite shape, although it does resemble a bird with a large wing span. But it would be a very large bird, given measurements of distances and estimated cloud ceilings.

One researcher, Andy Roberts, suggested a heron. Checks were made into this possibility – raised back in 1982, you may recall, in connection with the pterodactyl sightings above Bradford – but no evidence emerged. Photo analyst Bill Rose argued against the idea that it was any sort of bird. The case is continuing – although quite how one analyses a video looking for evidence that it shows an 'extraordinary' bird is perhaps an unanswerable question!

So for now it remains only of possible relevance to Yorkshire's flying dinosaur, although still typical of what goes on within the Pennines.[4]

One important thing to note about these Yorkshire sightings is that palaeontologists have only recently found evidence of what these bird-like creatures would be like in flight. Although I call this creature a pterodactyl, (as witnesses did), in fact this was just one of a wide number of aerial dinosaurs that evolved over millions of years. Generically the creatures were called pterosaurs. It had been assumed that they could only glide, owing to their bulk, but new fossil evidence has revealed a fine bone structure in the wings of what were often only modestly sized creatures. They could flap for a short time (although probably awkwardly). It is likely, therefore, that they would move through the air much less gracefully than they are portrayed in the movies and rather more as 'really' alleged by witnesses seeing the animal flying over Yorkshire, flapping on take-off then gliding long distances riding thermal layers around clouds.[5]

However, even this does not end the story of the Yorkshire pterodactyl. Perhaps the weirdest postscript of all concerns the science fiction author Ian Watson. In 1977, just as Mr Harris (as a teenager) was witnessing his dinosaur over Yorkshire, the then relatively unknown writer was in Oxford putting finishing touches to his epic novel *Miracle Visitors*.[6] I was deeply impressed by this well-thought-out story when it appeared in 1978. It captures better than any other story the essence of what it feels like to see something strange and not know how much of what happens is real.

Watson meant the novel to address properly the issue of the paranormal, witness perception and the nature of reality. I know this because I subsequently corresponded with him and he confirmed that the book was stimulated by the ideas of French UFO theorists. Their ideas concerned the interaction between truth and fantasy and its role as the architect of reality. They told of how altered states of consciousness might even be able to bring what Watson called 'solidograms' (three dimensional holograms) into being simply by thinking them into existence. This concept – the creation of a *tulpa* (as these thought forms are traditionally called in Eastern lore) – is an age-old part of religious philosophy.

All of these seemingly bizarre ideas form an integral part of the actual UFO mystery and many real-life paranormal happenings within window areas are woven into Watson's story. Fate and coincidence also stir into a heady brew. The following chapters will show these same mind-numbing concepts as they pop up everywhere in real life and challenge our understanding of cause and effect, truth and fiction, and the nature of things. Sightings are not mere events. They can be life-changing experiences.

Watson told me that he noticed something odd as he was writing his book. UFOs seemed to home in on him around Oxford even as he was composing the story line about a young boy who was able to conjure up his own aliens.[7] Indeed, soon afterwards Watson moved to a small village near Northampton and – completely unbeknown to him – the UFOs followed! As I report in a 1988 book on alien contact cases, a sudden concentration of such tales appeared in precisely the same part of rural Northamptonshire soon after Watson's novel was published. I discuss several in the book and interviewed some of the witnesses. But just as Ian Watson did not know of the often unpublished events no witnesses had heard of him or his novel. Indeed the witnesses had not even heard of one another. This was an apparently random mixture.[8]

Weirdly this science fiction author was independently composing a fiction based on real theories about UFOs, the paranormal, reality and coincidence. He had chosen as his theme a young boy who could enter an altered state of consciousness (what we here call the Oz Factor) and then conjure up images of miraculous phenomena amidst a barrage of synchronicities and strange phenomena that had dogged his life. Meantime, as this novel was being written, a young boy in Yorkshire was truly entering altered states, experiencing odd things and seeing a pterodactyl glide over his garden.

In *Miracle Visitors* – by coincidence again (what else!) – Watson sent his fictional youngster to Yorkshire to conduct an experiment that would test his ability to forge reality out of imagination. He did so in an area just north of where four years later the real-life sightings of a flying dinosaur would occur.

As by now you will probably have surmised, Watson's character, Michael Peacock, successfully entered an altered state and was asked to manifest a 'solidogram' above Yorkshire. That entity – in the story – was chosen to impress a researching scientist and was to be a monster bird that swooped down from the hills and vanished back through a gap between realities.

Watson's young boy had made a pterodactyl appear in the skies over Yorkshire right in the midst of similar events really happening that the author surely could not have known about.

And so we come almost full circle to face the first awesome question about window areas.

They are magical places where normal rules do not apply. But can fiction create fact, does fact create fiction or do both run together – like colours in an artist's palette that blend imperceptibly as one?

We are going to face many such amazing questions as this book unfolds.

1

Legends, Myths and Mystic Origins

You might think that the myths and legends associated with the Pennines have nothing to teach the modern world. After all they emerge from a distant past shrouded in mystery when humans were grasping the first threads of civilization and – being deeply superstitious – not exactly 'with it' as we are today.

Of course, many people remain superstitious – about walking under a ladder, crossing one's fingers in the hope of attracting good or warding off evil, etc. Many things that we do, born of habits that seem culturally ingrained, have an origin so old that most of us are unaware of what we are doing. But, even so, surely these are mere foibles. If anyone took superstition too far and, for example, put their life in danger by refusing to walk under a ladder, we would likely regard them as the victim of some kind of compulsive behaviour disorder.

Yet at the same time, people who might feel sympathy for others behaving so irrationally may well say 'white rabbits' three times when midnight strikes at the start of every month. And why? Because it is what our parents taught us as a 'tradition' of good luck.

Regardless of what we think, these ancient beliefs remain remarkably strong as part of what it means to be human.

Yet the importance of very old myths and legends goes deeper than mere customs. There are two very different but significant reasons why we cannot ignore this emotionally powerful motif that drives the soul of mankind.

For a start, much of what we regard today as supernatural enters our world by way of a greatly updated version of how our ancestors adopted a folk tale. If farmer Giles reported seeing a fairy on his haystack then the story was spread around the village. It merged with the ethos of the community. If others saw similar things a folk belief evolved that rapidly transformed by word of mouth into a form of reality. To many of the people – not much over 100 years ago in the Pennines – these things were not tall stories or amusing anecdotes. They were actual events that revealed the hidden nature of the cosmos.

These days, of course, science and the age of reason makes most of us giggle when we think about fairies on a farm. And yet in the same breath we might wonder about the strange light seen over farmer Giles' hayfield late last night and ponder if we might not after all share the universe with similarly diminutive extraterrestrials. For UFOs and aliens are 'legitimate' scientific speculation. We are sanctioned to consider them possible – despite there being no more proof that ET is real than there is for an elf.

A moment's thought is all we need to realize that the aliens have become the space-age fairies. We have not lost our desire to look for hidden things around us nor to seek out powers that transcend the mundane. Nor has the lure of the mystical waned in the face of marching technology. We have simply shifted tactics, as our consciousness adapts to the new situation. New gods have subjugated the old – bug-eyed spacemen abducted the goblins and returned them to fairlyland. But how much more – or less – real are they than the creatures seen in a haystack 100 years ago? That is no easy question for anyone to answer.

Mythology and legends are not stranded in the past. They are dynamic and ever present in the modern world. We use different terms to obscure what we are talking about. But if a person from medieval Burnley was transported through time they would recognise familiar themes within the stories that fill the twenty-first century equivalent to the folk tale. And, in case you had not worked out what that latter-day equivalent might be, just think about the internet – alive with electronic chattering of myths in the making spreading space-age lore like forest fires across 100,000 web sites devoted to the supernatural.

However, there is another reason why we must pay heed to these stories from the past. Many of the obscure elements within ancient legends recur today amidst the techno-babble of modern paranormal phenomena. The things that were important in the legends of the past are often equally important in the supernatural wonders of today.

You have already seen one or two in the introduction to this book. If you stay alert as you read on then you will come upon many others, such as the importance of the balancing power of three (notice how often UFOs are triangular or have three balls or lights). In fact almost everywhere we turn, today is really yesterday. We simply have not woken up to the implications yet.

Other Worlds, Other Worldviews

The inhabitants of the Pennines before the Norman conquest were firmly ensnared by Celtic beliefs. To these people ours was not the only world. There were other realities that surrounded and enveloped us. Other beings in those alien realms also co-existed with ourselves. Most of the time we were not aware of what they were doing. But when *they* chose to do so they could make themselves visible and pop through a doorway from their world to this, before popping right back again to leave us wondering.

As I am sure you will realize, this ancient worldview is not a million miles from the concept of the window area – of which the Pennines is considered to be one of nature's finest. We may use words that make it sound vaguely scientific. But we are, by wonderful symmetry, really just saying pretty much what our ancestors apparently knew 'instinctively' in their daily lives 1,000 years ago!

There are signs of this everywhere in the Pennines, as in the Celtic god images found in heads that appear carved in stone – such as those around Hebden Bridge and Mytholmroyd. Folklorist Dr David Clarke has long noted that the image of the Celtic god on these carvings depicts a being with obvious similarity to the entities widely reported during today's alien contact. The most notable features – in both stone heads and alien visage – are the triangular shape of the face and the prominence of the eyes.[9]

Even more noteworthy is that these ancient symbols are often found on bridges and rock faces where the most intense activity happens in the window area even today – places like Ilkley Moor and Wharfedale, around the Calder Valley. Is this coincidence or does it tell us that these 'power centres' were equally active and instinctively recognized long ago? Do these carvings somehow reflect ancient awareness that the 'old gods' lived here? Indeed today many seem to think that the space gods still do!

Physicist and amateur archaeologist Dr Terence Meaden has reached interestingly similar conclusions about stone circle sites at Avebury and Stonehenge. He has noted the modern day appearance of crop circles in these locations. Whilst most of these markings are certainly hoaxes, a few do seem to be genuine – in the sense that records of them date back hundreds of years. Meaden thinks they are caused by unusual atmospheric forces – an electrically energized vortex. He further argues that the ancient Britons saw them form, thought them signs from the gods and built stone circles in their image at their place of origin. It is a fascinating idea, potentially supported by the location of stone heads in the Pennines.[10]

We can also see the remnants of these old beliefs in many names – even those that have been transformed across time from once obvious significance. I mentioned before the preponderance of 'devil' names where the activities of these other worlds were at their most intense. The Pennines is full of them. Sometimes, such as at Devil's Elbow in the High Peak, it is because strange lights and forces have long been known there. At other times it is supernatural spirits that are to the fore. Boggart Hole Clough north-east of Manchester, for instance, relates to the old Pennine demon, the boggart, which was believed to have lived in its spooky dell.

A few names may seem more obscure, such as Hob Tor in north Derbyshire. Hob is an ancient name for evil (as in hobgoblin) and the area's supernatural past is thus revealed. And on other occasions modern communities have rid themselves of the devil names altogether – such as the Devil's Bolt Hole near Peak Forest, where it was long believed a dark force lived at the bottom of the deep pothole. Today its evil meaning is obscured by the relatively recent name Eldon Hole (although this may itself derive from Elfdom, as several other locations in the Pennines with 'El' prefixes do have that basis).

By seeking out such markers within the landscape it is possible to get clues where the other world was once believed to conjoin our own reality. These passageways between universes are worth investigating since whatever forces cause windows to flare into life may still be active there today. And, of course, looking for common denominators between long recognized hot spots is the first step towards understanding what may cause the phenomena we still witness today.

Old Soldiers Never Die

One of the ways in which the energy that seems to soak the Pennine landscape leaves traces of its activity is by generating what we might term an 'action replay'. This often applies to ancient battles – although more correctly it applies to any powerfully emotive event, of which battles are obvious examples. Paranormal researchers have long suggested that something in the ether appears able to 'record' these things rather as a video signal is preserved for ever through changes in electromagnetic energy stored on tape. Since emotion is the key to most 'stored' phenomena, we may surmise this must have energy to leave as its mark.

The parish church at Chapel-en-le-Frith dates back in parts to the thirteenth century, although most of the buildings have simply been developed on an older site. In September 1648 it was still a small affair within a sprawling forest that surrounds what is now a small hilly town. It was to this place that no fewer than 1,500 soldiers were marched during the English Civil War after being defeated on the moors near Preston by Cromwell's forces. Unsure whether they were to live or die they were crammed into the small space with barely enough room to move arms or legs and holed up in quite horrendous conditions for sixteen days.

Before the nightmare ended forty-four of the platoon had died amidst the unthinkable crush and many others were so weak that they subsequently died when they were left, as the surviving prisoners were marched to meet their fate. But the terrible suffering of these incarcerated men took a toll that may have left its mark across the centuries. For today many visitors describe this otherwise ordinary churchyard as eerie and sombre. They sense a deep oppression even when they do not know the ancient circumstances.

Is it possible that those weeks of emotional suffering sent out some kind of mass 'psychic distress flare'. Did this permanently alter the 'feeling' or 'vibe' of this place, so that someone who is sensitive to atmospheres – just as some people appear able to detect the heavy pressure of a thunderstorm before it happens – might become aware of the dark secret that lurks in the air?[11]

Although this case may seem rather speculative it is far from the only example of this sort of thing. The Pennines has a veritable catalogue of events tied to powerful

28

emotions – of spurned love, trauma and sudden death – that all seem to have imprinted themselves indelibly across time.

At Eyam, in the High Peak, an amazing event occurred in 1665 as the great plague devastated Europe. It reached this tiny village through a bundle of clothing sent to the local tailor from the disease-ridden city of London. Once it took hold people started to drop daily for there was no cure – only, for a few, inexplicable immunity. The vicar, knowing the danger, persuaded his 350 citizens to make an astonishing sacrifice. They literally cut themselves off from the rest of the country and holed themselves up in the diseased village for thirteen months to let the plague run its course. They suffered awful hardship and 267 of them succumbed, but they prevented it from spreading beyond. Only one woman tried to escape by fleeing to nearby Tideswell, where she was attacked, forcing her back to reluctant exile. She died in Eyam and some visitors to the village can sense this emotive event. The ghost of that terrified woman has even reportedly been seen on the outskirts of town as if replaying over and over her failed escape bid.

Ghost Riders in the Sky

But this is not a pattern confined to the distant past. Modern tragedies seem to create the same phenomenon. David Clarke has made a study of the action replays from the Second World War that have caused bomber planes – such as Dakotas and Lancasters – to be seen flying in eerie silence over the moors and reservoirs west of Sheffield – in fact the same area where the Totley pterodactyl was seen.

David, a very capable investigator, has checked for flights by real aircraft and none of the type was near the location where these 'ghost planes' flew during the 1980s and 1990s. They behaved exactly like action replays of a war-time mission, since many planes *did* crash on such flights amidst the mist-shrouded Pennines, where visibility

29

can drop to almost zero very quickly. One can only imagine the moments of sheer terror that sudden realization would bring as you fly towards a mountain and there is nothing that you can do to prevent your certain death.[12]

There are guidebooks to the sites of the wreckage scattered on the moor tops. A number of people who have ventured onto these desolate hillsides and braved the swirling mist to look, speak of the eeriness and chill silence that they witness. Some have also reported seeing ghostly figures wearing flying jackets standing nearby – phantoms from the aircraft still floating near their shattered flight deck.

The common theme to all of these incidents is that a scene from the past – usually involving death, trauma and tragedy – is replayed if the right person chances to be in the right place at the right moment. Sometimes only a sense of mood is felt. At other times a misty figure is seen acting out what they once did, perhaps many centuries ago. But we can be sure that this is not some dead spirit literally hanging about before entering Heaven by noting the replays of air crashes. Presumably Lancaster bombers do not have souls to 'haunt' the sky. The only thing that sensibly explains 'visions' of inanimate objects is that somehow an impression of a long-gone event can become 'recorded' within the atmosphere of these hills.

Whilst it may here seem that only the southern part of the Pennines has these reruns, given their prominence in Derbyshire, that is not the case. They do focus around the area where light and energy phenomena are today most prevalent (the region where the so-called Longendale lights occur). But they also happen in another of the major Pennine hot spots – the Rossendale/Calder valleys.

One case that I investigated at first hand occurred on the moors outside Todmorden (ironically a town named after the ancient word for death, and where the mass murderer – the so-called 'Dr Death', unassuming GP Harold Shipman – began his unthinkable tally of up to 400 killings).

The isolated cottage that I visited was at the centre of a

series of 'action replay' events – not some dramatic battle or the death throes of an aircraft, but something of stunning triviality. Nellie, who lived there, described how she had heard on several occasions the sound of her son coming home on his motorbike. She heard a complete repeat of this event, as the bike drove up the hillside, parked in the yard, the door opened and her son entered. The only problem was that none of these things were *really* happening – at least not then. They *had* occurred years earlier and her son did not now visit the house on a motorcycle.

We might be tempted to think that this was a mother understandably pining for the return of her son and hearing what she wanted to hear. But that was not the case. I am sure from my discussions with Nellie that this was a genuine 'action replay' event. It had all the trademarks.

Indeed, there was an additional clue that this story offered. The house in which these replays occurred was an old stone building made out of local rock – as are many of the rural houses in the Pennines. This rock is a millstone that is rich in quartz crystals. These crystals vibrate when put under pressure. In fact they are used in some cigarette lighters, where the pressure of a button crushes the crystal, causes a vibration and generates a tiny surge of electrical energy which provides the spark that can ignite flammable gases. Some researchers, such as Paul Devereux, suggest that large masses of quartz-bearing rock where they are under strain (e.g. by the weight of reservoirs) can produce an electrical signal that may cause a chain reaction and trigger glowing spook lights that can be seen in the surrounding atmosphere.

More to the point, if electrical charges are being created can these operate like a VCR and 'tape' sounds or images of some actual event to be rerun in later years? After all a video recording is an electrical signal that is modified and stored. It is not magic. One important pointer from the house on the moors is that, unaware of any other cases, Nellie told me that she had suffered many strange electrical problems in the building. Indeed the power company had failed to discover why her circuits were draining so much energy and why electrical equipment such as TV sets and light bulbs burnt out so often. Of course, we might ask, if old traumas or motorbikes can be replayed in this way through time, is it possible that the flight of a dinosaur from millions of years ago could also be rerun?[13] ⊐

Broomsticks Old and New

Pendle Hill is perhaps the most famous name in the history of British witchcraft, holding a place similar to that attached to Salem, Massachusetts, in US folklore. In fact, it was not this 1,830 foot high peak north of Burnley, between Colne and Clitheroe, that was the centre of evil. Rather the wooded slopes around it had been associated with witchcraft long before the infamous trials of the seventeenth century.

Indeed there are stories of strange beasts and names such as 'Devil's Chair' appear in this area. At Hell Hole Bridge near Clitheroe the siege by rocks reportedly tossed by an unseen devil from the Pendle slopes has entered legend. The eerie nature of this region does not stem from April 1612, but that is when Old Demdike, a notorious witch whose antics in the Pendle Forest were reputed to have gone on for fifty years, was finally accused under strict new laws sweeping the country. Amidst claims of cursed dolls causing sickness and death no fewer than nineteen people were quickly arrested and tried as witches from what was believed to be a much larger coven. In the end ten women were found guilty and most were hanged.

Two decades later there was a new purge, including the conviction of some relatives of the first victims who were locally rumoured to be continuing the 'family business'. As at Salem it is known in retrospect that hysteria fuelled much of the tension and many of the charges were quite bogus.[14]

In some places alleged witches were rolled down hillsides in barrels to test their innocence. The problem was that if they survived the fall unscathed they would be considered supernaturally protected. If they were innocent God would claim them! The original case of damned if you do, damned if you don't.

Unsurprisingly these links with witchcraft have left the Pendle region with a legacy it is hard-pressed to shake off. We will later discuss the frightening poltergeist and aerial phenomena that haunt this area even today (p. 148–50). And there is evidence for some kind of strange atmospheric energy of the sort that we have noted as the trigger for supernatural events elsewhere.

You will recall that glowing balls dog the Devil's Elbow near Glossop. And we saw strange forks of electrical energy literally seeping out of the ground and climbing skyward at Totley (p. 16) – both in areas with a high supernatural quotient. Here is another example, this time from the slopes of Pendle Hill.

It occurred at Earby, a small village adjacent to the spookily named Foulridge which features later in the book (see p.148). The Ford family told researcher Jonathan Dillon about the many odd things that they had experienced over the years they had lived in the shadow of Pendle, including glowing red eyes that float disembodied in the bedroom and have haunted them.[15] On 19 December 1994 a formation of three white balls of light lined up into a perfect triangle and drifted past their house. The power of three, note, is a part of witch lore – hence three linked witches in many stories – such as the sisters who practise witchcraft in the long running TV series *Charmed*. But perhaps most interesting of all, football-sized ice-blue glows pass through walls and seem to seep up from the ground beneath the house itself. On one occasion this energy emerged from the floor, expanded like a balloon inside the room, promptly filling it with light. Another came from the rocks outside the door, seemed to climb skyward and then 'slowly oozed back into the land', as Melvin Ford said.

This seems a classic description of the so-called 'earthlights' phenomenon theorised by Paul Devereux and seen as being the power cell of a window area.[16] Indeed I have been fortunate enough to see one such event for myself (ironically not in the Pennines but climbing out of rock at the Berwyn Mountains near the village of Llandrillo). This was a smoky pale cream light that literally did ooze out of the rock face, before climbing upwards as if riding some invisible current, to form a discrete blob about the size of a beach ball that dissipated into the atmosphere. It was an entrancing sight.

That so many earthlights have been seen near Earby, accompanying other anomalies long associated with the Pennines, suggests a causal link. It may be that many of the supernatural phenomena that are reported are either driven by this earth energy or appear as the vaporous glow that acts as a template out of which all sorts of strange things are moulded. Two adjacent red lights might be seen by a witness as the eyes of a devilish creature. Not much imagination needs to be at work for that to happen. A cloudy mass with a glow in the centre would perhaps once have been considered a demonic beast whilst today it would inevitably be perceived as an alien spaceship. Perhaps what is central to all these things is merely the smoky energy out of which all sorts of oddities have long been woven by the human mind.

Another fascinating case from this area was revealed in the files of the Public Record office at Kew during research by historian Granville Oldroyd. Once again it shows this pattern at work.

The case occurred in the early hours of 24 August 1914 and involved police sergeant Tom Pope and a constable called Snowden who were guarding railway property in Clitheroe. At 2.50 a.m. they independently observed a light above Pendle Hill and Snowden said in his report that it was 'an airship, the shape of a sausage and that the light came from a platform underneath it. . . . There appeared to be white clouds about it, which in my opinion were smoke.'[17]

So we again have a strange object, claimed to be a Zeppelin, emerging from a smoky cloud on top of this centuries-old haunted hill. The Zeppelin was, of course, much in the news at that time because the First World War was about to erupt and the Germans were feared to possess such weapons by which they could invade and bomb the UK. These fears proved groundless, since German airship technology was not yet so advanced, so this thing was certainly not an airship. It was yet another of those ghostly lights within a swirling mist that was transformed by a human observer into some historically topical reality. We might indeed envisage a sort of equation at work here: energy phenomenon + cultural expectation = perception of an anomaly that fits the beliefs of the day.

Move forward half a century and we can safely predict what a smoky cloud with an energy glow inside it might look like to any modern witness who saw it rise over Pendle Hill. Instead of Germans in the skies our thoughts would surely turn to aliens. People these days would see a flying saucer.

In fact, we do not need to speculate on this fascinating question, we can actually *know*. In a truly astonishing case a near identical incident took place on the night of 9 March 1977 at virtually the same time of night (3.10 a.m.). And this one was indeed reported as a UFO! I was lucky enough to interview one of the two men who saw this thing, Brian Grimshawe. He was with his colleague, Jeff Farmer, near the railway on the other side of Pendle Hill in the deserted town of Nelson. They had just dropped off some canteen workers from a factory night shift when they, too, saw a glowing mass of lights emerge from within a swirling misty cloud on top of Pendle Hill.

What Grimshawe and Farmer saw, a dark cigar with a central mass of swirling colours blending together like a melting pot of neon fire – is a virtual rerun sixty-three years later of what the two policemen witnessed on the other side of the same hill.[18]

Yet these men could not have known about this earlier

case. The PRO file on the policeman's sighting was not released until several years after I documented the testimony at Nelson. These two accounts of the twentieth-century supernatural power of Pendle Hill were totally independent and are either an extraordinary coincidence or evidence that a genuine energy of some sort is being regularly created here – a power that witches may once have abused. If so, then it has the form of a misty light that is transmogrified by witness perception in different ways down through the ages but always in a culturally topical fashion.

Moreover, the Nelson case offers evidence of the physical power behind this energy – the electrical fields that might somehow interact with the earth's own electromagnetic powerhouse.

Grimshawe and Farmer described how the cloudy cigar caused their car engine and lights to fail as it floated at roof-top height over their heads. The electrical systems started to work again only after the thing headed away southwards towards Manchester and out of range. Leaping out of the car the two men also felt a downwards pressure as if the atmosphere was 'leaden'. And there was an electrical tingling causing their hair to stand on end, their eyes to water and their heads to throb – almost as if they were surrounded by some viciously strong electrostatic field – as indeed they might well have been.

Nor were they the only witnesses. The whole area surrounding this part of the Pennine window was seething with activity between late on 8 March and the early hours of 9 March 1977. My files show over twenty sightings from that time, and 75 per cent of these reports came from within 10 miles of Pendle Hill. I doubt that this is mere happenstance.

If we can understand why this long-haunted site suddenly became active on that one night in 1977 we may be on our way to figuring out what causes the Pennines to be special. For these window areas seem to be like volcanoes. They remain generally quiet as a picturesque part of

the landscape throughout history. They will always generate increased levels of activity (volcanoes tend to have
multiple earthquakes and small scale eruptions on a more
or less constant basis). But every now and then something
causes the delicate balance of forces to get disturbed and
the window (like the volcano) bubbles over into a frantic
period of intense activity, before settling back into
dormancy for the whole cycle to begin again. **⊐**

Fairy Stories

As with witches, so with fairies. Not only are there genuine
historical records of these strange ethereal beings but the
Pennine window is one of the places where they seem to
live on – albeit in a modern guise.

You will find reports of fairies throughout the Pennines
right up until the twentieth century (and I am sure reports
will go on being made during the twenty-first century too!).
But one of the locations where you find them often is in the
shadow of Ilkley Moor. This has already been identified as
an active part of the window. At Appletreewick, Cracoe and
Carelton Moor modern-day UFO encounters have
occurred, including three photographs taken at these locations. Nearby, at Thorpe, the aliens of today were the
elemental beings of yesterday (the 1820s to be precise).

A doctor named Dixon was walking over the moors
towards his home at Rylstone when he saw a 'tribe of fairies
dancing in a ring of moonlight' on a limestone ridge long
reputed even then to be the home of otherworldly creatures. Dixon tried to join their throng for a closer look but
they reacted with hostility and forced him to flee.[19]

Although most people associate fairies with the winged
beings flittering about in children's nursery tales they
would be wrong to do so. These romanticized beings are a
Victorian invention added in the mid-1800s to brighten up
the lives of often poverty-stricken families. Real fairies, as
reported widely in folklore and during allegedly real sight-

ings through the ages are more akin to what we would today think of as elves or gnomes. They are small, but not tiny, 2 to 3 feet being a typical height. They are also often green (by colour or clothing). Indeed they are the archetypal 'little green men' – not, as you might think, the exclusive province of modern space fiction but a symbol of this ancient belief about secret denizens who share our planet but reside in some alternative reality.

As you will see elsewhere (p. 163–71) the little green men of Ilkley and Wharfedale did not disappear with the death of Queen Victoria. They are alive (well sort of!) and seemingly busy. One of them was even photographed on the moors above East Moreton in 1987 and this case has been the talk of the UFO world ever since. For, of course, there are no 'unidentified fairy' researchers to study it these days!

However, the most celebrated fairies of the Pennines are those at Cottingley, a village between Bradford and Ilkley Moor which has a little beck near where these creatures have long supposedly been witnessed. In the years between the First World War and the early 1920s a number of photographs were taken by two teenage girls, Frances Griffiths and Elsie Wright, showing not only fairies but also gnomes that they claimed to have seen there whilst playing.

The photographs are not, by today's standards, convincing. The figures are not like real fairies but instead very much based on the idealized winged sprites that were then politically correct. The girls had books of such fairy drawings at their disposal. One of them was a gifted artist. The images look two-dimensional – and indeed that is no surprise because they were!

Although these girls fooled a lot of people,including Sir Arthur Conan Doyle, who took their story way too seriously, they admitted on television, when they were old ladies and close to death, that the photos were hoaxes using cut-out drawings. With the advantage of hindsight, you can even see the hat pin propping up one gnome.[20]

This hoax has been the subject of a recent big-budget movie, *Fairy Tale*, which politely leaves open the question of the reality behind the photographs, but otherwise tells the legend well. However, the story does not end (as in the paranormal it very rarely does!) with the confession of a hoaxer. For the two girls insisted until their deaths that whilst the photos were a fake they had fabricated them only to convince their families that they really did see fairies there! Cottingley Beck was full of them, they argued, and even today if you are in the right frame of mind (or state of consciousness?) you can see them.

Perhaps it really only depends upon personal perception. If you encounter the energy that oozes from the Pennine rocks then you may see within it what you want to see, or experience what you expect to experience – be that a glowing light, a UFO, a dinosaur or a fairy.

In that sense the fairies, and the dinosaurs seen only 2 or 3 miles from Cottingley (p. 14–16), or the little green man photographed five miles to the north, or the UFOs that overfly this area almost every week, are all 'real'. We simply have to define what we mean by 'real'.

2
A Gallery of Oddities

It is time to look at some of the strange phenomena reported in the Pennines which illustrate why this is a very odd place to live. In the course of exploring these different events – in alphabetical order for ease of reference – we will come across many weird encounters.

Again we will see patterns unfold and interactions emerge between what seem to be unrelated types of anomaly. As you will appreciate, appearances can be deceptive. Of course, some strange things do have explanations. Others remain a mystery. But above and beyond both these things the wonder of the Pennines survives.

ABC: Alien Big Cats

This might seem an odd place to start – as what is strange about the sighting of large cats roaming the hillsides? There may be nothing paranormal about alien big cats but, as this imaginative name conjured up by researchers might suggest – some think they could be interlopers from another world.

There are reasons why these creatures may have bizarre origins. The hunters who form posses that go to hunt for them hardly ever succeed. The big cats, which are not native to any part of the UK and have not been for centuries, seem to appear and disappear at will. They often have more in keeping with a ghost than with an animal from the zoo.

Yet throughout the Pennines there are areas where what researcher Andy Roberts has delightfully termed 'cat flaps' occur.[21] And, it may not shock you to discover that these centre on the familiar hot spots such as the High Peak of Derbyshire and the Rossendale Valley.

One of the more unusual events was the sighting of a mountain lion in the moors above Waterfoot and Bacup in the Rossendale Valley of Lancashire during the summer of 1984. Even as farmers claimed to see the light brown and massive cat from a distance across their fields the UFOs were flying above the same area – as indeed they often have. An object like a barrel with two lights was seen above a reservoir just outside Rawtenstall at the height of the big cat scare.

This was one of the earliest times that 'aliens' and 'big cats' were linked semantically – although it seems unlikely that anyone literally intended that ET was dropping off lions to wander the Pennine Hills. More properly it demonstrates that these disparate phenomena often merge.

The curiously phantom nature of the creature was well illustrated by a sighting at Whitewell Bottom on 16 August when a farmer was willing to shoot the animal – and did so, but apparently failed to wound it. Instead it escaped to appear again in the same general location days later where up to a dozen witnesses claimed similar confrontations, persuading the Bacup police that it was a real animal.

There was other evidence of this, in the form of several dead sheep and a mauled cow that seemed to have been attacked (but not eaten) by a large cat-like creature. Yet police were not easily convinced that a mountain lion was at large, although they took no chances and launched a search. They suggested that these witnesses were really seeing a wild dog that was posing a threat to farmers' stock.

Needless to say – as is usual with these episodes – the reports of the mountain lion quickly disappeared – although further incidents were to follow years later. And nobody ever found traces of the animal – be it lion or dog – not even a carcass. This lack of physical remains is the biggest factor against the real 'big cat' explanation. Sooner or later these animals must die. Why does nobody ever find a body? But that applies to large dogs mistaken for lions every bit as much as it does to a real big cat. And, of course, the alternative theory about some phantom creature still has problems. How does a ghost mutilate sheep?

There may be the basis for the idea of a big cat arriving from a realm where mountain lions are still indigenous to the Pennines. If ABCs can cross such 'frontiers' so can other creatures – like the Totley pterodactyl perhaps. Or, indeed, maybe big cats cross time, not space, appearing from the days when there were real big cats in these hills. Presumably, too, if 'alien animals' arrive via a crack between space-time realities, they can go back, making efforts to track them down rather pointless!

The big cats are not always so shy as to be incognito. They can be as affectionate as a domestic pet. The remarkable experience of Kathleen Topliff near Hayfield on 26 March 1992 is an example. Her Derbyshire home overlooked Ollersett Moor, between New Mills and Chinley, scene of the most consistent Pennine big cat sightings. Her view of the animal was no distant one – it came into her lounge! It sauntered around her house as if it owned the place, but seemed frightened when their eyes met. Indeed it started to hiss ferociously as Mrs Topliff chased it with a broom handle into her bedroom. She received a nasty hand wound before it leapt out of the window and disappeared.

It is hard to consider this encounter as being a phantom, since I have yet to meet a ghost that bites! Moreover, there have been sightings of the Ollersett cat in large numbers. It was even the subject of a dim and fuzzy photo from New Mills and farmers here have found cattle bitten by its teeth. The police have few doubts about its reality. They go after it suitably armed, with both tranquillizer darts and bullets, but it has long evaded capture.

From eyewitness accounts such as that of Mrs Topliff, we know that this cat is the size of a large dog, with jet black fur and yellow, staring eyes. It also often exudes a foul odour. Visibly it resembles a panther according to most reports. Of course, time-travelling or space-hopping ABCs would be very *real*.

The beast of Ollersett Moor is never away for long. On 6 November 1989 police saw it for themselves when it was cornered at Birch Vale but got away. However, this first-hand observation was enough for them to issue a warning to the many hikers in this area who walk the trail of the old railway branch from Hayfield to New Mills or the Pennine Way that passes through Edale. 'This is not a hoax' the ramblers were categorically assured. Inspector Graham Lomas reported that they thought the beast was best considered to be a black leopard!

On 15 January 1995 it was seen by a man on hills between Chapel-en-le-Frith and Chinley, walking brazenly across the moors carrying lunch – a rabbit held tightly between its jaws. Again, one would presume, ghost cats have no need of dinner, but maybe they do still eat in an alternative universe.

Moving to 30 May 1999 the big black cat was seen near a reservoir outside Whaley Bridge. Local resident Alastair MacDonald watched it through binoculars and said it was undoubtedly a cat, not a dog, but the size of a labrador. His description resembles a panther.

In 1999 and 2000 more sightings followed and the reports spread southwards, with the animal heading towards civilization. In Chapel-en-le-Frith one local wildlife expert saw it often in summer 1999 and said it was too large for a fox and too cat-like in motion for a dog. At Wormhill, just outside Buxton, Tony Whittaker found a paw print 5 inches across – much too large for any normal cat and indicative of an animal up to 5 feet long. Several badgers were found mutilated nearby and one had its hair ripped out by very sharp teeth. And in Buxton itself a large black cat was disturbed in bushes in midsummer and leapt away leaving heavy indents in a gravel path much deeper than any left by a dog.

Dove Holes, where I live, is midway between Chapel and Buxton and we do get a lot of wildlife such as hedgehogs and foxes. Whilst I have yet to see an ABC I think I did hear one in early 2000. Cattle in the field by the railway were disturbed by something and I heard a fearsome growling, spitting noise that sounded like a cross between King Kong and a cat on heat. This was in the dead of night and I was not inclined to brave the dark to investigate.

But the closest sighting occurred in Chinley on 20 October 1999 when a local businesswoman encountered the animal walking right next to her on a dry stone wall. As she closed in her assumption that it was a fox was shattered by its cat-like appearance and large size. It was a dark colour but had white markings on its face. She got very close to the creature and it stared her in the eyes.[22]

The white face markings in this case suggested to the Derbyshire Wildlife Trust that at least some of the big cat sightings were really Scottish wildcats. Panthers do not have such facial markings but these rare and indigenous wild cats (mostly found in the Scottish highlands but also in other remote spots) do. However, by no means all sightings fit this pattern and witnesses shown photos of wild cats and panthers usually choose the panther as the best match to what they saw.

Keith Wood, a retired Peak park ranger has chased the ABCs in Derbyshire since 1981 when sightings first began to escalate. Hard evidence is rare, but he says that there are numerous caves and potholes where such a beast could escape detection.

The question is, could one cat really be responsible for so many sightings across twenty years? Or is there a colony that has thrived – and if so, how?

Surprisingly there is a precedent. On the moors west of Buxton red-neck wallabies exist. These small kangaroo-like creatures are native to Australia but have survived in the UK partly due to the fact that global warming over the past fifty years has increased the ambient temperature just enough to adapt the environment. It is believed that a mating pair were surreptitiously released in the early 1930s and they eventually led to a colony of at least sixty. Sightings were common and park rangers kept a tab on them. But in 1997 the sightings had dwindled and worried wildlife experts said that they feared for the future of this small collection of 'out of place' animals.[23] This shows the fragile nature of even a fairly large colony when up against the common enemy of much wildlife – man.

So could a group of panthers have similarly survived on Ollersett Moor? Or are the sightings all misperceptions or a single stray animal?

In 2000 a worrying revelation was made by the retired owner of a private zoo. He noted that in 1976 the laws had changed making it illegal to own exotic pets without proper authority. Quite a few people who secretly owned big cats as pets were forced to release them or face prosecution. This man, confidentially, explained that he had driven out on to the moors between Glossop and Sheffield and released a panther into the wild hoping it would be able to fend for itself! Is this the beast of Ollersett Moor? Or were other big cats released by similarly frustrated owners and reintroduced to the wild this way?

Whilst the elusiveness of these creatures – not to mention their widespread sighting, without bodies or droppings being reliably discovered – tends to give strength to those who champion the 'supernatural' theory, some of the ABC sightings must have real zoological explanations. I have no doubt that some will prove to be Scottish wildcats and others misperceptions of large dogs. But the possibility that real big cats are on the prowl cannot be ignored.

In one case we can say that for certain. In May 1983 Margaret O'Malley got the shock of her life when a large black cat appeared on her shed roof at Adswood in Stockport. Was the beast of Ollersett Moor heading for pastures new? Had she seen a big dog? In this case it was neither. The brave woman approached the animal and found it to be a large puma that was happy to accept a saucer of milk! The police were called and the mystery was solved when a woman rode up on horseback with a rope to secure the friendly big cat. It had 'escaped' from a travelling fair which had an associated circus and had simply decided to go see the sights of sunny Stockport!

Alien Contact

Although the alien origin of these mysterious big cats is at best controversial, aliens do love the Pennines, for there are many cases where an extraterrestrial contact has reputedly occurred.

One place where aliens pop up with alarming frequency is the branch line north of Sheffield that forms the final remains of the windswept Woodhead line crossing the hills. Many stories have been reported locally,[24] but we have to be cautious as to how we interpret some of them, such as the following event.

There were two witnesses on this occasion – a mild night in mid-April 1977. Jill and her boyfriend had driven out to an isolated spot near Worrall, South Yorkshire, in order to sit in their car for the sort of peace and quiet appreciated by young lovers everywhere. But as they sat watching the world go by there was a soft rustling noise and they saw a bizarre phenomenon manifest through the rear window. It was a great big hemisphere virtually on the ground and glowing with a bright orange light that had a fuzzy edge to it. That this misty shape was somehow generating an electrical field is suggested by the fact that the car radio was filled with static and became impossible to hear at that point.

However, as this floating mass headed towards them, by far the most frightening part of the encounter was to follow. An image was standing inside the hemisphere. They could see only the silhouette – virtually black against the orange glow – of a powerful human figure. It seemed to be tall and broad and was inside the glow, moving with the floating mass and heading in their direction.

Needless to say Jill and her boyfriend were not going to stay and find out precisely what was heading for them. They sped off down the road, with the thing still visible behind their backs, determined to regain the security of other people. Looking back after a few minutes they were highly relieved to discover that the object had gone.[25]

If we take this sighting at face value we have a classic encounter with a hovering UFO that had an alien entity inside. But this interpretation, whilst of course possible, needs to be tempered with caution when the case is compared with others. For there have been several nearly identical incidents where less exotic explanations were forthcoming. At Bignall End in Staffordshire a woman reported seeing a hovering yellow/orange dome shape and inside it a dark 'alien' that was silhouetted. Investigation revealed that the moon was rising at just this position and a telegraph pole was between the house and the moon. Did this combination trigger a misperception? In my reading of the facts it seems hard to conclude otherwise.

In the other case a huge orange floating mass drifted over the Canary Islands and was photographed and witnessed by many people – including a doctor out on a call at a remote village who said that a tall alien figure was visible inside, silhouetted against the object. A Spanish military investigation took years to unravel the truth but when veils of secrecy were pierced this phenomenon was explained. A ball of gas had been created by a rocket launched from a submarine engaged in a secret test. The floating mass was therefore quite real. But the 'alien' inside it must have been an optical illusion – perhaps triggered by some object such as a tree – in line of sight between 'UFO' and witness.[26]

Is that the sort of thing that happened at Worrall? We can only surmise that the moon might have been rising in this position (because the precise date of this case is not known). But if this was the orange ball and a silhouetted tree or pole created the alien then what about the radio interference?

Might the UFO have been an energy emission squeezed out of the rock – as seen during other Pennine cases – thus creating an atmospheric glow? And, if so, was the alien similarly just an illusion grafted on to that?

Whatever the answer we face a less than simple choice here, because what looks at first like an alien contact may in reality be no such thing. ⌐

The way in which apparently simple sightings can turn out to be more confusing – almost bending reality – is well revealed by this next case from Alverthorpe, West Yorkshire. It happened on 13 March 1979 and exactly what took place is still open to debate.

Walter Parr* was an engineer who on this cold night had headed off to the pub to meet some friends. But he found himself in an odd state of consciousness, as commonly reported by witnesses during a close encounter. For no apparent reason he took a route across some mud-sodden fields – a 'short cut' that he would never normally follow. He just felt 'compelled' to do this. Notice how often you will hear this said in other cases. Then, halfway across the field, alone and vulnerable, he realized that a huge light in the sky was paying him undue attention and swooping towards him.

Baffled by this, but trying to dismiss the object as a security light that he had never seen before, Walter tried to rush through the wet field in the darkness. It was now about 8 p.m. but the 'thing' had placed itself at rooftop height dead ahead. Looking at it, he could see that it was a long oval or 'squashed rugby ball' shape and surrounded by a greenish mist. The mist was fluorescent and seemed to cling to the surface of the metal of the object, causing it to glow. Walter also now realized for the first time that he had been 'cut off' from reality in a very odd way. As I have said, I call this effect the Oz Factor. It is extremely common in such cases but witnesses rarely realize it or know that others have reported it beforehand. To them it is just an oddity. This appears to be an altered state of consciousness during which the mind 'tunes in' to signals from another reality whilst temporarily tuning out the sense of the world around.[27] During the Oz Factor a witness will often report that all ambient sounds disappear. There are no traffic or people or even birds singing. And time itself seems to stretch out and disappear – presumably a consequence of the altered state of consciousness in which witnesses reside.

In that field near the Alverthorpe pub Walter was aware of the sudden eerie silence and how the normally busy building was deserted. It was almost as if he was now in an alternative version of the world where all human life had vanished.

What happened next was impossible for him to describe. There was a 'jump' in reality. He was now inside the toilets on the edge of the pub. The UFO, of course, had gone. Time and sounds and people were back to normal. But how he got from A to B was beyond his comprehension. There was simply no transition – as if he had been dumped back into another world in a slightly different spot but instantaneously. When he entered the pub the landlord smiled and noted that it was a good job he was a little late because they had just suffered a power cut and were unable to serve beer for a few minutes.

Even more curious is that Walter left the toilet having forgotten all about the experience – rather as we forget our dreams upon waking. This incident dissolved like snowflakes in the sun. Moments later as he entered the pub to meet his friends (without noticing whether there was any obvious 'missing time') it was just a feeling inside his head. 'If you can imagine that you have a got a thought right at the back of your mind and you are very aware of the fact that something is there, but you don't bother to think about it,' he noted.

Then, three days later, the events came back – but only slowly and in bits and pieces with the confusion enhanced by this 'blink' in reality. It took Walter months to pluck up the courage to tell his wife and when sharing it with investigators his self-effacing testimony was obvious. Attempts to rationalize what had happened followed. He said 'I keep asking – did I really go out that night? But I know that I did.'

Surprisingly, trouble with memory, not to mention jumps in reality, are common features of such cases. I have dozens of examples, many from the Pennines. Again, presumably, this relates to the fact that these experiences are occurring within an altered dream-like state of consciousness.

Often cases such as that from Alverthorpe are the basis for subsequent full blown 'alien abduction' sagas. The UFOlogists assume that there is a period of time missing from the memory. This must be the minutes or hours during the 'reality jump' that is unrecalled. They use techniques like hypnosis to 'regress' the person to the incident and try to coerce a memory they expect to find lurking in the subconscious. Unfortunately regression is as capable of causing the mind to fantasize as it is to facilitate true memory and the stories of alien kidnap into starships (which differ from person to person) could well be convenient props that the mind slots in to fill this gap. There is rarely any evidence for their physical reality.[28]

In this case Walter was regressed by therapist Dr Sheridan King. He recalled an alien nature to the experience, but saw no aliens. He observed the UFO more clearly in this state but also emphasized the vital significance of the swirling fluorescent green mist that surrounded it. This in itself is very interesting because similar mists have often been witnessed in the Pennines (see, for instance, p.195) and are often tied to time lapses, Oz Factor states and odd memory recall. There is an undeniable pattern.[29]

If you want to encounter aliens then one of the best places to go seems to be Todmorden. This mill town on the border between West Yorkshire and Lancashire is right in the midst of one of the most active pockets within the Pennine window. Alien contacts are very common here. I have investigated about twelve of them within just a few miles of one another. No other area of the UK compares with that ratio.

The most famous occurred in November 1980 when a

police officer, Alan Godfrey, encountered a swirling grey spinning top that blow-dried the rain-sodden tarmac of Burnley Road as he was on an early morning patrol. His car instantly 'relocated' from the outskirts of town heading out to Burnley and under regression from several psychiatrists he later recalled a bizarre on-board abduction by entities the size of children. The case has made big headlines and appeared often on TV around the world.[30] However, it is far less well known that something else very odd took place on the same road just ten months earlier. Peter Hough and I drove over to meet the witness in his Burnley home and here is what he told us about the early hours of 14 January 1980.

Bill was a truck driver but his career since the encounter was put in jeopardy because he has had 'mini-black outs' (during one of which he rammed a car on the M62 without recalling how it happened). He ascribes these to his alien contact, but it is noteworthy that PC Alan Godfrey experienced mini-time lapses during his life, too, when no UFOs were seen. Indeed, one doctor has even suggested that some 'abduction' witnesses might suffer from a medical condition called narcolepsy because these seem so common. In this state the witness 'falls asleep' for no apparent reason and then awakens, sometimes unaware that they have been 'out of the loop' for minutes. There was no physical evidence in Godfrey's case for him having this condition. But we might wonder if more witnesses should have a check-up.

That winter morning Bill had a delivery to Hollingworth, near Oldham, and drove the route from Burnley through Heald Moor, into Todmorden and right through this hyperactive window zone. It was icy so he drove cautiously at around 6.15 am and he was close to the county border (still just in Lancashire) just before the village of Portsmouth. That is on the same Burnley road where Godfrey later that year came to be 'abducted' but about 2 miles further out of Todmorden.

At this point the road cuts through a cliff edge on one

side and slopes to a railway line through the Calder Valley on the other. There is a lay-by on the road here. As he drove towards it Bill heard a loud hum like an electricity generator and saw an object in the lay-by like a tortoise shell with three beams of misty red light emerging from the side. Next to it were two beings, one of whom was bending over. Thinking at first that these were workmen – perhaps gritting the roads before the morning rush – he slowed down to a crawl.

Moving past the object at very close proximity its total strangeness now became obvious – as did the fact that these were not gritters. The light rays were fuzzy and laser-like. The bracken on the cliff edge glowed curiously. And the colour of the rays varied in a strange way depending on the angle at which he looked at them. Of the 'men' one seemed to be wearing a uniform and the other a silver one-piece suit. But Bill had no time to take in more details because 'as if drugged or hypnotized' his mind started to fog over.

As he 'inched' past the spot time stretched out like elastic. Peter and I drove past the spot and even going very slowly, we did not take more than seconds to do so, but Bill says he took 'minutes'. However, as he was drifting past his truck suddenly drained of all power and the headlights cut out. As there are no street lights near here the road ahead was plunged into darkness. But the vehicle engine (diesel powered) continued to operate. Bill told us that he thought the fact that it lacked a spark plug was the reason it operated normally when a petrol-driven engine would have failed. He was sure there was an electrical 'draining' effect.

The very next thing Bill recalled was a sudden 'jolt' and regaining consciousness (still feeling fuzzy-headed) at an unknown spot further along the road somewhere on the edge of Todmorden itself (very close to where the Godfrey abduction was to occur). The truck was stopped, the lights were back on and the engine was still running but there was absolutely no sense of discontinuity in time or space.

Bill's mind gradually cleared as he drove on but he only vaguely registered that the sky was now growing light (as it ought not yet to be doing in midwinter). Also someone was present to collect a package he was to drop off in Todmorden. This prearranged delivery was in fact the reason he took the back road (a route through Bacup would have been more direct) but he had been told to expect no staff on duty that early. Continuing to Hollingworth in broad daylight he arrived at 9.10 a.m. (checked against a clock as he was not wearing a watch). All of this seems to mean, he estimated, that he lost about two hours during the 'moments' that he 'crawled' past the lay-by. Needless to say that is difficult to explain.

After his return, Bill was unusually tired and slept deeply. He experienced vivid dreams reliving the event but would not be persuaded by UFOlogists that he ought to be hypnotically regressed – commendably telling us, 'You cannot be made to remember things that you do not remember.'

This case is infuriating for many reasons. Whilst one can just about conceive of a fantasy built around a road-gritting machine and might wonder if the flashing lights induced some kind of epileptic seizure, these are, of course, pure speculation. And it is undeniable that this case fits the alien contact pattern well. Moreover, if Bill simply had a blackout and fell asleep at the wheel for two hours then why did his truck, which was blocking this narrow road, not cause serious traffic delays?

We did ask the only local inhabitants, at a nearby farm, if they saw anything. They had merely experienced an apparently puzzling temporary loss of electricity, which may support Bill's story.

Probably the best-known type of alien contact is the so-called abduction where a witness is reputedly taken for a ride inside a UFO. Whilst rare there are many from the Pennines and understanding what they mean is, as always, fraught with difficulty. Here is a typically frustrating example.

Wendy Jones* clearly distressed, told me what happened on 13 March 1990. She said: 'It was a dark afternoon but quite warm. About 3.45 p.m. I was near Rochdale railway station when I was suddenly aware of something to the side of me – a movement of air up and down.'

At the same time she almost sensed a 'metallic' sound and felt air pressure pushing down and then sucking her upwards, creating a noise like a vacuum cleaner. Looking skywards she saw 'an enormous and unusual cloud'. This was very dark but unlike the other clouds it was not moving.

Being a busy street it is difficult to understand why half of Rochdale did not see this thing. Wendy says that some people did. She saw one man staring at it and 'I will never forget the look on his face – it scared me more than the craft'. But in close encounters such as this it has long been recognized by researchers that a weird 'isolation' effect occurs. It is almost as if a fantastic experience is being played out for selected eyes. Indeed I report a very similar case to this from a busy high street in Cheltenham in another book. That too was real, yet impossibly isolated.[31]

This 'only for your eyes' effect is usually denoted by the witness describing the Oz Factor, as reported in Alverthorpe and Todmorden. Here again Wendy experienced this 'shift' in the state of her consciousness. She noticed the traffic and people slowing down as if time were 'on hold' and in the outside world nothing existed other than this strange object. Staring up at it Wendy described a hollow centre with a spiral shape around the edge and glowing beams emitted from the sides. This rather resembled a tornado in some ways, although it seems even more unlikely that such a phenomenon would go unnoticed over Rochdale!

It is not clear how the thing disappeared, except that it moved 'slowly'. But the after-effects on Wendy were profound. She shared some of them with me but was determined not to probe too deeply. As she told me, 'I cannot sleep at night. I do not believe in anything like this. Please forget this happened as I must do. I hope I will forget it one day.'

The reason for this concern was the 'crazy dreams' that were 'very real' that she had in the days and weeks after the experience. In these visions she recalled the encounter but then 'it went on' past the point where she felt the upward suction effect. For now she saw herself being pulled up and going into the 'cloud' where she met 'thin, skinny, sad-looking human-like people'. They reminded her of Japanese folk with Oriental features, but fuzzy grey eyes. They were human-sized but very slight in body. 'Their skin was very pale and smooth and there were no blemishes. Also very little hair.' Although she seemed not to know this Wendy is here offering a very consistent description of aliens seen throughout the world.

Wendy felt vertigo as she 'rose' upwards then found herself in a room where there was a large 'view screen'. 'I could see Rochdale as though I was looking down on it from above. The screen was just on the side of their wall. It was so unnerving. I felt disorientated and dizzy.' Then she was led into a dark room with flashing lights – like traffic lights – and lost all recall until 'floating' back down to the ground.

In the immediate period after this sighting Wendy had a terrible headache, was very sick and felt tingling pains in her toes. Her skin developed an itchy rash. These physical symptoms subsided after a week but coupled with the awful and persistently 'real' dreams it is easy to understand why she wanted to put this trauma behind her. Yet Wendy's story is much like those reported by countless 'abductees'. But how do we know if these dreams and visions, which turn an odd cloud into a spaceship, are triggered by an encounter with the atmospheric energy that seems prevalent in the Pennines? And can that somehow alter their state of consciousness in close proximity? Or are real aliens 'out there'?

Anyone unfamiliar with the data about alien contact cases would assume that this it is a very simple phenomenon: people claim to see aliens, and either they are deluded or there really are extraterrestrials visiting the earth.

Unfortunately such a simple choice is not supported by the evidence. By far the majority of witnesses that I have met are totally sincere. They believe that what they tell me did really happen. There can be other explanations – misperceptions that cause trees to appear to be aliens or potential medical conditions that might produce odd effects. And even when there are no such possibilities the encounter has bizarre features that seem to deny it as a real-world event.

Whilst the presence of an actual UFO (often some kind of energy glow and little else) tends to be well established – by other witnesses independently describing it, for instance – the close encounter phase involving aliens nearly always occurs in isolation. A witness has an altered state of consciousness (usually defined by the Oz Factor) and within this period of 'oddity' can get 'taken out' of normal reality into a magical realm. Here, for a short time, the witness experiences the alien contact that follows in a personal manner that shares cultural similarities with other cases but is individually unique.

A good way to illustrate many of these things in operation is with another case. It occurred on 15 July 1989 in Wharfedale, another of those localized hot spots within the Pennines that (like Todmorden, Rossendale and the High Peak) are the focus of long spells of intense activity.

Morris* lived in the village of Addingham between Skipton and Ilkley, looking north across to Ilkley Moor. In the middle of the night, according to the UFO group Connect, he went up on to the moor in response to a feeling that he should do so. But he saw nothing and returned home at about 3.15 a.m. Next morning it was discovered that at 3.30 a.m. (just as Morris was going back to sleep in bed), a neighbour, Stephen*, and his mother were both awoken by a noise like a vacuum cleaner and went outside to investigate. To the north, over Beamsley Beacon, they could now see a rugby-ball-shaped mass of red, green and white lights floating in mid air.

To Connect, this sounded like an aircraft heading into

Leeds/Bradford airport with engines throttled back. But they soon discovered two things to cause them to reassess that opinion. Investigator David Barclay, working with another Yorkshire group, had a sighting called in from 2.45 a.m. (whilst Morris was still on the moors further to the west). These people had seen a 'rugby ball' heading from Harrogate towards the Wharfedale area. Because David also suspected an aircraft the airport were immediately called. But they had no air traffic up at that time. The object was unexplained.

The other oddity came when Morris was met by his six-year-old daughter at breakfast to say she had seen a 'being' in her bedroom in the middle of the night – thus at about the same time as the UFO was hovering nearby but was not seen by the family. The girl only had a dim recollection of this until two days later (after seeing another entity at the top of the stairwell). Then the memory flooded back. It is interesting that she did not describe the beings as aliens but likened them to Anneka Rice, a TV personality famed at the time for running around solving riddles! This use of familiar imagery helps put the case into a 'normal' context.

The two entities were described as being the size of small humans (about 5 feet tall) with long, thin arms and very pale faces. Needless to say this is not the reason for the use of the description of Anneka Rice – that idea entered the child's head simply because of the dark one-piece jumpsuit that the beings wore (similar to hers on TV).

It is difficult to know how to link all of these events – or, indeed, to know if any of them *are* linked, beyond circumstance. But it is possible to perceive the object next to the tall mast on Beamsley Beacon as one of the energy glows we keep describing, then to ask how this physically real phenomenon might affect local people in different ways.

Did it cause Morris to get an almost psychic feeling to go on to the moors looking for answers, but finding nothing? And did it cause the little girl, as she slept in her bed, to dream an alien dream based on the awareness of her subconscious mind that something strange was out there?

Thinking beyond the simple confines of someone just seeing a spacecraft with alien occupants during so many of these cases is perhaps the key. It seems to act as a bridge between different phenomena. What may seem on the surface to be unique events may interconnect via the human mind.[32]

Apparitions

We can easily see how these separate phenomena blend into one another with this next case. It could be placed either in this section or the previous one, and has many similarities with the sighting at Addingham. Perhaps only the cultural context or our choice of words defines what we presume about its identity.

Mrs Nicholls from Bradford described the following event one night in spring 1977, during a flap when many UFOs were being seen locally. She awoke from a deep sleep at about 3 a.m. with her body suffering a severe 'jolt'. This 'bump' – as if falling to earth – left her wide awake and she could hear the bedside clock and her husband's breathing. However, her body was paralysed and unable to move. Despite this she felt no fear. In fact there was a strange, detached calmness that sounds rather like the Oz Factor at work.

From her position on her side she was able to see the bedroom door and through this she 'sensed' – at first merely as a feeling – that someone was coming up the stairs. Even now she was oddly calm and merely accepted this otherwise terrifying scenario – even more so when into view came a floating white apparition in the form of a tall being. It was clothed in a dazzling aura of white like an energy field.

As it stood in the door watching her, time seemed to be suspended, and it was impossible to know how long drifted by. She got the sense that whoever this 'ghost' was it was trying to tell her something, but what this was did not register. Her husband did not wake up. Mrs Nicholls made no attempt to disturb him – and she was still paralysed. Then the figure gradually began to fade away and so did her recall. The next she remembered she was waking up in the morning, but now with a clear memory of this encounter.

You can see how easy it is to consider this as an encounter with an alien. Indeed if you compare it with the story of the truck driver's abduction near Todmorden (see p.51–4) more than a few links emerge. Terms such as alien, ghost or monster – or even mass of energy – could all describe what was seen here. And whichever one we choose may dictate where this event is filed for analysis. But, of course, the main clue here (as with many other so-called bedroom visitors) is the circumstances under which they occur. They happen to a person alone in bed late at night emerging from a deep sleep.

How do we know that this was not simply a vivid dream? The witness is certain that it was not. Mrs Nicholls reported: 'I felt that a part of me that is usually asleep – in me and in all of us – had for a moment in time awoken and allowed me to see something which is maybe all around but usually not visible. . . . This experience was totally real and will always stay in my mind as a very vivid and beautiful [one].'[33]

However, there are more important clues: the sudden 'jolt' on waking and prior to the experience – for example. This is nearly always reported during alien abductions and out-of-body experiences when the witness 'comes to' after a period of missing time (as in the Calder Valley lay-by). Commonly the witness thinks that they have literally been 'dropped down' (from a spaceship) or re-entered their physical body after floating free in some way. But this same thing is also described by people when waking from a deep sleep and is more properly a symptom of a sudden shift in consciousness. Whether it has a physiological cause or a psychological one – or indeed whether the effect really does result from the 'psychic self' returning into the physical body – it happens in more mundane situations. I experienced it myself in August 1984 when heavily sedated after major surgery. I would drift off and 'jolt' as I awoke by what felt like falling a few inches back on to the bed. But like many others suffering these 'jolts' I did not see any aliens, only nurses!

Moreover, the 'paralysis' effect is also nothing to do with the supernatural. This is another clue as to the shifting states of consciousness. In fact sleep paralysis, as it is termed, is a recognized condition that we all experience every night. In the deepest sleep when we are dreaming heavily the body is naturally paralysed – for good reason. Otherwise we might act out our dreams, and if a dream sees us climbing a mountain then we could well wake up on the roof! Sometimes, as in sleep walking, this process becomes disturbed, but it is perfectly normal for the muscles to be paralysed. Usually we are so deeply unconscious that we are oblivious – much as drugs used during surgery also work to prevent the patient from 'twitching' whilst the scalpel is poised in a crucial area! But if the person emerges suddenly from sleep and becomes briefly conscious during this sleep paralysis then odd things can sometimes occur.[34]

In this state the soporific effect of sleep creates a calming sensation and the state of consciousness might superimpose dream images on to the background of the bedroom. The person will likely fall rapidly back to sleep and usually recall nothing the next morning. But when they do remember something they will probably assume that the experience was real.

Such happenings have been reported throughout the centuries. Long ago it was believed that a demon or ghost (called an incubus) was attempting to assault (or even rape) the victim in their beds. It seems almost certain that the physical sensations of such an attack were a consequence of the sleep paralysis and sense of presence (and a sense is often all there is) – nothing more than a waking dream.

Today our demons have become 'sex-mad aliens' or 'randy ghosts' according to personal interpretation. But the phenomenon is recognizably the same wearing space-age dress. A major study of this effect was conducted by Dr David Hufford twenty years ago, digging into folk traditions of a bedroom visitor known as the 'old hag', which was widely reported in Newfoundland. Hufford wisely noted that, even though the physiological causes can sometimes be defined, the reality – or otherwise – of the apparitions that occur cannot be assumed one way or the other.[35] After all, when paralysis is induced by drugs in a hospital the patient may experience odd physical sensations. But the sighting of ghostly ward sisters or alien surgeons cutting you open does not seem to happen then, as you might expect that it would if this effect was purely a psychological phenomenon triggered by the perception of sleep paralysis.

At first glance the next case may seem quite similar, but it asks deeper questions about the nature of these apparitions. Mrs Ellis* from Halifax told me what happened to her in the autumn of 1942 when she was only nine. Because it was wartime, blackout restrictions were in force and being ill with jaundice she was left alone in a dark room as the long evening wore on. Only a dim fire illuminated the surroundings as she looked out across the moors with the spectacular view that her window provided.

Suddenly the Oz Factor struck. We recognize this (although she did not) from her description of how everything became remarkably quiet and still, and time slowed to a halt. A brilliant blue-white glow had now appeared between the window and bed, and out of it stepped three figures. They were seemingly human but glowing a silver white. Looking and acting like ghosts they floated to the foot of the bed, seemed to look at the little girl and then promptly went up to the wall as if it were not there and walked right through it! At the same time the big white glow just disappeared.

This apparently frightening event did not instil terror – as under any normal circumstances it surely would do, even in an adult. There was an odd sense of calmness that filled Mrs Ellis.

She has, of course, asked herself across the years whether this was just a dream or hallucination. But as you can see such questions are impossible to resolve. All she can tell us is that to her it *seemed* completely real. However, the most curious aspect was the way that next morning her jaundice had completely vanished. She had been suffering quite badly and the prognosis was for a slow recovery with wartime medicines in short supply. But somehow or other, inevitably perhaps, she thinks her salvation came as a consequence of this visit by three ghostly doctors. ⏎

Before leaving this type of case, it is worth comparing these last two with one other, which might offer further clues. For again the witness was a child – 13-year-old Nina from Shipley, West Yorkshire. Late on the night of 8 March 1979 she was taken ill and, like Mrs Ellis thirty-seven years earlier, went to bed. She was an epileptic and had an attack. But about two hours after going to bed, at 1.30 a.m., she was disturbed by the sight and sound of a tiny being – under 2 feet tall – that just appeared in her bedroom!

The apparition looked human but was surrounded by a glowing, pale green fluorescent aura (as we have seen, this surrounding energy field is very common in Pennine cases). Just as with Mrs Ellis this 'ghost' moved to the foot of the bed and stared at the child. But Nina reacted swiftly, turning on the bedroom light; the apparition then instantly disappeared.

What happened here? Epilepsy, just like narcolepsy, is known to lead to shifts in states of consciousness. It introduces chemical changes in the body during which hallucinations can occur. Do such things imply that bedroom apparitions result from the altered states and changes in body chemistry that follow a medical condition and then might lead to the seeing of visions? And do these visions follow culturally directed guidelines, causing us to see ghosts, or demons, or aliens accordingly?[36]

Another clue that we must take on board is that there appear to be haunted personalities to whom apparitions are a regular occurrence, not merely a once-in-a-lifetime memory.

Mrs Noreen* from Leeds reported some of her experiences to me. They began when she was a teenager, but the first vivid incident occurred in 1971. Her father had died whilst she was still young and on this occasion she felt that he had returned. In fact what happened was much more in keeping with the cases already described in this section than an actual sighting of her dead father. She heard a noise like the wind coming up the stairs and then felt as though it 'enveloped the bed'. Whilst, of course, this could have been her father visiting from the afterlife (assuming that there is one) equally we see that this story has the same insubstantial feel with extra meaning grafted on.

This becomes more poignant when we hear about the next event in Mrs Noreen's tragic life story. Her sons were killed in a horrific accident and was so devastating that she considered committing suicide. But, she says, just as she was about to take the pills to end her suffering, a series of friends called around 'on impulse' – something that Mrs Noreen thinks was 'arranged'. Someone, perhaps her dead father, had 'sent' them to rescue her from her intended folly.

The odd experiences did not cease. Now she saw what looked like little balls of light floating about the bedroom – something that, understandably, was interpreted as another sign. In fact balls of light seen in bedrooms are yet another common feature in Pennine cases. Many of the witnesses I have interviewed who have had strange experiences have seen them, usually when they are younger.

Alan Godfrey, the police officer from Todmorden who was abducted in 1980, (see p.51) had such a bedroom visit from a floating ball of white light. Jenny, a woman who experienced both apparitions and alien contacts at Walsden, between Todmorden and Littlebrough, saw tennis-ball-sized lights floating around her bedroom as a youngster. And Mike Sacks from Bacup, a witness to several close encounters in the Rossendale Valley, reported 'green opal' like lights in his room when he was twelve.[37]

In June 1982 Mrs Noreen described another incident: 'I

saw on the wall [of my bedroom] a brilliant white oval. Through this oval – faded at first – came the face of my eldest son who had died. He was smiling with such love and happiness. It was marvellous.'

This apparition in a glow on the wall seems to have conditioned Mrs Noreeen to accept that her children 'lived on' and she heard her eldest boy's voice often after that. She has also felt 'electric' tingling sensations in her leg and noted static interference on the TV set that she relates to his presence. We might notice that many of these things are in the form of 'energy' phenomena such as we have seen occur during many other cases. Indeed glowing energies and associated electrical effects link many cases. ⅃

The encounters reported in this section may not seem to be traditional ghosts, but these bedroom visitors are actually more typical – often the interpretation of such amorphous 'forms' as actual dead people haunting a building owes something at least to the imagination.

✶ However, there are cases where a ghost is seen in the way with which we are most familiar – as an apparently indisputable human being. Harry and two friends report one such case in January 1985. They were visiting the Rivelin Valley west of Sheffield (an area at the heart of one of the active hot spots already noted) and walking near the Round Dam area of the water's edge. This affords a wide open view of the countryside.

The three men were trying to catch up with two other friends ahead of them when Harry spotted a stranger sitting beside the water apparently fishing. He describes him as being an elderly man with a beard, dressed in an old-fashioned blue velvet jacket and flat cap.

Intrigued by his curious appearance Harry pointed him out to his friends but, despite being only about 50 feet away, neither of them could see him in what were clear daylight conditions. Harry looked back and the man was still there. Astonished he led his friends to the water's edge, determined to prove that he was not going mad. Doing so meant losing sight of the spot for a few seconds as they went over a rise. Once on top of the hill Harry was shocked to discover that there was nobody there.

There was no way that this man could have vanished that quickly. They could see for a long distance around the spot and even running at full speed the man could not have fled in those few seconds. He had quite literally disappeared. Except, of course, that in so far as two of the three men staring at the water were concerned he had never been there in the first place. Somehow only Harry could see him.[38]

Does this imply that the 'ghost' was only ever there in Harry's mind? But why would it conjure up a total stranger wearing old-fashioned clothes doing something so mundane as this?

Not only human beings can become ghosts. The ghost aeroplanes of the High Peak have already suggested that and animals, too, seem to be capable of creating apparitions.

Joan from Liversedge, West Yorkshire, told me of her lifetime of strange experiences, which began in 1951 when she had an out-of-body experience during the birth of her first child. She floated up by the ceiling and in a completely detached manner, free from pain or concern, watched her pain-wracked body below as if it were another person. Then she had a sense of being 'needed' and shot back into her body moments before her daughter was born. I have heard similar childbirth stories from several other women.

However, the most relevant incident involved Tina, the family's dachshund, who sadly became terminally ill in 1979. In October, a few months after the dog had died, Joan returned home at dusk and through the long glass panelling in the front door saw Tina jumping up and down preparing to greet her mistress. This was a behaviour pattern that she had often displayed whenever Joan came home.

The event was so natural that Joan did not for one moment think that it was odd. She temporarily forgot that her pet was dead and opened the door as usual. Tina was still there, in view as large as life behaving excitedly. Then the dog ran into the sitting room and jumped on to a chair waiting for a treat – something that was a regular routine. So 'normal' was this that Joan apologized for the fact that she had nothing in the house for her. At this the apparition of the little dog just vanished.

On the one hand we would probably suspect that expectation and wish fulfilment might provoke such a sight. But could that really bring about such a complete hallucination, to the extent that it was indistinguishable from real life? Research into apparitions shows that it could. In various studies at the Oxford paraphysical laboratories they have found that the vast majority of ghosts seem utterly three-dimensional and completely real. If a normal person or animal is seen then the witness only realizes that they are not seeing somebody who is alive if they recognize that person as being dead – or if the 'spook' does something remarkable, like vanish into thin air or walk through a wall.[39]

However, this full-scale vision of Tina was not the pet's only post-mortem appearance. Joan reports how she and her husband also heard the dog on several occasions jumping off the bed – making the exact noise that she so often had during life. The clicking of her claws outside the door – a sign that she wanted to come in – was also heard a number of times.

Is this an important pointer towards what is happening in these cases? After all why would Tina's ghost appear in the form of mundane sounds? All of them have one crucial thing in common. They are reruns of actual events that did take place inside this house.

Indeed most apparitions of this kind are like a loop of film or a sound tape being rewound and played again for a new audience. This reminds us of the apparent video replay of ghost bombers over the High Peak, where witnesses see them flying as they might have done 50 years earlier, or the house where the sound of a motorbike was replayed long after the owner and the motorcycle had moved away (see p.30–1).

In Joan's case we might think that her mind was simply rerunning a familiar memory from her head so strongly that she thought it was real. But that sensible theory fails for two reasons. Joan's husband often heard the replayed sounds as well. And most witnesses who saw ghost aircraft over the moors had never seen them in reality (in fact were not even born when the planes flew), so somehow these events presumably have to be physically real and imprinted as 'time recordings'.

What this suggests to me is that there has to be some as yet unrecognized way that energy signals from emotive events can be recorded in the ether and that certain sensitive people can at times 'tune in' and replay them. If so, then this is almost like a time machine that is literally just a sophisticated version of the VCR. If so, perhaps such a real 'ghost recording' video machine can actually be developed – and in a few years' time rather than watching last week's episode of *ER* we might be watching (as live) the coronation of the other ER the Queen – fifty years ago.

Disappearances

We must now take a side trip into the Twilight Zone by considering reports of mysterious appearances and disappearances. Of course, people go missing all the time. Sadly there are many mundane reasons why this can happen – suicide, escape from a terrible home environment, murder and so on. We should therefore beware of assuming that there is a supernatural cause, even within a window area.

However, people being moved through time and space seems to be a recurrent theme during these mysterious encounters in the Pennines. And a few instances do seem to demand our attention.

That is certainly true with regard to the fate that befell Zigmund Adamski in June 1980.

To start with, this Polish surname could hardly be more famous in UFO circles; George Adamski was perhaps the first person to claim to have gone for a flight in a spaceship after meeting aliens. He became celebrated through a series of books in the early 1950s telling of his meetings with Venusians. He even had an alleged audience with the Pope, such was the fame of this would-be pioneer astronaut.

Zigmund Adamski was no relation to George. He worked as a miner in one of the many Yorkshire pits, but on the afternoon of 6 June he was enjoying a visit from Polish relatives and preparing for a family wedding the next day. He set off to the corner shop in Tingley on a sunny afternoon hoping to buy some potatoes. As he strolled down the street he said hello to a neighbour who was polishing his car and moments later should have reached the shop, but he never arrived. Nor did he come home. His disabled wife Lottie was distraught as the hours passed. When he missed the wedding and there was still no trace, everyone knew that something serious had happened. But what?

Police investigations led nowhere. This kindly man had no enemies and no major worries. He was, in fact, looking forward to retirement. His total disappearance from a sunny suburban street was a mystery. But it took an extraordinary turn five days later and over 20 miles away at Todmorden, the small mill town that, as we have already seen, may well lay claim to being the most supernatural place in Britain!

On the night before Zigmund's reappearance (10 June 1980) there was one of the regular catalogue of close-encounter events in this valley. A couple in a house on the edge of town heard a strange noise in the middle of the night. It was like the tide rushing in or air escaping. Looking outside they witnessed an ellipse in the sky pouring down red light before rising vertically upwards and out of sight at speed.

This was one of many such odd sightings in the area over the next few weeks. Police officers on nearby Withens Moor chased a bright light. A panda patrol on Soyland Moor to the south experienced fantastic radio reception (hearing broadcasts ten times further away than normal as a UFO hovered above – something which is only likely when unusual levels of atmospheric ionization occur). And street lights in Todmorden were extinguished then came back on again as a red light passed.

Hours after this latest wave began (the afternoon of 11 June) a macabre discovery was made in a coal yard by Todmorden railway station. There was a body on top of a coal heap in full view of the tracks coming from Manchester. It had not been there shortly before, when the yard was last checked. Passing trains would have had a good view if it had been there for even a relatively short time. But how this person had got onto the 15 foot high pile was harder still to fathom. There was no sign that anyone had carried the deceased and, in any case, who would lug a heavy body up a slippery coal heap in broad daylight with the enormous risk of being seen, especially with miles of open Pennine moor all around?

The dead man had what was described as a look of shock or fear on his face according to the police officer called to the site. A post mortem later that day in Hebden Bridge revealed that he had died from a heart attack and that he also had an unexplained burn mark on his body. A major investigation began to try to find out what had happened. The inquest was held, adjourned, reopened and dragged on for over three months without resolution. In the end the coroner, James Turnbull, expressed his total exasperation, in the records I have studied, pronouncing an open verdict and saying, 'I am not happy...but it may be that we will never know.' Both he and the police had to admit that they had no idea how this man had arrived in Todmorden and got onto the coal heap.[40]

In fact the mystery here was much deeper. The man on the coal tip was Zigmund Adamski. He had no connections with Todmorden, so how he had got there five days after his sudden disappearance *en route* to the corner shop was just one more puzzle in a growing list. However, the most extraordinary mystery of all was still to come.

Adamski had vanished on 6 June 1980. He turned up

again in Todmorden on 11 June (hours after the first UFO in the renewed wave). The inquest closed without answers on 25 September. And sixty-four days later, on 28 November 1980, the police officer who had gone to the scene of the body of Zigmund Adamski was himself abducted by a UFO from his patrol car on Burnley Road. This was less than half a mile from the coal heap. The police officer in both these incidents was Alan Godfrey.

You will recall how Godfrey had driven along Burnley Road that winter night when he encountered a swirling grey mass. He was then apparently 'sucked up' into some kind of spatial and temporal anomaly, coming to his senses 'relocated' further down the road without any memory of the transition. It was as if he was 'moved' through time and space, and some minutes were also unaccounted for. The same had happened, of course, that January on the same road to the truck driver passing Heald Moor (p. 52–4).

Godfrey was on Burnley Road just after 5 a.m. looking for some cattle. There had been reports that they had been seen from a nearby housing estate and whilst odd this was not considered too baffling given the farms that surround the town. Patrols had looked for them, but without success. Godfrey had tried himself earlier in the night but the cows seemed to have temporarily vanished.

In fact what happened to these cattle proved fascinating. Although Alan Godfrey never found them – his close encounter put paid to his search – they turned up at dawn. The farmer concerned was mystified as to how they had escaped. This small herd had simply 'moved themselves'. Moreover, they were rediscovered in a field only a few hundred yards from where the policeman's abduction took place – one that seemed inaccessible. The field was extremely muddy because it had rained heavily during the night, but daylight revealed no hoof prints to indicate how these heavy animals had reached the place where they now stood. It was almost as if they too had been 'picked up' and relocated into another field a few hundred yards across this oddly haunted road.

In 1981 a body was found on Soyland Moor in a similar condition to Zigmund Adamski. The man was never identified, nor was it explained how he got up onto this desolate moor – before or after his death. He was found at a spot long associated with the supernatural and known as Fairy Springs.

On 15 July 1995 yet another curious episode took place at a house in the Calder Valley between Todmorden and Hebden Bridge. Four people having a summer barbecue found themselves surrounded by a grey mist and, just like Alan Godfrey fifteen years before, lost all sense of space and time and 'came to' some time later with the environment around them inexplicably different. Their recall was, as one man put it, 'like a video tape cut to pieces and reassembled out of order'. They felt physically sick and also 'out of sync' with reality for a time.[41]

Odd as these symptoms sound this description is quite common in such cases. It is as if the person is taken on a journey through multiple universes to one which is not quite identical to the one they left behind. The journey causes them to feel 'out of phase' until their body readjusts, leading to physical symptoms which range from burns to nausea, giddiness and loss of body control.

According to modern physics there is a strong likelihood that there are 'parallel' universes, each differing slightly from our own. If there was a way in which travels through space-time could occur – perhaps as a consequence of some unknown atmospheric anomaly not unlike a small black hole, one might not emerge in the same place from which one left. In fact one might travel to a universe that is not quite one's own. And if one did, would one ever know – other than through the sense of disorientation? For example, when someone totally disappears and is never seen again, have they fallen through a hole in space-time and reappeared in another universe? Do witnesses who report that they encounter strange swirling mists and then suddenly find themselves in a slightly different time and place (such as further along Burnley Road) actually return to a closely similar but not identical universe to the one that they left? Are people who disappear or are 'abducted' not journeying into outer space but to a parallel version of their own universe – unaware, in fact, that they have not returned to the reality they call home? Is there some version of the universe 'nearby' where Alan Godfrey vanished but never came back?[42]

Energy Fields

Leys were first identified (or rediscovered) in the British landscape some seventy years ago by the pioneer researchers into what today are called earth mysteries. Believed to be straight tracks across the countryside linking ancient Celtic or Druidic points of worship they owe something to similar beliefs long held by the Chinese. To them mystic power flowed in channels of energy within the earth.[43] These lines of power are also thought to cross the human body and can be tapped with needles by acupuncturists in order to let healing energies flow.

Today, of course, this concept seems less strange because we know that the earth has a metal core and spins in space to generate a magnetic field. So there are real lines of electromagnetic (EM) energy that we cannot see but which are none the less present, and can have tangible effects. Where these energy lines intersect they can boost or negate each other's power, providing, for example, notorious 'dead spots' where EM communications are disrupted or boosted (as on Soyland Moor – p.72). The human body also contains channels of electrical energy and even magnetic particles. That it could also follow such rules is reasonable.

Our ancestors were much more in tune with the land. They relied upon it for survival. They may have been instinctively aware of locations where these invisible energies were at their most powerful because, as we have seen, the human mind does respond to natural radiation. Some people are particularly sensitive to changes in atmospheric pressure and electrostatic charge in the air. In the past these people became tribal shamans who experienced visions or intuitions (today we call them mediums or psychics). And if a shaman recognized some location as special the whole tribe would take notice.

Such hot spots were often recognized because strange things had happened there over many years – hence the ascribing of appropriate supernatural place names (see p.14). As a result, worship or ceremony might be focused here, which may explain the ancient markers such as stone circles and megaliths and, much later, churches built on the same spot to benefit from the energy believed to be at its strongest.

Ley hunters retraced this ancient art and have since found countless examples (popularly miscalled 'ley lines') which cross Britain, and other parts of northern Europe, linking ancient monuments and often featuring place names with the 'ley' suffix.

You can also find evidence of similar beliefs elsewhere – such as the straight lines etched into the South American landscape and covering many miles of Peru in and around the Nazca plains. They were also constructed – about 1,000 years ago – as pathways leading towards ceremonial special sites.

Whether the leys are genuine energy channels or simply act as marker routes like the pathways at Nazca, they do depend upon the recognition of a 'living earth'. This clearly ties in with the concept of window areas where these powerful forces seem to be at their peak. Unsurprisingly, therefore, the Pennines are filled with 'ley' place names and perceived lines of power.

We have already seen examples of the visual power of the earth, such as the forks and balls of energy rising from the ground at Totley (p. 16–17) and Earby (p. 33). Here is another example from Yorkshire.

Witness Jim Bolton reports what he saw at Ravenscliffe near Bradford on several occasions. One morning in 1983 at about 5.30 a.m. he observed a 'shimmering energy' rising

from a field near his house. This was not like a heat haze –
it was an actual energy emission coming up from the
ground. 'It rose about 30 feet into the air [and was] quite
transparent. It appeared to wobble or spiral until it reached
the top where it spun and sprayed into the air, dispersing or
disappearing . . . It was visible for a minute or two.'[44]

He also saw similar effects rising from the ground at
nearby Shipley and Idle Hill. Both have been scenes of various strange phenomena, ranging from the sighting of
demons to bedroom apparitions. Research by Paul Bennett,
who investigated the leys in this area, found that not only
did several lines cross at these sites but a standing stone
had been placed at the active spot thousands of years since,
indicating that there was something special about this place
long ago.

Paul Bennett also noted that local dowsers (using rods to
magnify the body's sensitivity to these changes in the local
EM field) had reported sensing unusual energies here in the
form of several rising spiral paths – which seems to be the
effect that Jim Bolton had visually observed. Bennett
believes that the neurones in Jim's brain were extremely
sensitive to this energy leaking from the earth. In psychics
these brain cells, he postulates, may act like miniature internal dowsing rods.

* These 'explosions' of earth energy activity also seem to
occur during 'flaps' and it is worth looking at some of the
clues that they offer as to what is going on.

In late February and early March 1977 a series of lights
were seen rising from the hills in the area between Burnley
and Skipton. These glows seemed to climb out of rocks,
split apart and rush across the sky like opposite poles of a
magnet repelling one another (possibly an apt comment).
This two-week burst of activity ended with the spectacular
'car stop' at Nelson in the early hours of 9 March (see
p.35–6). It also included a strange event over Ilkley Moor
where four members of the Royal Observer Corps saw
something floating over a stone circle site. Paul Bennett
climbed the moor to visit the spot after talking to witnesses

and claimed to get a mild electric shock when touching one of the standing stones.[45]

Moving on a year a similar outbreak occurred around Menwith Hill, to the north of Ilkley. Here the spectacular lights over a few days around 28 July included glows beside transmission towers on hill tops – notably a blood red one that flooded light over the countryside. This is very like the phenomenon witnessed over Todmorden the night before the discovery of Zigmund Adamski's body (p. 70).

✱ In autumn 1981 there was an interesting outbreak of lights in the Rossendale/Todmorden area. At Weir on 15 October, for example, the glows were seen to 'spark' off electricity pylons and then drift into the sky as if electrical energy was leaking into the atmosphere through this conduit. At Walsden near Todmorden a witness and her dog 'sensed' a strange charge in the air and looked up straight at a hovering glow that split apart and shot in different directions – one section towards Bacup, another towards Rochdale.

And in April 1982 the same moors around Todmorden were subject to a three-day flap when all sorts of odd phenomena were reported. Lights, dubbed 'a disco in the sky', were seen on 17, 18 and 19 April. Many locals went into the hills to watch these aerial displays that appeared from cracks in the ground. Just as at Walsden they were seen to split in two and 'repel' one another across the sky. One skywatcher returned to town from a trip up the hill with all the fuses blown in his car as if a power overload had occurred. Local street lights dimmed then brightened again during the appearance of these lights.

There were no sightings on the night of 20 April, but something else occurred on that afternoon. A loud explosion filled the sky and the ground shook. This was later traced to a small earth tremor on the Craven Fault, a split in the rocks that crosses this hyperactive part of the Pennine window.

Putting together all the various clues from these (and countless other) small flaps that have occurred in the Pennines suggests a fascinating picture.

There seems to be a real physical energy concentrated

within the rocks of these hills. This 'leaks' out into the atmosphere through suitable release points (upright stones, transmission masts etc.). It can be 'sensed' by some people who possess greater acuity – perhaps via the neurones in their brains. Jim Bolton apparently could visualize them as well. Others have to wait until these electromagnetic energies create visible changes in the sky – probably by triggering ionization effects in the molecules of the air. The resulting energy fields can create radio or TV interference, or cause power overloads and temporarily disrupt street lamps. They also cause air particles to be charged and to glow, leading to 'disco lights' in the sky. As some ions are positively and some negatively charged they can repel one another just like magnets, causing these glows to shoot across the sky in opposite directions. ⌐

Can science explain some of the things that have puzzled thousands of Pennine witnesses? Hills, towers, pylons and standing stones may work like lightning conductors to distribute the flow of ions into the air. There is also evidence that pressure on rocks can 'squeeze' the charge into the air. Experiments crushing crystalized rock in the laboratory both in Boulder, Colorado, and in Britain by geochemist, Dr Paul McCartney, have proved this can happen. This would explain why these phenomena are common around quarries and reservoirs where the rock is put under stress. The reservoirs of the Longendale Valley in the High Peak is one perfect illustration. This has generated so many strange light effects that a permanent web camera has been set up, called 'the Haunted Valley'.[46]

However, the most significant clue may be this link with earth tremors, as in the Craven Fault (and similar lights seen in January 1974 as an earthquake struck the Bala fault in the Berwyn mountains). Earthquakes occur when fractures in rocks slip against each other and slowly build up strains. Destructive earthquakes happen when massive tension accumulates, perhaps across several years, then 'erupts' in a catastrophic slip. These are amongst the most dangerous natural disasters that still plague humanity.

The experience of numerous small tremors in the Pennines (often too small to be noticed) shows the other extreme of the same effect. Here the strain gradually leaks over a long time and the energy is transformed not into destruction but into glowing effects in the atmosphere. As we saw in April 1982 with the Craven Fault, replace this gradual leakage with a sudden slip and an earthquake may stop these lights.

This poses a fascinating question about the earth energies which apparently power the strange phenomena in the skies above the Pennines. If we can understand the principles by which these events occur can we discover a way to 'defuse' more deadly earthquakes in other parts of the world where thousands are killed by them each year? Is it realistic to hope that we can channel the stress from somewhere like the San Andreas Fault in California into a much more gradual transformation of leaking energy that creates an ongoing atmospheric ionization ? If so then terrible natural disasters might be tamed and replaced by spectacular light shows that could even become a new tourist attraction!

From all the evidence it seems certain that these glows are very real light effects, and if someone is in the right place with a camera then they ought to be able to photograph them. Similar lights have been witnessed and filmed in other active window areas all over the world. The Pennine glows are virtually identical to the so-called Marfa lights regularly photographed in Texas, and the Min Min lights seen in Queensland, Australia, have drifted through the outback for centuries.[47]

However, as yet we are restricted to occasional chance photographs taken from these windows, such as the curious phenomenon captured at Appletreewick. This small village is on the moors north of Skipton and Ilkley and is surrounded by many strange events (the light effects often seen to the west of Menwith Hill are close by). It sits right on the Craven Fault. Nigel Mortimer, investigating the case, found countless relevant stories. Researcher Alec Macellan, for instance, had claimed to hear a strange rumbling and see a green glow rising from rocks inside a disused mine less than a mile away. Local legends tell of a monster with glowing red eyes (the barguest) that roams the moors. And most specifically there were sightings of orange light phenomena only four days earlier from a camp site in the valley below the hill slope visible in the odd photograph taken by Jane, landlady at the Craven Arms, from the front of her pub at 2.30 p.m. on 30 May. She was filming a group of morris dancers and 'sensed' a rapid motion across the viewfinder, (although she saw nothing) just heard a noise like displaced air.

However, on processing the shot, a spectacular pinkish orange ball, several feet in diameter, appeared behind a tree above the valley. None of the dancers saw anything, but the photo indicates that all in shot were facing away from the object.[48]

Extensive efforts were made to find an answer. Nigel Mortimer submitted the case to me at the British UFO Research Association (BUFORA) and attempts were made to find a hot air balloon (as there is some similarity in appearance). However, this solution fails on many grounds, not least because balloons move very slowly and someone would surely have seen anything that was visible for more than a few seconds.

Several analyses were conducted by photo labs, including Kodak, as it was considered possible that this might just be a film fault. Extensive efforts to reproduce the effect failed. The leaves and branches of a tree directly in front of the object are clearly superimposed onto it. Whatever the thing was it looked physically real and floated above the valley. Kodak told Mortimer that they could think of 'nothing conventional' to explain this image. Sadly the brother of one of the dancers died at home at almost exactly the same time that this photo was taken.

This case is typical of the evidence that can be fortuitously obtained by someone in the right place when one of these earth energy effects occurs. But it also shows the potential for a full scale monitor exercise in the Pennine window, one designed to provide us with scientific evidence.

That potential is well revealed by Project Hessdalen in a valley near Trondheim, Norway. Here multiple sightings of lights provoked a joint UFO/scientific/military operation in which researchers spent two weeks camped out in a remote area, in sub-zero temperatures monitoring the sky and using sophisticated equipment to track and film the occasional light effects. This was highly successful and produced several good photographs and accompanying data, such as spectroscopic readings. This hard-won evidence gives cause for us to be sure of two things.

First, these are the same phenomena witnessed over the Pennines and they do result from ionization within the atmosphere.[49] However, the conditions in the Pennines are much less severe than in Norway. The area is nothing like as remote and surrounded closely by major universities at Manchester, Sheffield and Leeds (all under an hour's drive from active window hot spots). And, indeed, the Pennine lights are seemingly more active than those in Norway. All that was needed was for a serious research project to come together to set up operations within the window and we could make enormous scientific strides.

Project Pennine, as this venture is called, was initiated during the writing of this book and the BBC set up a small-scale exercise in November/December 2000 near Glossop. It was short term and limited, but has pointed the way. The project hopes for bigger and more scientifically minded ventures in the near future, if university departments can overcome their understandable prejudice. The problem is that they perceive this as a public-relations minefield because of silly media chatter about little green men.

✳ Seeing these energy balls at a distance can be unnerving. Witnessing them close at hand can be terrifying. Andy Clarke* from Dukinfield on the western side of the Pennines contacted me via the science centre at Jodrell Bank to report the following event on 4 April 1986. 'I was walking

home from work when I heard a strange noise. It was something like a low-flying helicopter and came in waves. I
could hear the distinctive whoomph-whoomph sound on
my eardrums.'

Looking up, Andy was surprised not to be able to see the
aircraft. But he did detect a fizzling or sizzling sensation in
the air as if it were 'charged with electricity'. It was then
that he spotted the blue/white globe of light with a fuzzy
outline that was heading slowly towards him from
Glossop. ⊐

Investigation by Georgina Mills failed to find any explanation for this phenomenon and whilst we did consider ball
lightning – a rare form of atmospheric lightning – there
were no obviously consistent weather conditions to point to
this. What we did find was that the area beneath where the
blue light appeared was riddled with fault lines in the rock.

What was also intriguing was the sound on the ear
drums that apparently caused the witness some pain. This
effect has been reported on other occasions and is obviously
a little-known clue. At Hook, Hampshire, in October 1967,
for example, a van driver felt his ears 'clicking' as his
eardrums were depressed in and out with great rapidity by
the proximity of a glowing light.

Amongst various other examples is one that I followed
up on site. A Scottish couple lived in a beautiful villa up a
mountain above San Antonio on the island of Ibiza. In
August 1978 there had been a wave of strange things (local
shepherd children witnessed an angelic being floating in
the trees, for example). Then this couple faced their own
nightmare.

At 2.30 one warm night the couple were awoken by a
'whoomph-whoomph' noise boring into their skulls. They
went to the window and watched a ball of orange fire
bathing the mountainside and climbing majestically
upward whilst hugging the rock-strewn slopes. The glow
pulsed in and out to the rhythm of this noise. When the
glow vanished, as it did after a few seconds, the noise
stopped.

This couple demonstrated how to reproduce the effect by cupping their hands over their ears and moving them to and fro rapidly in order to create a series of pressure changes. For this is what they – and other witnesses – are surely describing here. The ball of light somehow displaces air in rapid waves and creates changes in pressure that depress the ear drums. On Ibiza the couple woke next morning with pounding headaches, feeling nauseous. These 'illness' after-effects are commonly described by witnesses to these encounters, usually without knowing their cause. They may well be a consequence of the trauma affecting the ears, which control, amongst other things, our sense of balance.

You might also have noticed how in cases from the Pennines physical after-effects can be linked to unusual sounds. Note, for example, the sound like the tide coming in and out that was reported at Todmorden in 1980 the night before Zigmund Adamski's body was found – or, indeed., the near identical auditory effects reported by the two men during the Nelson car stop case in March 1977 (see p.35).

✷ Sometimes the sighting of such a light can have entirely different physical effects, such as described to me by Joyce* from one Pennine suburb just west of Sheffield. In April 1979 she was amazed to find a ball of blue/white light inside her bedroom. She watched in awe as it grew brighter and illuminated the entire room as it hovered just a few feet in front of her, swirling in a misty fashion. 'As it started to spin like a top,' she reported, 'it gave out a humming sound. Then it got faster and faster and as it did so the light became more intense . . . All of a sudden it burst, seeming to scatter thousands of pieces all over the carpet.'[50]

Joyce was so stunned that she searched the bedroom looking for shattered glass – until she realized that this was some form of energy and not a glass bulb. However, she became convinced that this event was a portent, perhaps even a guardian angel. A few weeks later she was struck full on by a car whilst crossing the road and knew nothing more until twenty-one days later when she awoke from a coma. Her injuries were severe and she spent nine months in hospital. Doctors later told her she had to be revived from near death; they were amazed she had pulled through. Joyce ascribes this 'miracle' to the blue ball.

Hauntings

Many a place would seek to lay claim to the title the most haunted house in England, but there is really only one place that can claim to be *the* most haunted building in the Pennine region: Chingle Hall in Goosnargh between Preston and Longridge Fell to the west of Clitheroe. It has been visited by countless ghostbusters (often spending the night to raise funds for charity) and is perhaps as regularly haunted by paranormal researchers as it is by its resident spooks. It has a long history of weird events.

Built in 1258 this modest but ancient manor house, with a now mostly filled moat, is a delight to visit, although it is privately occupied these days. It is believed to have been constructed from shipwreck timber dating back to the days of the Viking raiders. Although much altered (the draw-bridge has gone) it has had a bloody history, sheltering priests in small concealed 'hides' when the state was seeking out those loyal to the Pope after the Reformation. Even in the late seventeenth century the house's owner, Sir John Wall, was hanged for retaining his religious beliefs. His head is reputedly buried under the house and is thought by some to be the trigger for the long association with haunting there.

Researcher Terence Whittaker has spent much time documenting the sightings of ghostly monks that have been reported in this building for centuries. He has also used a 'spectre detector' here – a device that records changes in the local electromagnetic field and sounds a buzzer when these happen – because, you may by now not be surprised to hear, these energies are a major part of the experience at Chingle.[51] Footsteps (as if these are temporal recordings of the echoing ghostly monks) and buzzing noises have all been recorded. An especially weird event was taped live by BBC Radio Lancashire during a Christmas 'ghost watch'. They had recorded loud rapping noises coming out of thin air coincident with the room temperature plummeting. One of the crew saw a dark shadowy form and Whittaker's detector recorded alterations in the ambient conditions inside the room.[52]

Aside from tape recordings there have been numerous reports of electrical interference blocking the operation of cameras and other equipment. All tests have indicated that some kind of EM energy field is soaking Chingle and causing these effects.

During 1996 the Northern Anomalies Research Organization (NARO) made several trips to Chingle to make video and other recordings with the assistance of the then owners. I have found the place strange and eerie and the atmosphere undoubtedly intense, although the building is unexpectedly small. To be honest I would not stop the night there! But other intrepid NARO members have and experienced for themselves the power of the building. The team of eight researchers who spent two days there in January 1996 were rewarded with a number of phenomena. They heard rapping sounds on the ceiling of the room where John Wall had been born, the smell of lavender suddenly filled the air, and they taped what appeared to be the faint music of a choir – all fairly typical low-key Chingle events.

At about 2.15 a.m. on 26 January Tony Cranstoun and Mark Glover were in the chapel sitting in the pitch dark when Tony saw an orange glow across the room, which gradually shrank in size. He called to Mark, who saw nothing. But as they continued to look to see if it recurred, a line of flickering lights appeared in the corner by some timber beams. Mark scuttled out to bring in the others who had monitoring equipment set up elsewhere in the house. Tony, who had a loaded camera, snatched a quick shot. By the time everyone arrived the lights had ceased, but Tony

Cranstoun's photograph was successfully developed. It showed a spectacular array of lights – much more obvious than those he recalled seeing with his eyes. No camera fault revealed itself on investigation.

Interestingly, Tony reported afterwards that when they checked the voltmeter they found that it read high levels of electricity in the room and he also noticed that the clothing he wore that night retained an unusually high level of static charge that persisted for several days after the event. This is something connected with other Pennine episodes (see p.196).[53]

The strange lights recorded at Chingle are far from uncommon. The internet is full of sites with such photographs that have been taken at haunted houses and even graveyards across the world. But professional photographer Phillip Carr believes he has at least part of the answer.

He notes that often these lights are not seen at the time when the photograph is taken and that they merely 'turn up' on film. This, he argues, results from the compact nature of modern still and video cameras, with many moving parts to the lens system which distort images. Thanks also to the fact that a flash is often necessary in buildings at night, some odd effects may appear. Small particles of dust, even raindrops or moisture in the atmosphere, can be illuminated to create out-of-focus blobs that are assumed to be supernatural.[54]

There is no doubt that the increase in efforts to record ghostly happenings is a significant factor in the number of cases that are flooding in. Another cause of ghost sightings, in several cases that I have investigated, is the accidental intrusion of jewellery in front of the camera lens. In one case, where a witness sent me a photo of a ghost light in a haunted inn at Stockport, it was soon obvious what had happened. A necklace must have dangled in front of the lens as they were shooting the room and, being so close to the camera, was recorded well out of focus on the developed picture. So the photograph revealed the room in focus but complete with an eerie chain of blurred lights hovering in shot.

NARO were also called in to troubleshoot strange images that were recorded by the security video cameras at a shopping mall near Warrington in 1991. Much investigation finally revealed the answer here. The ghostly balls of light that were moving around the deserted centre in the dead of night were in fact only present when an infra-red spot beam was being used. This projected forward from the security camera to help illuminate an area that would otherwise be pitch dark. But something was interacting with the infra-red light and causing a previously invisible object to reveal itself. The image was an insect. Risley Moss Nature Reserve was nearby and creatures from here were occasionally producing this decidedly eerie effect.

In 1999 there was a not dissimilar story that made the TV news when security cameras at a large building in Leicestershire recorded what appeared to be a spectral light floating past the camera. But this too proved to have a simple explanation. It was a combination of several of the forces at work in the cases above. Rain and leaves falling close to the camera, which also used a spot beam to illuminate, were made to seem strangely fuzzy, leading to the idea that a phantom had been recorded.

Of course, whilst we need to be aware of these lessons and seek rational answers, particularly when a witness has no other evidence, this is not the complete solution. Witnesses see – or sense – as well as film these strange lights at haunted locations. And when other equipment records the presence of some kind of energy field, it is reasonable to assume that something else is taking place.

In order to get an impression of what a typical haunting is like, here is an account told to me by Janet from Macclesfield in the southern Pennines. 'My brother and I were visiting my aunt, who lived alone in her terraced house,' she explained. 'We had knocked on her door and, receiving no answer, I peered through the sitting room window. I could see quite clearly into the room and the small kitchen opposite the window. Here I saw a 'person' who seemed to be washing clothes.'

The woman was facing away from the window and Janet assumed that it was her aunt. So she told her brother to bang harder as she was obviously busy and could not hear them. This he did. Looking back through the window to see if this had attracted their aunt's attention Janet was stunned to discover that things had altered in just a couple of seconds.

'The kitchen door was bolted from inside the sitting room and a heavy table was placed in front of the door – a precaution that I knew my aunt took when she was going out. This task could not have been achieved in the seconds that it took me to speak to my brother. Also the person who had locked the kitchen door would still be in the sitting room as the only other exit besides the kitchen was the front door where my brother was standing.'

She had a complete view of the room through the window, and it was obvious that there was nobody inside the tiny house. Utterly baffled by what she had just seen Janet and her brother went down the street and met their aunt, who was returning from a trip to the cemetery. She confirmed that nobody was at home.

This case is difficult to explain in any rational manner. There can be no doubt that nobody was in the house when Janet looked through the window and that the person she is adamant that she 'saw' was not actually in there. Janet assumed it was her aunt, but it cannot have been. The woman engaged in the washing was simply an ordinary person in slightly old-fashioned clothing. Moreover, the scene was not macabre, but a very mundane event. This is invariably what is reported in ghostly encounters. The figure seen is simply doing something totally ordinary, such as walking across a room.

In cases that I have investigated 'ghosts' have haunted rooms by doing such 'frightening' things as walking across the carpet with a bowl of soup, cooking dinner, doing the washing up and flower arranging! From this it seems pretty obvious to me what hauntings are not. They are not visits from the afterlife by some eager spectre returning to convince relatives that they 'live on' in a heaven which has a fondness for home economics! Nor are they tortured souls aiming to spook the living. Instead these stories come across as simple 'action replays' of ordinary happenings that might have occurred in real life.

We seem to be dealing with replayed scenes, in the sense that we touched upon in earlier cases. Otherwise the spirit of a ghost would surely be superimposed onto the modern scenery – because, presumably, you would not have a phantom kitchen door, table or bowl of soup. So the fact that these things were witnessed suggests that the haunting is an 'action replay' of an entire scene, either in the mind of the witness (as a form of hallucination) or as some actual time-travelling replay.

This possibility is further enhanced when we see how modern technology has become the focal point for space-age hauntings, as if the phenomenon responsible finds it easier to make its mark through interaction with new technology that uses electricity.

In one case spectral voices were picked up through a baby alarm set up to monitor a young child left alone in the nursery. The alarm transmitted whispering voices coming from the room where nobody other than the baby was present. In another incident a ghostly voice was recorded on a telephone answering machine. The strange noise imposed itself on to the tape in this Manchester house.

Another answering machine saga occurred at 2.23 a.m. on 28 November 1999 at High Green in Sheffield. The phone was not heard to ring, despite being positioned only feet away from the sleeping witness, Stephanie Nettleton. On this weird recorded message she heard the sound of galloping horses followed by an elderly woman's voice saying, 'I am lost' and 'Can you hear me?' When played the recording the next door neighbour recognized the voice as resembling that of the previous occupant of the house, who had died there a few years earlier.

BT checked the records and found that no incoming or outgoing phone call had been made at that time. They had no idea how the machine could have picked up this message.[55]

However, it is not merely audio messages such as these that appear to be recorded 'out of time' – the same is becoming true of video images. There are now several cases of dead people's faces being seen on TV screens – usually when they are not tuned to any channel. Indeed a whole cottage industry has been created involving paranormal researchers who attempt to use sophisticated video recorders in an effort to contact dead scientists in the after-life! They claim some success with a few fuzzy looking snatches of 'contact' from some heavenly laboratory presented in evidence.[56]

Spontaneous cases tend to be more interesting. For example, in 1995 there was the extraodinary case of Shaun Paterson. Killed four years earlier aged eighteen in a motoring accident, his presence was felt by his mother, Sue, around the house. She noticed a tickling sensation on her skin and interpreted this as the presence of her dead son trying to be close to her. Other evidence of odd electrical energy around the house came when the TV set kept switching channels on its own and the house lights went on and off.

Her husband Trevor took photos of Sue when she felt these 'sensations', hoping that something might appear on film. A faint misty light was visible on one occasion but in several shots there were images on the blank TV screen in the background of the room. One odd photo appeared to show Shaun's face. Another seemed to be a scene from Devon, where he had been visiting shortly before his death.

There are a growing number of these post-mortem TV 'appearances' and a whole new field of paranormal research seems to have opened up. Where it will lead is anybody's guess. Perhaps to a new reality TV series – *This is Your Afterlife!*

Monsters

There have been reports of monsters associated with the Pennine hills for thousands of years and these are no thing of the past.

At Troller's Ghyll near Appletreewick, scene of that morris troupe photo (see p.79), the Viking invaders considered the place to be haunted by the apparition of a small, squat creature (the 'troll' of the place name). This was gradually transformed over the years to become seen by medieval folk as a 'barguest' (or boggart in Lancashire, boggard and barguest in parts of Yorkshire). This apparition was of a beast whose shape was largely perceived (not seen) behind glowing red lights, which were often assumed to be eyes. The entity was thought to be shaggy-haired and foul-odoured – interestingly the same description often given by witnesses to Bigfoot or the yeti that is seen in mountain areas around the world. But Yorkshire's 'mountain beast' was smaller – more goblin-like.

As late as the 1880s a series of deaths to walkers on the moors were ascribed to the same creature. Indeed, one man, killed by unknown means in 1881, was alleged to have been discovered with strange burn marks on his body – a story curiously akin to the events that befell Zigmund Adamski ninety-nine years later. (see p.70–1) The generic name boggard (or boggart in Lancashire) is usually given to these monstrous creatures in the Pennines (a derivation of *burgh gaist* or 'borough spirit' in old English). Usually they are not ghosts or spirits in the traditional sense, being regarded as imps or demonic beasts and having the ability to change shape or to manifest out of nowhere into any form desired.

At Boggart Hole Clough, a wooded dell between Manchester and Oldham, the creature is rarely seen but heard to reflect laughter from those who play in what is now parkland. It exhibits its devilish pleasure with these sounds, which in former times would be taken out in mischievous ways on passers by through this then rural area. Tossing stones was another common form of boggart assault.

The moorland area between Sheffield and Stocksbridge has also been the focus of numerous modern day boggard-style encounters. In fact there is a road called Boggard Lane at Oughtribridge near the scene of various frightening experiences (see p.193–5), including familiar-sounding Pennine phenomena such as strange lights, replays of scenes from the past, floating apparitions and missing time.[57]

The fact that highway construction work was underway at the time when one major flap of activity occurred near Stocksbridge in 1987 is interesting, because it fits the unfolding pattern (see p.194). It has long been believed by those interested in folklore that disturbances to the ground cause evil forces to be unleashed. Scriptwriter Nigel Kneale brilliantly incorporated this idea into his 1958 BBC TV series (and later Hammer Horror movie) *Quatermass and the Pit*. Here building work at an underground railway triggered sightings of a small imp-like entity at a place long known as Hob's Lane. The name, his story argued, derived from centuries of encounters with hobgoblin creatures at this spot – and historical records showed that they were especially prolific when a new well was dug or the railway had been constructed.

And so it was in real life with the building of the Stocksbridge by-pass. This major earthworks seems to have disturbed the balance of forces. The same effect has been commonly reported by home owners when repair work or major reconstruction to an old building causes the spirits to 'become restless' – some say because the ghosts do not like the changes to their environment. But we can now see a more reasonable explanation.

Earth energies are apparently stored in the ground and are clearly associated with quarries and reservoirs, fault lines and earth tremors – all natural major disturbances to the rock. Building a new road through an area where there are these natural energies seems to be virtually inviting a new outbreak to occur.

It is also noteworthy that the boggards seen in this area

are often reported to be misty and to transform themselves into various shapes – just as the orange lights near Appletreewick become 'eyes' on a 'demon hound'. In other words, lights and shapeless mists are all that exist – the physical product of the earth energies. These are then made manifest as monsters by way of humam expectation, cultural forces, legend and suggestibility.

✷ The matted hair and shagginess of the monsters in the Pennines is a curious feature, especially as reported by witnesses on the boggy moors. A modern case was reported by Mr and Mrs Singleton who in 1995 were returning home from York to their home and were east of Shipley at about 1.30 a.m.

Passing a 'gentle hill with wide grass verges' whilst crossing the River Aire they saw a very dark 'shaggy shape' mass, well over 6 feet tall, with an extremely broad girth and without any sign of limbs or facial features. Utterly overcome with dread, Mrs Singleton saw it 'shuffle off the kerb' towards the spot they had just driven past and was filled with a strange foreboding, believing that it would be a very bad move to look directly at this monstrous form. Similar evil impressions have long been reported from boggards and are one reason why these monster sightings have long had a supernatural interpretation.[58]

Nigel Mortimer has researched the traditions of a smaller but similar creature seen in this same area, between Shipley and Ilkley. Known as the water wolf, its first encounters date to the time of the Roman conquest and it is said to be rough skinned and greyish in colour. Some reports talk of a flat, straight body but often it is formless. The entity was seen in association with bodies of water and believed to be another of the many shape-changing goblins that manifest in the Pennines. It spawned a legend that parents taught children about – not to go drink from rivers unsupervized for fear of attack by the water wolf. Nigel found a case as recent as 1909 where a young girl called Judson supposedly accidentally swallowed a water wolf at Haworth. It stayed inside her for several weeks and then leapt out of her throat and into the hearth where the fire consumed it, giving off a smell reported to be the same as bad eggs.[59]

It is certainly most interesting to compare these events with another extraordinary case in the same area, just above the village of East Morton on Ilkley Moor, in 1987. A former police officer actually took a photograph of what he saw on the slopes. This photograph certainly looks rather like one of these mythical goblins being described in these monster sightings (see p.170).

Poltergeists

Poltergeist outbreaks have much in common with the monsters and goblins just discussed. Whilst in modern times we often tend to connect these cases with visits from the afterlife you will spot interesting patterns to the stories that follow that could suggest otherwise. They may be a manifestation of the same strange energies already met operating *inside* a house rather than out on open moorland.

A good illustration from 1995 was reported to NARO. It comes from the Lancashire Pennines near Manchester (I cannot be more specific to protect the identity of the occupants of the affected house). Michelle Hickman reported how she would take her daughter to visit there and would chat to the mother whilst her daughter played with the family's own girl of similar age. Michelle also took her toddler (less than a year old) and one day she 'vanished' after crawling off unnoticed whilst the women were gossiping. As the house was a large, old structure there were plenty of places to hide so a search began for the missing child. When she was finally traced, on a low landing, she let out a shriek and stared ahead into the gloom. Michelle followed her gaze and observed a tall, dark shape that she 'sensed' to be a man.

'It was stood just behind the top of the banister . . . The figure was stationary and struck me as standing to what I estimated as being well over 6 feet tall,' she reported. 'It was also very dark, in fact almost black, which meant I was unable to distinguish any detailed features . . . Its composition was dense enough to black out the background but at the same time it failed to be as solid or "real" as a person. I also experienced an overpowering sense of intimidation, almost as though it did not want me to be in the house.'

Compare this with the encounter on the roadside near Shipley (p. 92) and you see the similarities right away. This shapeless, ghost-like monster exudes a sense of presence peculiarly common during such poltergeist attacks.

After seeing the figure Michelle screamed and fled downstairs with her child. Her friend rushed to see what was wrong but the entity had gone. However, both Michelle and her young child were emotionally disturbed by this encounter for some time afterwards.

This event led Michelle to investigate the history of the house and it proved to be most illuminating. Her friend's parents had bought it in 1967. The couple they purchased it from had only lived there for two months. They were very nervous and seemed desperate to sell on first meeting, but when asked why they had stayed so briefly in their new home – in other words what was wrong with the house – they rather lamely replied that they liked 'moving' and preferred not to settle down anywhere for long. Yet curiously they moved only a short distance to another house in the same road!

Soon after settling in with their large family, the new occupants felt decidedly uncomfortable, as if some presence was watching them all the time. It was much as though they were squatters in their own home.

During the next twenty-three years, as Michelle's friend and her family grew up in the house, countless odd things happened there which constitute a very long poltergeist outbreak ('poltergeist' being taken from the German for 'noisy spirit'). Minor events included room lights switching themselves on and off (again suggesting an electrical energy field at work). More curious were echoing footsteps in empty rooms, the way small objects kept disappearing and relocating themselves in parts of the house where nobody had put them and odd 'vibrations' that caused the house to shake inexplicably and the coat hangers in a wardrobe to rattle. Again, many of these experiences readily tie in with reports from various other kinds of phenomena that we have already met elsewhere in the Pennines.

The tall, dark shape which was seen by Michelle and her young daughter had been reported several times before they first described it (although Michelle did not know this, of course). Even strangers visiting the house had seen it, and it was always visualized in the same way.

When Michelle's friend and her husband took on the building from her parents they decided to do major reconstruction work. Predictably, this was when the new burst of psychic activity began – perhaps suggesting once more that earth energies were disturbed. Curiously the 3-year-old girl who lived in the house (and who knew nothing of the apparitions) claimed she had a 'friend' called Alec, who said he had been stabbed but came down from heaven to live in the attic and often just visited the top of the stairs!

These things proved too much for this family. In December 1995 they sold up, deciding not to tell the new occupants of their sitting tenant occupying their new home. And so, perhaps, the story may go on.

This case very much illustrates what happens with poltergeist attacks. Although the term is associated in most people's minds with outbreaks of violence where evil spirits rage or wreck furniture, this kind of aggression is not normally the main focus. Indeed poltergeists are really channels of unseen energy that move small objects, create sounds and smells and only rarely bring visual apparitions. In addition, the invisible forces that can move a chair are also known to tidy up the house. Neatly ordering shoes on the floor or coat hangers on the bed have been reported.[60]

An investigation conducted by Andy Blunn and reported by Phil Bradbury for NARO was in fact carried out on behalf of the Society for Psychical Research (SPR) to whom witnesses often report poltergeist attacks on the assumption that a 'spirit world' visitation is occurring. The witnesses were the Moor family (parents and 18-year-old daughter) from Mossley near Oldham. The presence of a teenage child is another common thread in these cases and it has provoked suspicions that the emotional angst and growing pains of that age can leak through into the house, 'priming the pump'. Indeed some poltergeist outbursts act almost like a psychic temper tantrum.

Interestingly this case was not confined to the Moors' home. Their neighbours, who shared an adjoining wall, were also ensnared by the events. Lynn had a 2-year-old daughter and she was seen looking at the wall, talking to thin air. When asked what she was doing she claimed a 'man' was standing there, but nobody else could see him. However, Mrs Moor had seen the familiar dark silhouette shape of a formless man – basically a shadow apparition.

The main poltergeist events were typical – small objects being moved, a sense of someone present but not seen, and knocking sounds in the walls. But there were also manifestations of a house-proud spook, putting small objects away in neat order. And the main outbreak of activity had occurred in January 1996, some months after the family moved in, just when the Moors started to renovate the building. At the same time, according to the NARO report, 'Lynn appears to have become prone ... to depression, emotional outbursts and fits of temper which seem to be uncharacteristic.'[61] This again suggests that the poltergeist is a combination of the people in an odd state of mind within a location that has a powerful energy field that can be disturbed.

The geophysical forces that seem to be involved in poltergeist assaults are shown very clearly in an extraordinary episode that occurred on Hill Top Close in Rochdale and was first discovered by Alicia Leigh of NARO. She, Stephen Mera and Peter Hough spent frustrating days trying to understand how, in the midst of a major drought, when local reservoirs were running dry, it was raining *inside* this Pennine bungalow!

Many hills in the Pennines have names associated with the supernatural. These were given because of age-old links with strange phenomena and the presumption that the Devil was to blame. Hob Tor in Derbyshire is one such spot, Hob – as in hobgoblin, being a demonic name

The Devil's Bolt Hole, or Eldon Hole, is accessed by winding tracks rising from the village of Sparrow Pit. In this part of the Pennines there are many caves, pot-holes and grottos where earth spirits are thought to live

At Chapel-en-le-Frith in Derbyshire the church is believed to have a 'psychic atmosphere' based on a terrible act during the Civil War when many soldiers met their death on the spot. Such 'time replays' are common in the South Pennines

The Pennine village of Peak Forest is steeped in history. There was a period when this Derbyshire location rivalled Gretna Green for the performance of instant marriages. During the eighteenth century it attracted doomed or fated lovers from all across the north

The picturesque village of Tideswell, a frequent winner of best-kept village competitions, is full of apparitions. These include a headless cow and a woman who fled from the nearby village of Eyam to Tideswell. Eyam had voluntarily sealed itself off from the world to try to stop the spread of the plague. After capture, the woman died. She now haunts the area

Ollersett Moors near Chinley are where alien big cats have most often been reported within the Pennines. In this spot between Chapel-en-le-Frith and Chinley one large cat-like creature was seen with a rabbit in 1995

Within the Pennines, rock outcrops, such as this at Peak Dale, often generate floating lights. The limestone rock here runs in a fault line alongside quartz-rich grit. It is in such locations that energy from inside the earth is believed to trigger flowing particles of plasma

At Chinley the Hope Valley railway runs past steep slopes. It was on this very embankment where the passengers left the train after the tragic crash – an event foreseen in a dream

Jenny Randles investigates the track at Walsden, West Yorkshire, where her namesake 'Jenny' had an extraordinary encounter with a glowing mass of light

The Vale of Edale is popular with hikers and balls of light have been witnessed passing low over fields here

Quarries abound within the Pennines and there is a close correlation between them and the lights, humming noises and other paranormal phenomena reported in the area. It is argued that the mining and blasting work disturbs the ground and kicks earth energies into life

The police boot of Todmorden officer Alan Godfrey following his November 1980 encounter with a glowing mass. He had no memory of how the boot was split, but under regression hypnosis later 'saw' himself being attacked by a beam of light and floating out of his patrol car

Poltergeist attacks in the Pennines are commonly linked with building work that 'disturbs the ground' and releases the 'boggart' spirit. Here, on a sandstone outcrop near Stockport in the Pennine foothills, a group of martial arts students felt the wrath of the poltergeist as it manifested in bushes by the waterfall as a floating mass. Several lost control of their senses and one was dragged from a lake where he was about to commit suicide. Major excavation work in the adjacent woods had produced a sudden 'earth tremor' – still unexplained – that was temporarily holding up completion of the building work as the poltergeist attack occurred. Only when the foundations were considered safe did work resume and the attacks come to an end

Jenny Randles surveys the location in the Calder Valley, between Todmorden and Hebden Bridge, where apparitions and time-slip visions were reported. Note the on-going building work which is often tied to bursts of activity within the window area

Investigator, Roy Sandbach, who has worked with Jenny Randles chasing many strange cases in the Pennines – including this haunted house near Burnley

Rossendale Valley witness turned hunter. Mike Sacks is surveying a witness sketch beside Ogden Reservoir at Helmshore, scene of the object seen beneath the water that terrified two fishermen

The events that plagued the Gardener family began in October 1994 when a damp patch appeared on the wall of the bedroom used by their daughter, Jeanette. Despite the local authority being called in, the house went on oozing water and no source could be found. It was not coming through the roof or from an underground river; it seemed to be emerging out of the air just like a storm. As the months progressed the 'indoor rain' became more severe, even creating rivers that ran across the ceiling from wall to wall. Back came more council workers, then electricians, all seeking answers, but as the family literally sheltered under an umbrella inside their own house nobody could explain how water was getting there, let alone find a way to stop it.

Before long the perplexed housing authority suggested, probably in despair of finding any other answer, that the Gardeners were using a hose to douse the ceiling in order to get themselves moved to a new home. Vera Gardener was furious at this suggestion, saying they had lived in the bungalow since 1980 without problem, they were very happy there and they only wanted to move as a consequence of the wet attacks.

By summer 1995 the family were thoroughly fed up. They spent day after day mopping up the water that soaked carpets and ruined bedding. Attempts by the council to reduce condensation using extractor fans also failed, even though these would cure normal levels. Jeanette switched bedrooms in the hope of escaping, but the water appeared in the new room that she adopted. The council then installed a hydrometer. This measured atmospheric water vapour levels and proved that there was a big increase in the building, but not how or why this was happening. Indeed, the long, hot weeks of baking temperatures that summer evaporated the moisture from just about every other house in Rochdale, but not Hill Top Close. It was still raining there.

The suspicion that more was going on here than anybody could guess grew when these periods of intense 'watering' were found to match outbreaks of other poltergeist effects, notably doors opening and closing and a smell of liquorice in the hall. Vera's first husband (who had died from a heart attack in the house) had smoked cigarettes rolled in liquorice paper. This 'odour' seemed to be replayed in the room, much like the sounds and sights of past events have done in other cases reported in this book.

Peter Hough reported observing the indoor rain at first hand, when water began to pour from a light fitting. He went up a ladder with a torch to investigate and said, 'The air was choking, hot and dry . . . The loft was well insulated, but the fibreglass layers were rucked up where council officials had searched for leaking pipes.' He found that the loft floor directly above this shower was bone dry. The water was not coming from above or leaking from outside through the loft. It was within the room itself.

Whilst Peter was hunting for the leak, Alicia noticed something important. The room temperature plummeted and she went ice cold just as she got soaking wet. She also observed droplets of water forming on the kitchen door in a matter of seconds. Nobody was in the kitchen and no cooking was being done. Even more oddly, Stephen then witnessed water on the ceiling almost defying gravity, as the Gardeners had said that it did, creating an instant river that rushed along the ceiling.

NARO conducted a first class investigation here. They interviewed neighbours, some of whom had seen the effects and all of whom considered the family sincere. They spoke to Michael Smith, a priest who had tried to bless the house, and had also seen the indoor rain. He was sure a poltergeist was the cause. The investigators took samples to compare with the house tap water. They photographed the effects and arranged for the Gardeners to let them stay in the house alone overnight to take measurements. Prior to this vigil on 5/6 September 1995 there had been a burst of more violent activity in the house. Scissors and even a hair dryer had been seen to levitate and fly across the room without anybody touching them.

The night of the NARO sleep-over was far from uneventful. Members of the team heard coughing and wheezing (Vera's dead husband was a chronic asthma sufferer and these sounds had often been heard in the building before his death). But most remarkably a small statuette of the goddess Themis appeared out of nowhere, standing upright on the floor as Alicia Leigh watched. Checks with the video record of the house taken at the start of the vigil so as to locate all objects proved that the statuette had not been there before. The video camera was active during this sudden 'appearance'. But for those few seconds, it was frustratingly pointing in the opposite direction!

Whatever the cause of these events they could not be blamed on the Gardener family this time, because only the NARO team were present in the house during their occurrence.

The sample of the indoor rain was tested by North West Water and the results were dramatic. In comparison with tap water from the house there was eight times the level of calcium, sixteen times the level of sodium, eighteen times the level of chloride and the water was six or seven times more conductive of electricity. So this was *not* tap water and these impurities could not have come from the water seeping through the roof and absorbing chemicals that way.[62]

Water poltergiests of this type are not uncommon. Another impressive investigation was conducted by Roman Bugaj for the SPR in 1996. This struck a house in Sosnoweic, Poland, whose location was in a geologically active region with high quartz content inside the rocks and numerous fault lines running through, very much what seems to be the basis of the many strange events in the Pennines. In Poland the indoor rain only struck when 12-year-old Arthur Matura was present. Pools of water would collect inside his house as water droplets formed around him. The SPR team even bound him with ropes to prevent trickery and still the water soaked the ceiling and poured into the room. The puzzled water authority failed to stop the downpour from happening even by cutting off the water supply to the house!

With the Matura family it seems clear that Arthur was the focus, and he was going through the emotional trauma of puberty at the time. The rain-making was briefly replaced by a series of more aggressive poltergeist events (such as lights switching on and off and household items moving about on their own). These also died down and the house returned to normal as if the energy had run its course. Most poltergeist outbreaks are similarly short-term. In Poland, as in Rochdale, temperature changes (another common feature in poltergeist cases) accompanied the indoor rain.[63]

I think we can reasonably infer here what scientific processes are occurring. These events all depend upon energy transfer. When temperatures drop heat energy is being extracted from the room and, because energy can never be destroyed except in nuclear reactions (just changed from one form into another), this lost energy reappears as kinetic forces causing objects to move.

Some 'balance' is at work between the energy within the house – perhaps related to the emissions created by the geological terrain – and the emotions of whatever person is at the focus. The water that appears during these outbreaks is presumably what Rochdale council measured through the hydrometer readings. All rain is condensation – water literally being squeezed out of the atmosphere by environmental conditions – but this was occurring *inside* the house. The balancing energies that 'draw' heat from the room must trigger this event, forcing extreme levels of water condensation to take place indoors. That these physical forces match our knowledge of atmospheric science and yet fit bizarre events reported in a paranormal context is good evidence of a real phenomenon at work.

Precognition

Time is a very strange thing – by no means just a steady progression from the past, through the present into the future. Both psychologists and physicists speculate that at the heart of the universe there is *no* time; all things simply exist in a timeless, spaceless reality.[64]

This bizarre experience reported by Mrs Shelley* from the foothills of the Pennines near Burnley, Lancashire, well illustrates how we can ill afford to take time for granted. It was summer 1990 and she awoke to find the house oddly quiet. This was unusual because she had two young sons and the area nearby was a busy estate with people and traffic active at all hours. She got out of bed to investigate what was happening. Her digital alarm clock said it was 11.22 a.m. So why was it so quiet?

Going downstairs Mrs Shelley followed her normal routine, including visiting the bathroom and examining the front door to see if a letter she was expecting had arrived but, to her disappointment, there was no post waiting for her. Tottering into the kitchen she poured herself a glass of water and then swilled it in the sink. It all seemed a perfectly ordinary few minutes – except that it wasn't.

Deciding that it was a quiet day with nothing urgent to do Mrs Shelley went back to lie on the bed. The next thing she knew her husband was rousing her from a doze, waving the expected letter in front of her bleary eyes. Perhaps the post had been late that day. Or, she asked him, 'Did we have a lunchtime delivery today?' Mr Shelley looked nonplussed. 'Lunchtime? What are you on about?' he asked. 'It's only ten past nine,' and he pointed to the digital alarm.

An interesting discussion ensued over this baffling experience because Mrs Shelley tried to persuade her husband that she must have experienced a 'time-slip', moving forward some two hours before returning to her normal timeline. But he noted a flaw. 'You could not have done. Why was the letter not on the mat at 11.22, if so?' She smiled. 'Because you had already given it to me at 9.10!'

When 11.22 a.m. really did come round, nothing strange occurred. No spectral Mrs Shelley wandered down the stairs or into the kitchen. And, in fact, there is a recognized name for this phenomenon: the false awakening. People have been known to get up, get dressed, get on the train and go to work in a recall lasting more than hour, only to wake up suddenly and find they are still in bed!

Psychologists argue that the false awakening is, in reality, an extremely vivid dream that occurs in a brief period directly after the person wakes and then immediately falls back to sleep. This happens close to the time when you would normally get up. During the moments that your consciousness was briefly alert, it apparently thinks, 'Ah, it is time to go to work' – but because you instantly go back to sleep again the routine act of getting up then only occurs during an ensuing vivid dream.

It is likely that this strange experience is the cause of a number of seemingly paranormal phenomena, including the sighting of bedroom apparitions. Even some UFO encounters that are witnessed from the bedroom in the dead of night display signs of being false awakenings. They may involve seeing a bright star or planet through the bedroom window during that brief moment of lucidity before going back to sleep and this 'event' continuing in a dream.

With Mrs Shelley's 'time-slip' she could justifiably wonder what its cause might be, because, if you have a false awakening that begins and ends in the same place (e.g. whilst you are in bed), then any experience that occurs in the 'gap' will seem real.[65] Time and consciousness weave strange spells as they somehow forge our experience of events.

We can compare these reports of strange dreamy experiences with proper time-slips – such as the ones we have already met regarding phantom aircraft over the Derbyshire peaks (see p.29–30). ⏋

In 2000 Derek Gibson from Cornwall related how he had a fascinating experience in the winter of 1983. He had visited north Manchester for a family wedding and, being unfamiliar with the area, went to the church the day beforehand in order to check it out. He was not terribly impressed, describing it as 'rather dilapidated' with 'rusty railings, very long grass and what I took to be a chapel with a square tower'.

But as he watched, the image in front of his eyes altered. Now he could observe newly painted railings, clean brick-work and a cultivated garden. Indeed, even the overcast weather had been replaced by a sunny day (surely para-normal in Manchester!). As he watched more closely he could see figures wandering about near the church, includ-ing a woman about thirty years old, wearing old-fashioned clothing, carrying a parasol and with her hair clearly not in a modern style. Various other people, equally quaintly dressed, were nearby and although they were talking they were too far away for him to hear what was said. Looking at them in bemusement he saw the scene simply vanish to be replaced by the picture that he witnessed moments before – a run-down, unmanicured church on a typically grey Pennine day. This was, in fact, what the scene was really like in 1983.

About ten minutes later Derek experienced a similar 'time shift' when he saw a block of nearby modern shops suddenly change. Now a series of wooden tables were in front with a group of poorly dressed men wearing grey flannels and flat caps sitting before what were much more spartan looking shop fronts than had been there before. Again the men were talking but their conversation was distant and muted and he could not hear what they were saying. Then, just as earlier, the scene evaporated in front of his eyes, to be replaced by modern stores and the surround-ing streets, and the noise and bustle of a busy road that passed directly in front.

Derek made several interesting observations about these time slips. He described somehow witnessing this area as it was perhaps a century earlier. He said that the scene had a flatness and dull colour, rather than the vividness of the modern world that it temporarily replaced. There was also a curious sense of 'familiarity' to what he was seeing that he could not pin down. And as the phenomenon was occur-ring he noted that all the ambient sounds were replaced by a feeling of detachment and 'unworldliness'. This sounds rather like our old friend the Oz Factor once again.[66]

There are many time slips where scenes from the past briefly 'dub over' modern reality. Often, such as in a collection gathered by Joan Forman, there is a silvery, misty 'sheen' which resembles the 'lifelessness' described here. It as if the mind superimposes an image from the subconscious about the scene many years ago and places it on top of the reality as it is right now – something like a film that is filtered on top of the proper scenery before it is snatched away again. This is not unlike the 'real life video recording' idea that we speculated about earlier and that might cause other time slips to occur.[67]

It seems improbable that Derek Gibson really visited the distant past and then returned home again on two successive occasions. More likely this was essentially a phenomenon of consciousness – rather like the false awakenings just discussed. He was seeing the past inside his mind as part of a waking dream and this was dubbed over the top of present reality to create a persuasive facsimile of the past in the form of a three-dimensional running video.

✱   Past and future intertwine. That is self-evident because in some senses a time slip into the past is also occurring forwards to the future (for the past event is interacting with *its* future). But that both past and future can somehow be detected is very clear from this extraordinary story reported by Paul Willoughby from London. It certainly intrigues me because it involves a train journey that I often take and a station that I travel from regularly, as well as a spot on a road along which I pass at least once a week.

At the time, 2 March 1986, Paul was a student in Stoke-on-Trent. He had what he calls a 'disturbing dream', in which he was standing with a group of people in an unfamiliar country road when he saw a man walking along an electric power cable as if it were a tightrope. Suddenly, the man slipped and fell, and the power shorted, electrocuting the man. A woman next to Paul sobbed hysterically, 'He's dead! He's dead!' as he, she and others were led into the country lane where there was a line of police cars and ambulances. All Paul wanted to do was find a phone to call his father, but he kept getting a busy tone.[68]

This weird dream shook Paul at the time, but he put it behind him when nothing untoward happened. Then, a week later, he went to see his father in Doncaster. After the visit, on 9 March, he returned to Stoke, catching a train from Doncaster to Sheffield, then one from Sheffield to Manchester and another one on from there to Stoke. All throughout the first leg of this trip Paul felt 'fear and sadness', but he reached Sheffield without any problems.

The train from Sheffield to Manchester proved to be the same one on which he had arrived, simply extending its journey. Paul decided to get up from his seat in the front carriage and stretch his legs. On his return he passed the relief driver entering his cab and Paul recalls feeling real sorrow as they crossed paths. Paul was about to return to his seat at the front but changed his mind and walked back from this spot immediately behind the driver, entering the third carriage instead.

The train left on time and within ten minutes was passing through Totley tunnel, which carries the Hope Valley line under the Pennines. At around 6 p.m. they reached the small Derbyshire village of Chinley, where the freight branch lines from Buxton and Dove Holes limestone quarries converge on the through-valley passenger lines. Paul's train, although slowing after a signal check, was still moving at a fair speed when there was an enormous crash and it derailed. Chaos ensued as the passengers strove to grasp what had happened. In shock and with minor injuries, Paul noticed a young woman standing nearby and how she reacted as news filtered through from the front of the train that the driver had been killed in the accident. 'He's dead!' she screamed, just as in Paul's dream seven days before.

I researched the background to this accident and the details of what happened add a remarkable new twist to Paul's 'precognition'. In fact the Sheffield to Manchester early evening express is the same train that I have travelled on several times on the way home from the city, alighting at Chinley. The day it crashed, it struck two light engine freight locomotives that were waiting for the express to pass. Such was the impact, even at only moderate speeds, that the driver's cab was smashed and he died instantly – only half an hour after Paul had passed by the man on the Sheffield platform and felt a sense of overwhelming sorrow.

Some thirty-one passengers were injured in the smash, two very badly. All the more serious injuries occurred in the leading carriage, as this bore the brunt of the collision. Totally wrecked was the seat where Paul had sat from Doncaster – the one he always used and had almost returned to but for his sudden change of mind. If he had sat there then on the trip to Manchester he would at least have been badly injured.

Paul said that the scene that greeted the shocked passengers as police and ambulances lined up along the road by the side of the track (actually the lane between Chinley and Chapel-en-le-Frith) was identical to that in his dream. Although he was virtually unhurt, he was still ferried to hospital, and his first thought (again as in the dream) was to find a phone and call his father. This he did, but he could not get through, finding it engaged as it was in his precognition. The reason for this unavailability was that his father was desperately trying to learn of his son's fate, having heard of the accident on the news.

So most of the details of Paul's dream match eerily well with his terrifying experience. And his subconscious mind, seemingly aware of what was about to happen, made him change his long-established routine that night and consequently may have saved his life. But why in his dream did the man die by walking on a power cable to be electrocuted? The only person killed in the accident was the train driver and he died in the impact. However, the underlying cause of the crash was only much later discovered. An electrical circuit had shorted, which caused a break in the signalling system at Chinley, which then malfunctioned.

The express was wrongly routed onto the track on which the two heavy locomotives sat waiting for a clear road, causing an inevitable collision. So in fact the driver *had* died as a result of an electric power cable – just indirectly. Somehow Paul's dream not only saved his life but identified the complex cause of a fatal accident a week before it happened and months ahead of the official investigation that eventually resolved the circumstances.⌐

It is worth looking at one case of precognition in more detail because the witness, from the Rossendale valley, has offered a wealth of information about her background, which explains how these time anomalies can occur during life.

Pamela Taylor* was born in the same small Pennine village where I was raised and at almost exactly the same time during the early 1950s. I left Stacksteads, which nestles in the steep valley between Rawtenstall and Bacup, just before I started school, owing to my father having a long rail commute to work each day into Manchester. Had I stayed there a little longer Pam and I would almost certainly have been in the same small village school class together. As it is we have never met, but we do share a fascination with the paranormal spawned by strange experiences that occurred in this area, now known to locals as 'UFO alley' but in the 1950s not even recognized as a window area.

Pam, who now lives elsewhere in the Pennines, has a very artistic temperament. This often seems to facilitate psychic ability. In her case it manifests as a pronounced musical talent and is also noticeable in her 'artistic' writing. There are centres of the brain which not only control human creativity and the capacity to manipulate visual images. They seem prominent in people who have visions of the future on a regular basis.

Enhanced imaging abilities may simply exist within the brains of such gifted people, since extrasensory perception (ESP) operates as a visual medium through dreams and often uses symbols and vivid images to make itself memorable. As a child Pam had a number of interesting experiences in Stacksteads. In fact her ability to relive her childhood in stunning clarity remains. A certain sight or smell will trigger a flood of images that then wash over her and almost transport her to that scene from a long ago age. This may be how what are taken to be actual journeys through time also occur. If they happen to people with an extremely strong ability to store visual images then some simple trigger could cause an association within the memory store of the brain. This then presses the right button, releases the flow of images and becomes so powerful that to the witness they seem literally to have stepped back in time. They are immersed within the recollection as if they are truly there.

Pam noted of her own suddenly triggered memory images – which she did not claim as literal time travels – that they were like a 'flash photograph' thrusting a scene from years ago into vivid reality. What is interesting is that during brain surgery, which is often done with patients at least partially conscious, it has long been known that if areas of the brain are electrically stimulated vivid flash images like this take place. They are, in fact, long-stored memories – recall of absolutely every trivial little thing that has been retained within the myriad energy cells that form the mind. Somehow the electrical charge reactivates them and they replay as if they are happening all over again.[69]

It would appear that people who tend to experience time anomalies (such as Pam) also get these flashes from time to time. This implies that a similar electrochemical process may occur within the brain to make memories more available to them than to others. Which brings us back to the idea of time slips as replayed events that are stored in some kind of electrical field within a window area. Sudden visions of a church as it was 100 years ago may just be landscape-sized versions of this same kind of memory flashback.

Time slips differ, it seems, only because they are memories being awoken with such clarity that to visually creative people they actually seem real. In a time slip the memory may apparently be of an event that you did not personally witness but that is somehow stored in the electromagnetic fabric of a location. It is just like signals encoded on the magnetic strip of a video tape that can then be replayed years later.

Stimulate the brain and we see our own past. Trigger an encoded event memory within the energy framework of a window and a time-slip vision occurs. Both happen within the brain as 'waking dreams', probably not as actual time travels into the past. Both are powerful enough to seem real. Both apparently have a kind of 'aura' surrounding them (which may be associated with the electrical stimulation that is going on in your brain). Interestingly, just as with time slip cases where sound is often not heard during the replay, so too Pam said of her flashbacks: 'Never, so far as I can remember, were these visions accompanied by the sound of the event within my memory.' This strikes me as an important clue. The brain stores sounds and visions in separate places.

Research into memory also indicates that emotional events are 'tagged' by a chemical and so are more readily stored. Indeed in March 2001 research at the University of Liverpool revealed that the brain can be trained to enhance its capacity by using such a memory tag to trigger recall of data. A 20 per cent increase was found in a series of experiments by clinical psychologists.[70]

It is surely noteworthy that time anomalies seem to have strong associated emotions. Precognitions also tend to be of events that create an impact (for instance tragedies) and time-slips like the crashing of wartime aircraft or the ghost of a condemned man seen in a building that was once a prison again fit this rule. Perhaps even with time-slips that are recorded in the electromagnetic 'atmosphere' of a window a tragic or emotive event will somehow get that added 'tagging' to make later retrieval more feasible.

At the age of twelve Pam experienced another incident that may be significant. She suddenly became aware that her mind was detached and floating at a different position to her body. This process, known as 'dissociation' is the basis of the widely experienced paranormal phenomenon of the out-of-body experience and is often found in conjunction with premonitions.[71]

Pam's dreams are also extremely vivid. She described how at one point, in 1984, after her father had died, she was in a depressed state of mind and missed his ability to help her. That night she had a long, very realistic dream in which her father returned, they talked for a couple of hours and he did indeed resolve her problems, allowing her to wake refreshed. Pam was not suggesting, as no doubt some people would, that her father' spirit visited her that night. She sees this as another example of the amazingly powerful creativity of the mind and how reality and time can be manipulated.

In 1976, during the birth of her first child, she also seems to have radiated her feelings as if they were radio waves. Her mother, who was 20 miles away and unaware of what was happening, told her that that night at 8.30, three fingers on her left hand went numb and this sensation remained for the next six hours. But there was no physical cause. These times coincided with the anaesthetic being induced via a drip into Pam's left hand and then later the drip being removed. Somehow this highly emotive, physical and sensual experience of childbirth was transmitted across time and space. It may be that paranormal experiences happen as often as they do between closely bonded people (notably mother and child, just as here) because of this emotional empathy.

Of her many precognitions, here are just a couple that Pam described to me. The first is typical of the trivial but emotionally bonding experiences that pepper examples of this phenomenon. Pam's husband was a doctor. In September 1971, soon after they got married, he started a new job. In her dream Pam saw him return with a new white coat for the job and ask her to take it up at the hem. She stared at it in the dream and said that it was already waist length. The dream ended.

Within hours of waking she related this dream to her husband, who looked at her astounded. He went out to the car, brought out a parcel and showed Pam that he had indeed just bought a new coat and he was about to ask her to shorten it because when he had tried it on in the shop it was too long. So, he commented, she got that part of the dream wrong.

Only she had not. He opened the wrapper and to his amazement found that the shop assistant must, without telling him, have swapped it for a short length jacket just like the one that Pam had seen in her dream and that did not need shortening after all.

But there can also be much more significant cases of precognition, such as this one. In midsummer 1982, with Pam's young daughter now toddling, she sat idling at the piano in a sort of daydream that seems typical of the onset of these experiences. In fact I think the Oz Factor state (where the mind detaches itself and tunes out external input) is one way of inducing this necessary 'blank slate' onto which a premonition can then be forcefully written. Here, as Pam idled at the piano keys, she was aware that her toddler was in the garden safely playing and well away from danger, but she did not really pay attention to this.

Suddenly she was swamped by a smell of bleach. 'It was just as though someone had put a bottle under my nose,' she told me. Puzzled and concerned she went to check the one bottle of bleach that she knew they had in the house. To her relief she found that it was safely sealed and locked in a high cupboard. So she went back to the piano but the powerful odour returned. Now she *knew* something was wrong.

Going outside she found her daughter dipping her fingers in a bucket at the end of the garden. It then struck Pam what had happened. A week before she had used a bleach solution in the bucket to clean the greenhouse. It was a pretty mild mixture to start with and she had used most of it in the cleaning. But it had rained heavily since then and the bleach-soaked bucket had filled with water over the past few days. This was the bucket in which her young child was now playing, completely oblivious of its contents. The solution was by now very weak; even dipping her nose into it Pam could barely detect the odour. From a long way across the length of a room and the full garden there was no way she could have smelt it. But her mind seemingly *was* aware of what was happening and made sure she took notice by conjuring up the smelly memory so forcefully that she had to act.

This is how many precognitions occur, I believe. They are replays of past images, sensual experiences or memories being used constructively by our minds to forewarn of danger. We 'see' the future but we do so by being offered images from the past.

I have records of mothers plucking children from their cots moments before a heavy shelf collapsed on to it, of a woman backing from a window seconds before a rock tossed into the air by a freak lawn mower accident shattered the glass, and many more like that. Clearly some process occurs whereby the mind can see ahead of time. It ensures that you pay attention by incorporating the images into a dream or seizing on a moment of reverie when the mind is 'blank'. Then it can prod your conscious mind via a form of powerful hallucination such as a smell of bleach or a simple urge to get out of the way. In fact what we call gut instinct is often much more than that.

Synchronicity

I am fascinated by coincidences – events that seem to occur by chance but appear so fantastic as to boggle the mind – and I am satisfied that they can indicate what we otherwise call the supernatural at work.

Synchronicity literally means the occurring together of events in time. It was coined by Carl Jung, a brilliant psychiatrist who defined the collective unconscious, and Wolfgang Pauli, a leading quantum physicist who sought the innermost workings of reality through the chaos of subatomic matter.[72]

That a psychoanalyst and a physicist should work together is strange enough. That they should do so to define what they called a 'connecting principle' that helps to put paranormal events into the context of both hard science and psychology is not far from amazing. But their idea – that coincidence underpins the fabric of reality at its basic level – was not guesswork. It is proven by repeated experiment. Deep within the structure of matter – and the essence of those electromagnetic waves that form our brains and minds – all events occur by way of laws of probability and chance.

In fact, synchronicity is the thread that weaves the universe together. Paranormal phenomena such as precognition are much like coincidence by another name. And synchronous experiences are in turn often low-level manifestations of the statistical laws that govern the universe. In a sense everyday events happen like dominoes randomly falling into meaningful order.

As a typical example, you may suddenly think, 'I wonder what has happened to old so-and-so' – a person you have not heard from in ages. Moments later the phone may ring and there will be so-and-so saying he just decided to give you a call 'on the spur of the moment'. Such things happen all the time. But what has occurred here? Did your desire to contact your friend beam out and cause him to call you? Or did his decision to phone you telepathically transmit itself across the miles as he was dialling? According to Jung and Pauli this was a synchronicity – where the statistical forces that rule the universe simply caused both events to occur separately and yet together.

It is interesting that phone calls often feature in synchronicities. Even the Sting song about this topic (a global best seller in 1983) features the line, 'A star fall – a phone call – it joins all – synchronicity.' When someone dials a phone number a series of events occur causing electrical circuits to fire in sequence and finally put us through.

If these 'trip' correctly we are connected. If they do not we get a wrong number. Synchronicity is a phenomenon that literally allows the statistical variations in events to trip in such a way as to be arranged into a meaningful coincidence. This process might well become most visible via a medium where countless connecting events are the routine, as they are with a phone call.

Certainly you might be forgiven for thinking that some weird 'connecting principle' was in force in a case from Droyslden, Lancashire, on the Pennine side of east Manchester, which occurred in 1996 to three generations of one family – Margaret, her daughter Lynne and Lynne's own daughter Gemma. They had arranged to visit the grave of Margaret's husband, the father and grandfather respectively of the two girls. He had died two years earlier. But just as they were about to leave the house the phone rang and Margaret answered to hear a man's voice say 'Hello, is Gemma there? This is her granddad.' Needless to say Margaret nearly dropped the phone in shock, but it was not her deceased husband back from the grave. It was, by 'coincidence', a man with the wrong number calling *his* grandaughter, also named Gemma. Here the dominoes fell in such a way as to create an apparent synchronicity. Perhaps it was just one of those things – except that it became *two* of those things soon after.

Margaret phoned some friends in Manchester. She spoke their name, and the man at the other end identified himself. A conversation lasting several minutes then ensued, during which they chatted about family matters without either party realising anything was amiss. Then Margaret said, 'How's your son?' to which her bemused 'friend' replied, 'I don't have a son.' Only then did it become clear to them that Margaret had another wrong number. Again the person to whom she was wrongly connected had the same name as her real friend and had a friend called Margaret who sounded sufficiently like this Margaret that the mistake was not spotted. Moreover, both her real friend and this stranger by 'chance' had wives with the same name, meaning that it did not seem odd when they had a two-minute conversation about what they both thought was the same woman!

We all get wrong numbers from time to time. Often the digits involved are similar, but there was no such confusion here. This misconnection involved the tripping circuits at the exchange that routed these calls. If you put these events together and ask what the odds are that so many coincidences could occur to make two wrong numbers seem correct, you start to see how powerful synchronicity can become.[73]

In the above case the event could be a pure fluke. After all someone always wins the lottery, despite odds of millions to one against. On the same principle millions of phone calls are made every day. Some are bound to be misdirected, and most will be quickly forgotten. Yet here the event takes on significance, because of how the call had apparent meaning. If it were a one-off incident we would be justified in accepting it as chance at work. It only seems truly odd when it happened again so soon afterward.

But if trivial events are *ordered* into a synchronicity, who orders them and why? Is God the architect of reality? Was some outside force trying to send a message (maybe Margaret's husband in the afterlife seeking to prove he was still 'out there')? Or do we do it ourselves as part of a symbiotic relationship between our mind and the cosmos? Are coincidences like waking dreams of reality that use trivial events as the symbols that paint pictures to spell out psychologically relevant patterns?

This last idea might seem fanciful but it is somewhat borne out by the many coincidences that occur. For example, in one case I can personally vouch for (since it happened to me) we can see 'creativity' at work. I was walking down the street, desperate to remember the name of my last family doctor before we moved house. Try as I might I could not do so – except that I knew it was an 'odd' name. But I needed it to fill in a form.

I might have 'slept on the problem' and, according to

psychologists, could have resolved the matter through a dream. In that dream my mind, which subconsciously knew the answer, of course, would create an image powerful enough to make me take notice upon waking (if the doctor was called Snow, for example, then I might have dreamt of a blizzard). There are many cases of this happening. The chemist Kekule, for example, dreamed of coiled snakes as he wrestled with the structure of a complex molecule – only to awake and realize that his dream had solved the problem for him with this image.

As I strove to recall my doctor's name I was in a street on a run-down Merseyside estate and it was the middle of the day, but I believe that my subconscious acted much as it would have done in a dream and shuffled reality in order to guide me to the truth. All I can say is that I was suddenly overcome with a completely weird sense of certainty. I just 'knew' in a feeling that came out of nowhere that if I 'let go' and did what my subconscious was telling me I would find the answer. It was one of the most eerie feelings I have ever had but it was not at all frightening. I succumbed to the certainty and walked across the street, letting my feet take me into a building. It was a library. I had no intention of going there or any idea what to do when I entered. I just walked towards the desk and within seconds saw the first woman in the queue put a book on the check out counter. The name of the author was Pattinson. Instantly I remembered that my doctor had been called Pattiniot.

I smiled, not even surprised, and left. I had been spared the task of trying to find the name of the doctor. But how? By this incredible two or three minutes in which I seemed to be 'led' towards the answer to a hardly earth-shattering question. It is very much as if my subconscious mind somehow tripped the fall of the dominoes that led me to take a whole series of little decisions and experience a sequence of seemingly random events in such a way that I *made* reality happen in a suitably appropriate fashion.

One type of synchronicity is even harder to comprehend – when the coincidence just seems to happen without meaning at all. It is as if reality is literally gathering into extraordinary patterns just for the sake of it. Here is an illustration that depended on three intriguing close encounters spread over several thousand miles but all occurring on one weekend in December 1980. Two are very famous, but one much less so. Being in the Pennines it links these others together by a seemingly extraordinary synchronicity.

Perhaps the best known case struck in Rendlesham Forest, Suffolk, a pine wood near Ipswich. Various strange lights were seen between 26 and 29 December, involving a glowing conical object that descended from the sky amidst a fiery aura and was witnessed by people driving through the forest as well as a military patrol from the nearby US Air Force base. Several witnesses, at 9 p.m. on 29 December described the arrival of the object saying that it had a faint fluorescent lime green colour.[74]

On the same night, and at the same local time (just after 9 p.m.) another major case occurred, 5,000 miles away in Texas. Again it involved a pine wood, this time near Huffman, and three people in a car (including the young grandson of one of two women). On this occasion a huge fiery mass descended from the sky and hovered low over the road. It spewed out heat and radiation, leaving the witnesses physically ill and the eldest women hospitalized for some weeks, during which she almost died. Her hair fell out in clumps and she developed blisters on her skin.[75]

Two events, both in forests, separated by the Atlantic Ocean but occurring on the same date at the same local time. And they are linked together by a third case, making a triangle of oddities, which interests us most specifically because it took place in the Pennine window.

At 9 p.m. (again) on 29 December 1980 Robert Harrison* was driving home to south Cheshire on the A523 Macclesfield to Leek road. His young son was travelling with him, and his wife and other son were immediately behind in a second car. They had just arrived at a part of the road that passes a canal, some reservoirs and a road rising steeply to the east towards Macclesfield Forest. Suddenly,

117

in the south east, over a quarry, appeared a fiery glow. It vanished for a few moments as the road snaked around, but spotting a lay-by Robert stopped and watched as the dome-like object hovered above the hill near Wildboarclough. Getting out and climbing the hill slope for a better view he watched as the craft moved slowly and silently across the road to the west. He reported that it was moving so slowly it seemed as though it would fall out of the sky. As it headed away the perspective did not alter, indicating, Robert believed, that it had a circular profile. When it was closest, a faint low noise was heard.

Robert called me and I suggested it might be an aircraft heading into Manchester (these are often the cause of UFO sightings in this area). But living locally Robert watched aircraft frequently passing this area and said this was completely different.

Exactly twelve hours later, at about 9 a.m. on 30 December, Robert was driving at the same spot, heading into Macclesfield, when he saw a similar object, this time glowing metallic in the daylight. It rose from a field to the west and crossed the road before descending over the reservoir. If you take time zones into account, these four sightings (in Suffolk, Texas and the two in Cheshire) spread evenly at six-hourly intervals. And all four were at 9 o'clock locally. But the coincidences do not end here, nor with the links with forests in each case. There is an extraordinary connection between place names too.

At Huffman, Texas, the sighting occurred on a road leading to a small place called Eastgate. In Cheshire both objects were seen to move in a line towards a place called Warren and above a place called Lyme Green. And in the Rendlesham Forest case a lime green object was witnessed and the only witness to have written his story into a book was a man called Warren. His sighting began at the military patrol point in the forest known as East Gate. Indeed Larry Warren's personal account appears in a book he called *Left at East Gate* – linking these cases together in quite bizarre fashion.[76]

UFOs

If there is one thing for which the Pennine triangle is well known it is sightings of UFOs. Indeed, the most active zone, between the Rossendale Valley in Lancashire and the Calder Valley in West Yorkshire, is called 'UFO Alley' by the locals because of the massive number of sightings that have taken place in this moorland region for many years.

A small Scottish community called Bonnybridge has been pursuing the 'diplomatic coup' of twinning themselves with that most famous of UFO centres, Roswell in New Mexico. And whilst Bonnybridge is a window area, in the sense of recent activity at least, and its idea to create a UFO theme park there is fun, it is not the same kind of window as is the Pennines. In fact Bacup and Todmorden would probably be well advised to apply to twin themselves with the Outer Limits!

However, there are sincere moves in Rossendale to take advantage of its location. Local businessman Roger Markham is keen to revitalize the once thriving cotton and shoe-manufacturing town of Bacup. He sees Bacup's position at the heart of UFO activity in the Pennines as an opportunity. He has begun an initiative – not to create a tacky 'UFO Land' gimmicky attraction, but to try to set up a research, resource and information centre that could become a home of serious interest. Such a place could host a museum, a conference centre, an observatory, informative exhibitions, and a reference library, for example, putting Bacup on the map as *the* place to do UFO research, with the added bonus that being right within a UFO hot spot you have a very good chance of seeing something whilst staying there. This sensible approach is a step up from building 'big green men' rollercoasters.

Although genuinely curious things are going on in Rossendale, it is also home to a particular kind of IFO (*identified* flying object). Since 95 per cent of all reported UFO sightings are resolved in mundane terms it is important to look at at least one case where investigation has revealed the truth.

On the evening of 2 December 1983 two 12-year-old girls were grooming horses that they had just been riding, before setting off to walk down the hillside to their homes on a Bacup estate. Suddenly they saw what they described as flashing white and red lights and an eerie glow behind them – all coming at them low across the misty sky. Fearing this thing was about to crash into them they actually leapt to the ground in an instinctive response. The horses also panicked as the glowing lights glided in silence over their heads, moving away southwards towards Bury.

Two days later, at a similar time in the evening, a white glow with a red light was seen heading south over the town by a local man. And then it returned on 6 December as a farmer saw something similar. Together the three reports formed a pattern suggesting that something strange was taking place. The Manchester UFO group NARO sent an investigator to find out.

Armed with a suspicion as to the cause we set up a monitoring operation that even involved putting an investigator into the radar control room at Manchester Airport. In this way we tracked the UFO; it was a cargo aircraft heading from Scotland to Manchester. The jet belonged to an airline with a red colour scheme and its flight crew were, on certain nights, throttling back the engines over what they thought was an uninhabited moor, and practically gliding for a few miles. This caused them to lose altitude (they were naturally descending by this point anyhow) and to be almost silent. They also dimmed the lights, making only the illuminated tail fin prominent – hence an eerie red glow appeared. Eventually, when the lights of houses around Bury came into view they throttled back up and accelerated away, having enjoyed a nice view of the sky in the meantime!

'Gliding' cargo planes were creating a mini-wave over Rossendale. It is not surprising that local residents were scared by the ghostly red object swooping down with the sound of rushing air. It was quite remarkable that this practice was occurring just outside such a densely populated area. But we trapped the culprit by catching it on radar (where a NARO member sat watching the screens even as the UFO flew by).

If this story sounds a little familiar, then that is probably because you have seen it dramatised on TV. The popular series *Heartbeat* (set in North Yorkshire during the 1960s) built an episode around the famous abduction of a Todmorden police officer 'UFO Alley' (see p.51–2). In 1999 they did another featuring a reconstruction of the NARO investigation. On the TV show a retired police officer solved the riddle of a swooping UFO that was frightening farmers around the fictional town of Aidensfield – perhaps the oddest recognition there has ever been for the work of a UFO investigator!

Moving a little further north to Settle in Yorkshire a report from bus driver Walter Burgess described a different kind of UFO – of the sort that is rather more difficult to resolve.

It was a day in July 1960 and he had driven through the Yorkshire Dales from Kendal in Cumbria towards Leeds. At about 6 a.m. on this bright summer's morning, after passing Clapham, he saw what he terms 'a large chain of circles hanging very high in the sky'. Walter stopped the bus and urged his passengers (about fifteen of them) to get out and see 'something wonderful'. They were entranced at the thing they watched in the fine blue sky.

Walter likened the object to a watch with a dangling chain. The circle was a deep gold and the twelve smaller circles hanging beneath it were yellow. The sun was back-lighting them and so probably creating the colours. Each ring had a hollow centre and the whole thing hovered motionless throughout the entire observation before they had to continue their journey south.

During the sighting Walter and several passengers all felt 'inspired', as if this were a 'spiritual experience'. He also claimed that there was a warm fuzzy sensation and that 'time was somehow different' as they watched. In fact 'time seemed to stand still'.

These, of course, are symptoms of the Oz Factor, such as we have met in Pennine cases several times already. They suggest an altered state of consciousness at work – but how could it be instilled into a whole busload of people?

Walter considered various possibilites, such as spiralling smoke rings caused by an aircraft vapour trail. But he had flown planes before becoming a bus driver and was sure that this was not such an effect. He claims this chain was a solid, constructed object of some kind, not a vapour trail. And it did not dissipate as such vapour would do. It appears to have been some sort of weird natural phenomenon, perhaps even a rare optical effect triggered by the sunrise. It demonstrates that some UFO cases are what we call UAP (unidentified atmospheric phenomena) and might well extend our knowledge of the wonders of nature rather than tell us anything about little green men.[77]

Most people think of UFOs not as weird atmospheric glows (although most sightings are of that ilk) but as strange aerial craft seemingly flown by another intelligence. This next case is no misperception. Nor is it any kind of atmospheric effect. In fact, to be honest, it is one of those UFOs that defies categorization altogether.

Eric wrote to me – 'against the wishes of my wife who says I should just forget it'. He had been a skilled trades-man until his retirement, initially an aircraft engineer working on servicing RAF bombers. He then spent many years as an electrical engineer keeping power stations operating. In April 1975 he was crossing a now disused railway line at Adswood where the bridge and rusting track still stood. To his right was a familiar geological feature in Pennine cases – a large quarry excavating clay for brick manufacture. Ahead were the Pennine foothills that surround Stockport.

It was early evening and there should have been some traffic, but a deathly silence had descended. This may have been the Oz Factor, because not only could Eric 'hear a pin drop', but there were no people, birds or cars around at all during the entire incident. Suddenly he saw, 'a little to my left and about 3 or 4 feet above me' what he called a 'brilliant green streak of light getting gradually wider as it passed'. The thing had come from the west along the railway track and above the bridge parapet and was now hovering right in front of him – so close that he could practically touch it. He was stunned by the precision engineering displayed by this object.

He described the device as clearly some kind of machine. It had a smooth, black lozenge shape without any sign of doors or windows. The green light was a glow coming from within through a shutter like an eyelid, which seemed to have opened up gradually as it passed by. After a few seconds the 'eye' had opened fully, revealing a fluorescent green glow. He said that the full 'eye' – which was several inches across – had the feel of an early TV screen from the 1950s about the way it glowed. Staring at it and realizing it was only just out of his grasp he could not help thinking that it resembled some fantastic hovering camera, but with such futuristic capabilities and amazing appearance that he was utterly bemused as to its origin.

After about ten seconds, during which the 'eye' remained wide open it began to close again, narrowing the green screen to a slit. As soon as it had closed completely – suggesting that observing Eric was its main agenda – 'the object left the scene with the speed of a bullet'.

By far the most puzzling feature to Eric was that, despite the close proximity and obvious moving parts, not to mention the object's instant 'braking' motion and hover capability, there was not the slightest whisper of sound. He had no idea what kind of technology could do that. The thing headed out towards the south Pennines and next day at work a woman took Eric's wife to one side and reported that she and her husband had seen something odd at about the same time. They had gone up into the hills between Macclesfield and Bollington to visit a favourite country pub when they had observed a glowing disc hovering over adjacent fields. It then shot away at great speed. If you plot the course taken by the flying camera after Adswood it was heading for Bollington.[78]

The next case is an interesting example of a 'vehicle inter-ference' encounter. Usually, as in the 'car stop' event in the foothills of Pendle Hill (see p.35–6) this means that the vehi-cle is impeded in some way; many such cases are on record.[79] But there are several cases where the reverse effect seems true – the car is effectively 'powered up' by the UFO.

In this particular incident, the location may also be important. It occurred only a few miles south across the moors from where the 'watch in the sky' episode had been reported. And it also happened looking eastwards straight towards Pendle Hill – scene of the car stop case. But rather than on the Nelson side of the witches' hill, this incident occurred on Waddington Fell, to the west of the slopes.

Alison Hampson* was returning from a party in the village of Newton-in-Bowland, which sits on the moors to the north-west of Clitheroe. It was 12.40 a.m. on 12 January 1992. As she reported, 'Everything was covered in a thick frost and extremely cold, but fortunately the (very hilly) road was well gritted.' On the moors as she headed south-east she saw a 'big blue star' – a glow that hovered extremely low and bright ahead of and to her right. She thought it might be a Russian spy plane, but suddenly noticed that her car was behaving oddly. 'I had a terrific surge of power.' Her engine swelled and 'my car lights became brilliant so that it looked just like broad daylight. I also felt as if it wasn't me who was driving the car. This effect carried on until I reached the edge of the village [Waddington] and everything then returned to normal and remained that way until I got home.' The big blue light had also now disappeared.

Alison was at the time taking university courses in psychology and law and had a close relative in the highway patrol section of the Lancashire police. The next day she took the car and asked him for an explanation as to what had just happened. He could offer none. Her car was a previously (and subsequently) very reliable Volkswagen.

Sometimes UFO cases just seem to defy any attempt to find solutions, even in terms of weird earth energies. When witnesses have what we call a 'close encounter', as in the next incident, it can be very puzzling indeed. It took place in another of those areas that is 'special' – to the north and west of Bradford in Yorkshire. It was mid-evening on 28 January 1985 and Mrs Castleton* was walking her dog on its regular exercise in fields at Allerton. Whilst it was sniffing (unaffected by anything) she observed a white light and a red light in the sky. They were next to one another and she tried to decide what these 'stars' were (they may, in fact, have been the planets Venus and Mars, as these were both bright at the time).

Having now focused on the sky Mrs Castleton realized that something else was up there. It was very big and dark and it was stealthily moving towards her. It was very low above the fields, about the size of a house, and resembled a saucer with a slight cupola on top and a flat base. Across the middle was a line of square windows from which a red glow emerged. Utterly amazed Mrs Castleton took off her woolly hat and could just hear a faint noise as the object approached. It was a combination of a whizzing and a whirring – nothing like the sound of the aircraft she had often seen. It appeared to be linked to the rotation of the object, which was very slow and deliberate.

As she stared, literally open mouthed, at this amazing sight, she realized that something else rather odd was happening. There was a total silence – all birds had stopped singing and traffic on the passing road had ceased. The world had seemingly come to a standstill. Indeed time smudged into one long blur and she felt a total calmness, the like of which she had not experienced before – the Oz Factor again.

After some time the speed of rotation of the disc increased and the object moved away to the north (towards Ilkley Moor). About a minute later it was swallowed up by the darkness, leaving her with a long battle to try to understand what she had just seen – a quest that was never to be resolved. The dog was later reluctant to go 'walkies' in this same area![80]

Let us return to Rossendale and a first-hand account of what it is like to come face to face with the impossible on the moors late at night. The witness was a local tailor from Stacksteads, Mike Sacks. He and his wife had already had a remarkable encounter on 24 February 1979 – a date that must go down in Pennine legend (see p.225–9). Mike spoke to me literally as he was watching the UFO, having obtained my number from a science observatory. Although we came from the same village I had left Stacksteads as a child so we had never met. But we have stayed in touch since then and Mike has always impressed me as a completely sincere witness whose testimony is beyond reproach and who clearly saw something that I cannot explain.

Following the initial sighting, during which Mike's account was backed up by four independent witnesses, including two Bacup police officers, the life of this ordinary family man was altered for ever – he had witnessed something beyond his comprehension but had no way to prove it to anybody. So he made up his mind to stalk the moors in search of that proof. He joined forces with his brother, Ray, who had just missed seeing the February UFO, and a photographer with the local newspaper who had become equally convinced by all the strange events in 'UFO Alley' that were being reported.

After weeks of frustration wandering the hills around Rossendale in the early hours (and seeing lots of stars, meteors and passing aircraft) their perseverance paid off on the night of 19 May 1979 – or, at least, to a degree it did. It had been a miserable night, with spring rain, but they stuck it out and were rewarded when the weather cleared at 1 a.m. Indeed it is surprising how often this is a factor in UFO sightings (some researchers speculate that the change in barometric pressure accompanying the passage of a weather front system might be a trigger). At 2.27 a.m. on the moors to the south of Stacksteads the momentous event occurred. Mike, Ray and John were debating whether to go home and get some sleep when Ray said, 'What the heck is that sound?'

Mike said, 'We were all immediately aware of it. The sound was a muted whining-whirring howl. We all turned around and looked upwards. The noise was being emitted by a brilliant light descending vertically.' It was 'like a lift out of control', Mike told me later. As the thing fell, causing them to edge away in fear of an impact, the event took an even stranger turn. 'As it revolved the brilliant light extinguished and as it did so the howl changed to a high pitched hum descending in tone as [the thing] rapidly eased its descent. It stopped virtually above us.' It was now silent, and they were looking right up to the underside of a massive structured object so low down and close that they could probably have hit it with a stone.

Mike is a visually creative person with artistic flair and some interesting psychic experiences (as a child he was saved by a sudden intuition from getting caught in a flash flood that swamped the spot where he was standing). He has drawn the object that the three of them witnessed in stunning detail.

He described the UFO clearly:

It had three sections – dome, midsection and rim .... Electric blue light was displaying on [the dome] from a gap or well all around ... Two appendages were clearly visible jutting out below the dome at 45 degrees and angled back ... The underside was concave with [many] multicoloured lights. I couldn't try to explain them but what could easily be seen were triangular pads (about 3 feet by 3 feet and approximately 2 feet deep). Set above these were rectangular pads slightly smaller. On the inner perimeter were glowing orange rectangular things spaced evenly around the underside.

So close did this thing hover that the three men had no problem defining its size (35 feet by 18 feet deep) or seeing that 'the flange was translucent. It looked like dullish aluminium but light could easily be seen shining from within.' After hovering there, simply observing them, the object then just seemed to tire of the game and accelerated away from a standing start – increasing speed and hugging a little gulley created by a mountain stream. It vanished over the hills and was gone, leaving three stupefied witnesses who had just seen something that could not possibly be explained away to their satisfaction.

John, the newspaper photographer, aware of the amazing opportunity, was busily snapping away with his professional expertise as they stood below the object. At this proximity he was the luckiest photographer in the world. He took twelve shots of the hovering UFO – pictures that ought to have changed the world. But they did not. Despite the fact that he processed them himself and all the other pictures on the roll came out perfectly, these twelve revealed only complete darkness. The UFO that they had all so clearly witnessed simply was not on the photographs.

Some will scoff, saying this must be fiction. If the UFO was visible to their eyes then it should have been captured on film. But knowing Mike I have no reason to question his testimony. And it brings us to the heart of the entire UFO mystery. Did these three men see a real craft that you or I might also have witnessed? Why did others in the valley not see it as well? How could something that was really there fail to appear on film? Was this some extraordinary kind of visionary phenomenon – real inside the mind but not in the outside world – rather in the way that time-slips may be? Was this a time-slip vision not of a past scene such as an old church but of a craft from our own future?

We can speculate endlessly, but we cannot know. All we can do is feel the intense frustration expressed by Mike after this sighting when he said: 'If only I could make you believe what I saw. It was there. I know it. There is not the slightest bit of doubt whatsoever. UFOs are real. UFOs are solid, physical craft. Nobody could possibly convince me otherwise after what I saw that night. It is just terrible *knowing* this and yet being unable to prove it.'

I am sure hundreds of other Pennine witnesses would echo these sentiments.

X Files

Some cases from the Pennine window just do not fit into any obvious category. They are like the 'X files' of the TV series.

For example, in the early hours of 9 November 1984 the people living on East Crescent in Accrington, to the south of Pendle Hill, found themselves the subject of an unusual bombardment. There have been cases of rock-throwing poltergeists in this area across the centuries, and stones, bits of iron, even coins have from time to time been reported as crashing onto the rooftops of affected houses. But this night the people of Accrington faced a new hazard – falling fruit. The apples – all apparently of good quality and edible – came descending from the air without any visible source.

Derek and Adrienne Haythornwhite described how they were awoken by what sounded like giant hailstones hitting their roof but on going outside they were amazed to see full grown cox and bramley apples falling onto the lawn, the hedgerows – in fact everywhere within sight. Although they clearly came from above there was no sign of how this was happening. One might think of apples being blown from nearby trees, but that could not explain the sheer quantity or their fall onto an area without trees. They did consider that it was cargo falling from a jet but this theory was discarded when the shower went on . . . and on. Any hoax would also involve remarkably persistent (and rich!) vandal, as the blitz lasted over an hour. Next morning, in fact, apples were found across several gardens and over 300 were eventually counted.

The aircraft theory for these bizarre rains has long been popular, since it seems well suited to the most common form of falling debris – the ice bomb. It is easy to image that when a gigantic glob of smelly frozen water falls on you from above it has originated from either the waste system of an aircraft or the wings when de-icing equipment has malfunctioned. In fact, this explanation does sometimes apply. Between 1987 and 1994 I lived directly under the flightpath into the very busy Manchester airport that crosses southern Stockport. During that time two cases happened within less than a mile of me. In one incident a huge mass of discoloured ice fell onto a garden in Edgeley (seconds before the aircraft that was blamed flew over my head!). Luckily the ice struck nobody on the ground but a young child in the family had a narrow escape as it fell near their garden swing. Whilst it seems likely that this *was* an accidental drop from an aircraft that was never proven.

Another disturbing incident occurred on 22 April 2001 when Steve Barton returned to his home at Glossop in the Derbyshire Pennines. An 18-inch wide crater was dug in his garden by a huge block of ice that smashed there. A neighbour saw it fall just after an aircraft passed low overhead and retained a fist-sized chunk in his freezer. Steve was shocked, saying: 'There's no doubt that if it had hit someone on the head it would have killed them.' And the Civil Aviation Authority at Manchester Airport confirmed that about thirty ice falls per year are reported in the UK and they always try to trace the culprit aircraft, but only sometimes can they prove a connection with a faulty system on board. Living near an airport can have dangers that your insurance brokers might like to know about!

But ice bombs cannot be blamed entirely on the aviation industry. In fact the number of instances where a connection has been proved is small. Most often something else seems to be going on. We know that has to be the case at least part of the time for one pretty devastating reason: the same type of incident happened before the aeroplane was invented! In May 1889, for example, there were several recorded cases of these huge blobs of ice falling from clear summer skies on to the UK and at that time they could definitely not be ascribed to man-made aerial craft.[81]

A fall worth noting in the Pennines occurred at Broughton Copy Farm, at Skipton, Yorkshire, on 26 May 1984. Owner John Taylor saw it and had a lucky escape. He was walking his fields when he heard a noise like rushing wind. As it grew louder he stopped and looked around to see something smash into the grass a little way behind him. It was a large beach-ball-sized mass of dark blue ice that had caused a small impact crater. As he touched it the outer bits crumbled away releasing a 'chemical' smell. He called the police but by the time they arrived the warm weather had melted the ice bomb.

Although we cannot eliminate an aircraft in this case, it has more than a passing similarity to an amazing chance event in West Didsbury, Manchester on 2 April 1973. Then an enormous ice bomb fell on to Burton Road near the River Mersey, just 10 feet from a man who was then walking past. The man was Dr Richard Griffiths, a research scientist at the local university.

Aware of the unique opportunity given to him by fate Dr Griffiths collected a large sample, preserved it in his freezer and was able to analyse the lump at work. This revealed that it was not detritus from a plane. The mass had formed from atmospheric water and gathered layers around itself as it fell a very long way through the bitter cold skies. Hailstones do this, but their size is limited by the distance they fall, giving less time to 'grow'. The Manchester ice bomb had gathered fifty-one separate layers and seemed to have fallen virtually right through the atmosphere to take on this jumbo form.

Thankfully most ice bombs fall harmlessly to earth well away from people, but if a lump this size hit your roof then it would smash right through it. There are plenty of cases of ceilings being demolished in ordinary homes and of the ice even falling right through to the floor. Only one man – a roof worker in Switzerland, is a possible victim of an ice bomb strike. This is not known for certain because he did not survive to describe his experience after the ice bomb, which fell like a spear, skewered him to the roof.

Dr Griffiths's close encounter suggests that the ice bombs might fall right through the atmosphere from space. US researcher Louis Frank has gathered further evidence for this. He has spent a decade using images from orbital satellites showing ice bombs. There are signs of frequent impacts to the upper atmosphere. He believes these tiny comets, as miniature iceballs, strike the earth at a rate of thousands per day. Most evaporate due to frictional heat, but some fall all the way to earth, gathering protective layers. A few reach the ground to form ice bombs, and if they strike near populated areas they produce these reports.[82]

But although these attempts to explain falling objects in scientific terms are sensible and often persuasive they cannot be the full answer to what is going on, as the following case proves. Fred Swindon, an industrial officer in Sheffield, was about to drive to work on the morning of 23 February 1981 when he found something odd scattered on the driveway of his Stainborough home. It was a small shoal of fish that had very recently dropped from the sky – falling onto his car. There were too many to have been dropped by an overflying bird, but no other obvious explanation could be found. The fish were about 3 inches long but were not surrounded by water or wet themselves, and so nobody had simply put the fish on the drive as a joke. This would have left some evidence, given that the fall was *very* recent.

After he left for work, Fred was amazed to find another of the same fish flopping on his bonnet. It must have been lodged unseen on the front of the car and been disturbed by the wind as he drove off. It was alive, like the others, and he managed to keep it by putting it into his windscreen wiper water bottle. The fish appeared to be local, probably from a nearby river. But how had they dropped from the sky in this way?

Curiously, falling small animals are not much rarer than ice bombs. Fish are common, as are crabs, frogs and even more bizarre things like worms. Again such things have been reported throughout history (some Greek and Roman scholars recorded them and the fall of 'manna' in the Bible is backed by a number of historically verified tales of similar falls of organic 'goo'). The writings of journalist Charles Fort, who collected such oddities from the late nineteenth and early twentieth centuries, are full of falling items.[83]

The most commonly argued explanation for these events is that they occur as a result of an atmospheric vortex akin to a whirlwind. This creates a small zone of low gravity that 'sucks up' small creatures and carries them aloft a short distance before depositing them to earth. This makes sense of the fact that relatively small things are always involved in these cases. You do not get cats and dogs raining down, presumably because they are too heavy to be carried upwards by these forces. What remains uncertain is whether this is simply an ordinary whirlwind, such as can form in certain weather conditions and cause grass and hay to rise up gently, or something more complex.

From time to time there have been red and yellow rains falling over parts of Britain, coating everything in their path with a sandy deposit. When analysed it has indeed been found to be sand – all the way from the Sahara desert. It is sucked up by an atmospheric vortex and then dropped 2,000 miles away after drifting across Europe for several days.

That animals could travel long distances in such a whirlwind and survive the fall to earth alive seems harder to understand. But some of the frog falls recorded, for example, have been of species that could only originate thousands of miles from where they drop. How does this happen?

There have been many fanciful theories to try to account for such events. One enduring idea is that some kind of vortex can literally 'warp' time and space as a side effect of the electromagnetic energy that it generates. Things like fish and frogs may then be 'teleported' from the point where they contact this field, moving 'instantly' to the location where they are found – therefore being still alive. Was this what moved the cows in Todmorden in 1980? The rotating dome that PC Godfrey saw on the road caused the trees to shake and blow-dried the wet tarmac in a spiral pattern, suggesting that it might be.

There are numerous cases on record of what I call 'time

storms' in which human witnesses describe encountering glowing energy clouds as they drive on a lonely road and then being pulled up in a gravity-free environment to be deposited elsewhere after apparently moving through time or space. These appear to be some kind of natural energy fields that occur at certain locations and these locations often seem to be window areas where other evidence for these fields is widespread.[84] Dr Griffiths, for example, described the presence of localized atmospheric electricity that resulted in one single and enormous burst of energy immediately before the ice bomb fell near to him.

There are cases where a fantastic energy field in the Pennines may not only have been seen – as lights in the sky, discharges from the ground glowing balls with sparks emerging but also felt by witnesses as sensations. We might now have to contemplate even odder explanations such as teleportation and time distortion.

There is another group of cases that seems to suggest that this energy field can even be heard by some people. You will have noted how UFO witnesses often report a faint sound like air whining or a humming or buzzing. Indeed likening a UFO to the buzzing of bees on the distant breeze is one of the most common descriptions. Whilst to some researchers this appears to be a clue about the propulsion system of an alien craft, others suggest that it reveals the energy field that flows within the Pennine window.

In fact the humming/buzzing sound has long been regarded as a phenomenon in its own right. When there was an outbreak of reports of such sounds in south Manchester during the late nineteenth century the term 'hummadruz' was coined to describe its humming, buzzing, droning resonance.

Research suggests a number of important features about this sound. It is very persistent and can really upset people who are sensitive, while others nearby often do not hear it. This suggests that it is something that affects some people more than others. As we have seen, witnesses to the supernatural phenomena that occur regularly in the Pennines do commonly have a gift for visual creativity. Modern brain mapping reveals that these abilities depend upon specific areas being active. So it is possible that such people sense or hear the phenomenon because it stimulates the electrical circuits of their brain.

Maurice Giffen, whose daily environmental patrol caused him to monitor the Welsh mountains, was the first man to map locations of the hummadruz. His observations do bear out reports from the Pennines. The phenomenon is common on high ground, most often occurs on calm, dry days (the very same kind of weather that tends to produce atmospheric vortices) and it seems linked to local geology. In the Pennines there have also been a number of reports of the hum occurring 'raw', without other supernatural consequences, that fit this pattern.[85]

There were reports of a buzzing noise in the air above Poole's Cavern, a geological feature of Buxton, Derbyshire, in August 1997. Indeed the couple visiting the site who heard it clearly spent a while looking forlornly for the nest of a thousand wasps which they assumed must have been the cause.

Another report, again from Derbyshire, came from Winster. Brenda Ray described hearing the sound in the southern Pennines as long ago as the late 1960s. At Robin Hood's Stride in the Dark Peak region she heard the sound build up gradually over several hours. It was, she said, 'as if the hillside itself was vibrating ... a pleasant humming, like an orchestra tuning up but on one note'.

Brenda suggested that this might be a geological phenomenon – a resonance within the crystalline structure of the rocks – as these seem to be present in areas where the hum is at its strongest. This interesting speculation matches the arguments we have already noted that rocks put under strain at window area sites can squeeze out electrical signals from their crystal structure and ooze into the atmosphere. Perhaps these signals give off an electrical buzzing noise – much like transformers and power lines.

It is also worth noting how these sounds are often heard

at sites renowned for thousands of years as 'holy' and special – quite possibly because even ancient man was aware of these bursts of activity.

Strange buzzing noises generated by the energy fields within a window area are innocuous enough. Even balls of light that render people unconscious are not permanently threatening. But if there are concentrations of power that create floating earthlights and electrical discharges that earth into mountains or people inside a window area, can these prove deadly?

They may do, for there is some suggestion of a relationship between the Pennine window and a frightening supernatural phenomenon known as SHC – spontaneous human combustion. I have researched this mysterious effect and there are now about 200 recorded cases where people allegedly 'burst into flames' and are literally consumed to ash through no apparent cause. Police, fire officers and coroners have documented them. In these cases there are often hints of powerful electrical forces surrounding a victim and possibly entering the body itself. The fire may just be a freak (and very rare) consequence of this energy build-up, causing the combustible gases within the body to erupt like a spark inside a room filled with flammable gas.[86]

Although SHC is a seemingly random phenomenon and rare enough for data to provide few meaningful statistics, here is one that is curious. There was a major wave of close encounters in the Pennines during 1980 (especially between June and December), and three of the eleven globally recorded instances of SHC in 1980 come from the Pennines.

On 4 March fire officers at Chorley, Lancashire, were stunned to find the remains of a woman who died whilst urinating into a chamberpot. Although there was little sign of an external fire – the carpet below her being unaffected and only smoke from her burning body causing any damage – only the lower legs of this woman's body were not completely consumed by fierce heat during her terrible death. Several other 'urinating' victims appear in the annals of SHC. In one case from Hungary in May 1989 a man was 'fried' after spending a penny in bushes next to his car after he drove through an electrical storm. Here it is believed the electricity earthed through the stream of urine that was flowing into the ground. Not a pleasant way to go!

We have already discussed the utterly bizarre death of miner Zigmund Adamski who was found with mysterious burn marks and dead from an induced heart attack (p. 68–71). This was on 11 June 1980 in Todmorden, right in 'UFO Alley' and during a flap of local sightings with attendant electrical effects. And on 4 December, only days after the highest point of activity of the 1980 wave, an SHC victim was reported at Lockwood near Huddersfield. Here a woman died in her kitchen during a localized fire that only left a small hole in the rug beneath her body.

One should not overreact by becoming fearful of bursting into flames, and much can be gained by studying the energies within the Pennine window. If SHC is indeed a real phenomenon (and that is still arguable) and if it is linked to the energy that appears so intense within the Pennine window, then it is a very uncommon occurrence. But it just might provide another vital clue to the powerful forces that are involved.

3

Magical Mystery Tour

A Regional Guide to the Pennine Window

In this part of the book we will take a closer look, region by region, at the character and variety of magical things happening in the Pennine Hills. During this trip around the Pennine window you will discover that there are several real 'hot spots' – the key places to go hunting if you are keen to see something strange for yourself. This cannot be guaranteed, of course – the supernatural does not run to a timetable (rather like the British rail network). But these hot spots, such as the areas around Todmorden, Glossop, Ilkley or Stocksbridge, are clearly the places to start. Even if you see nothing paranormal the Pennine scenery and fresh air are worth the trip.

North Yorkshire Dales

The northernmost region of the Pennines is largely bereft of large towns, with rolling dales located between the towns of Richmond, Harrogate and Skipton. It is very popular with hikers and there are scattered hamlets, quarrying activity and some beautiful scenery. But the low population density means that reports of paranormal activity are not as common here as they tend to be further south.

139

However, there are two very interesting pockets within this region where strange phenomena have become a way of life. One of these focuses around the covert base at Menwith Hill north-west of Harrogate. This base, operated by the National Security Agency (NSA), one of America's most secret surveillance operations, uses giant golf-ball-shaped radar domes to intercept electronic communications across the country. Strange lights have been seen often in the moors around here and villages such as Dacre have been the scene of reported bizarre light phenomena, like electrical storms in clear skies.

The other hot spot is a few miles to the west and has already featured in several cases in this book. The region north of Skipton on the border with Lancashire provided the mysterious Appletreewick photograph (see p.78–9). Images of glowing orange balls traversing the landscape have also been recorded in and around Carleton Moor – including some intriguing photos taken in 1998. And at Cracoe Fell a quite extraordinary light reflection from the shiny rock face created major consternation amongst local police in the mid-eighties at times when the environmental conditions were just right. This is an IFO (*identified* flying object, although in reality it was not even flying), but a remarkable-looking one even so.

Skywatching in either of these locations ought to bring rewards with sufficient patience – although it is not advisable to get too close to the base at Menwith as the NSA are *very* security conscious! Indeed, in one case, that of a dancer and her husband who were driving back over the moors here after a show on their way home to Stockport, the repercussions were stunning. Sanda and Peter Taylor encountered a very strange fluorescent glow, shaped like a melon, in the early hours of 16 August 1972. They stopped briefly to observe it and noticed a strange 'aura' emerging from the field. Time and space were disrupted but they drove off. Yet on arrival home in the pre-dawn hours a police car greeted them to ask what they had been up to! Their encounter had been officially logged without them knowing. Later the Ministry of Defence even sent an officer to their home to send the curious media politely away.[87]

But this is by no means the only interesting case in the North Yorkshire Dales. Here is another. Nigel Watson followed up letters sent by witness Thomas Adams to myself. Mr Adams was in the RAF as a 30-year-old serving at the complex of military bases north of Ripon, which includes the army camp at Catterick and an RAF station at Topcliffe. In fact Topcliffe was to star in a major incident in September 1952 when, during a big NATO exercise, 'Operation Mainbrace', an RAF jet chased a silver dome-shaped object that first hovered then shot away in broad daylight above Dishforth. The perplexed Air Ministry sent intelligence officers to Washington on the orders of Prime Minister Winston Churchill to work with the USAF and CIA on future policy after this event. Several others took place during an exercise in the North Sea, including a similar disc above a US nuclear-powered aircraft carrier.

The Dishforth object sounds to me like a weather balloon (although one would assume the RAF would know what these looked like!), but in June/July 1947 Thomas Adams saw something stranger. He was at the nearby RAF unit at Scorton, and was on guard duty with a colleague at a munitions dump just outside the main base. This was a lonely posting that he sometimes had to endure for several nights at a time. The USAF had operated this store during the war but now it was RAF property.

At 2 a.m. one summer's night both men were asleep in their little hut, when Thomas found himself suddenly dragged from his slumber and rushed outside to investigate what he called 'a terrible noise' that was grinding into his head. It was an eerie pulsating and vibrating sound that appeared to compress and decompress his eardrums, causing some pain. What was very odd was that, despite the nature of this sound, the second guard remained asleep inside the hut. Going outside, Thomas hoped to discover what kind of 'aircraft' was paying them a visit. Jets were fairly new but he had never heard

141

anything that could penetrate into the skull quite like this.

Once in a position to look at the hills to the west his confusion was only increased. The throbbing noise boring into his skull was coming from a blue glow hovering beside a clump of trees. It was extremely intense – an electric blue colour like a lightning bolt condensed into a tiny package. Staring at it for about a minute he then noticed that the light was fading and taking the sound with it. Both disappeared quickly and faded away but did not fly off. When the sound ended there was the most deathly silence.

Curiously, Thomas now returned to the guard hut and chose not to wake his colleague. Indeed a very strange state of mind had inexplicably descended upon him, almost as if he had been hypnotized. 'I just had this strong impression that I must not speak of this to anyone,' he said. And so powerful was the sensation that it was over thirty years before he confided in me.

You will recognize the pattern, which is consistent with other Pennine cases. In a completely independent case one witness described the effects on his (and his girlfriend's) ears to me as follows: '[Our] ears felt as if they had been closed – like when you fit your fingers in them...There was a feeling of heaviness [to the air]'. Later 'our ears began to pop like they do when on an aeroplane'. This seems to prove that changes in atmospheric pressure are a key part of these glowing energy balls.[88]

The other hot spot in the North Yorkshire area is revealed in this case from June 1965. Mrs Whitehead, a legal secretary, was grooming her dogs on the steps of her house at Flasby, in the Yorkshire Dales National Park between Cracoe and the scenic Malham Cove. She first noticed that the animals were attracted to something in the air. Following their gaze she spotted a huge silver oval hovering low and rotating. A slight 'swishing' of air was the only noise. On the base were a series of 'blobs'.

Mrs Whitehead told me that she felt a strange sensation during the slow drifting passage of this object. We would recognize it as the Oz Factor – 'I felt oddly calm and isolated from reality as this thing flew over me,' she said. The oval moved gently over the woods and she gave pursuit but never saw it again. 'I have tried over the years to explain it away as something recognizable, but cannot.'

As with the object over Dishforth this seems unlikely to have been a balloon. Taken as an isolated incident you might think it was some form of alien craft. However, it takes on a new dimension when you appreciate that very similar sightings have occurred elsewhere in the Pennines and other windows. On 15 June 1988 at Marple Bridge on the Cheshire/Derbyshire border, a large grey oval mass, also rotating, was seen to drift overhead. It also had 'blobs' on the underside. However, this began to break apart, falling in large clumps over a hillside golf course. From the more extensive observations available in this case we know that the oval was created by loose grass that had been sucked up from a field by an air vortex. A complex interaction of forces was happening and had caused this mass to stabilize as it rotated, creating a solid looking oval 'UFO' that could drift laterally with the wind. It only broke apart as the momentum lessened and the balance of forces altered. There was an upwards air suction, a horizontal motion, electrostatic attraction causing the clumps to come together and, of course, the force of gravity that ultimately caused them to 'rain' down when this became the dominant force in the equation.

Paul Fuller and I have published a detailed account of this case.[89] One witness here saw it drift across the sky as Mrs Whitehead did. But witnesses also saw the initial phase (when the oval was formed by being sucked upward) and the final phase (when it rained hay). The same thing may have happened at Flasby, but we have no added sightings. It is worth noting that Mrs Whitehead described the weather as warm and sunny – perfect conditions for this complex balance of atmospheric forces.

Another Pennine case with obvious similarities occurred in UFO Alley at Walsden, West Yorkshire. Jenny, a children's home care worker, had been horse-riding on the moors in late November 1978. As she walked down the steep path she noticed that her dog stopped frolicking and looked skyward. Following its gaze she saw, at a very low height, an oval mass with dark blobs in a circle on the base, all sheathed in a spectral mist glowing an eerie silver-green.

Jenny told me that seeing this thing was rather like walking over the moors and spotting the QE II liner at rest. You know it 'cannot' be there yet your eyes show to you quite plainly that it is. She further described the Oz Factor that typified her altered state of consciousness – how she felt in 'communion' with this thing and 'joined at the soul' as she put it. All other reality disappeared.

Jenny then felt an internal 'tickling' of her mind – possibly as a consequence of the electrostatic field given out by this thing. Indeed, the glowing cloud that is so often seen around such phenomena is, in my view, a major clue – perhaps dust attracted to the object by electrostatic. Here the energy field was intense enough to produce an internal glow and it was her proximity to this force that made her feel strange and probably alerted the dog too. Charged ions likely filled the air much as they do when a thundercloud is waiting to discharge its lightning bolt. This also can create a tickling or prickly sensation.

Often, as here, I have heard Pennine witnesses say, 'I don't know why I looked up – something just made me do so.' This is no premonition. It is a reaction to a sensory awareness that you have become immersed within an electrical field, the same field which in other cases – such as the Nelson car stop (see p.35–6) – can probably make your hair stand on end and your eyes to water and in extreme cases do worse.

The conclusion of the Walsden incident offers further insight into the complex balance of forces that is at work when these glowing phenomena appear. Jenny noted: 'The thing split into two – repelling each other like poles of a magnet . . . There were showers of sparks like electricity as it broke up. Moving like stones shot from a catapult the two

The field beside the school where a strange vortex sucked up loose hay from beside the fence. Rising to a height of about 20 feet the disc of dark matter then moved horizontally towards the left. In fact, numerous floating lights have been seen over the hills to the north and east

The lens-shaped mass now drifted at rooftop height across the school field and over the buildings in the background. The children playing underneath felt forces pressing down on them from above. The energy then slackened causing hay to rain down from the sky over a golf course and hillside towards Stockport

The steep sides of the Rossendale Valley have had so many sightings of glowing lights that this small part of Lancashire has acquired the nickname 'UFO Alley'. It was near this spot that police officers chased an orange blob up the moors to the right

On the trackbed of this long disused railway, through the Rossendale Valley in Lancashire, strange lights have often been seen, such as here at Waterfoot where the lights traverse the valley floor at speed

The windswept Pennines are perfect for the attempt to harness energy from the atmosphere. But the wind farm at Coal Clough between Todmorden and Burnley is in the heart of Pennine light country. On these moors there have been over a dozen reported cases of alien contact, time lapses and abductions

Haunted inns are common within the Pennines, but The Ash Tree at Butley near Macclesfield is one of the strangest, with its collection of ghosts, poltergeists and UFOs in one hot spot of activity within the surrounds of Prestbury – the so-called village of the dead

pieces went in different paths – one part went south towards Manchester, the other over the hills towards Bacup. Then it was gone and I stood there and I cried. I felt like I had just lost my dearest friend.' ⌉

One last case will illustrate the strangeness of the Yorkshire Dales. We return to the military encampments around Scorton, where Barry King helped me to confirm the information from letters that I received. This event occurred in late May/early June 1973 when two soldiers from Catterick, Lance Corporal Mike Perrin and a young trooper called Carvell, were engaged in a field exercise on Bellerby Moor north of Leyburn. They had headed out with a convoy of around twemty vehicles and had separated, the plan being to co-ordinate their positions by radio.

At 11 p.m., when Perrin had parked the Landrover in an isolated spot, they were awaiting further orders when the radio contact began to deteriorate. At first there was severe interference marked by static, then the set went stone dead, and at the same time their vehicle began to 'die' on them too, as the headlights failed. (The engine was already switched off.) They tried to rectify the problem by switching radio channels but this made no difference. They were miles from anywhere and with no idea how close they were to the safety of any colleagues.

As they debated what to do a strange glowing object headed towards them from the east. They had the Landrover window wound down as it was a warm evening, so they had an excellent view of this thing as it silently approached, apparently about 10 feet off the ground. It was shaped like a rugby ball and about the size of a car. It had what looked like glows or windows on the side and a mist or vapour was emerging from the base. As it came closer they heard a faint buzzing noise. Staring at this utterly unexpected sight the two men noticed that a small herd of cows in an adjacent field were equally transfixed, staring dumbstruck at the object.

Time stretched into an eternity (no doubt the Oz Factor affecting their state of consciousness), but eventually the object moved over some woods and vanished. As it drifted away the vehicle headlights came back on and radio reception returned. The two men continued the exercise until 4 a.m. and only reported the event on return to base. They did not tell me until they were out of the Army!

Accused of being out of contact the men requested permission to check with nearby radar stations to get proof of their story and to report to the Ministry of Defence (MoD) but were told that the MoD were not interested in such stories. But the men searched the woods in their own time and found a circle of burnt scrub close to where they had last seen the object, on military property where no public were allowed.[90]

North-east Lancashire

Moving south from the hot spot around Carleton Moor and Appletreewick, we come to a part of north Lancashire that is rather more densely populated, thanks to a cluster of semi-industrial towns around Burnley. As a result there have been more reports of strange things made here – as far back, of course, as the international furore over the witches of Pendle. The Pendle area remains today one of the most active parts of the Pennines where supernatural trickery happens today. But another pocket of strange phenomena can be found a little further west in the area surrounding 'Britain's most haunted house' – Chingle Hall at Goosnargh (see p.83–5).

Chipping, in the forest of Bowland, has long produced strange tales. The local pub, the Sun Inn, is haunted by the apparition of a woman in a long dress, who is seen to frequent the kitchen area. Objects also move about of their own accord, notably those associated with cleaning such as brooms. Legend links this haunting with servant girl, Lizzie Dean, who killed herself on the premises 150 years ago. Even more modern versions of an apparition include sightings of a cloudy spectre walking near the Ribble bus route at West Bradford. But there were supernatural ties with this area that went back even to activities of the Pennine boggart, to which I have already referred (see p.90–2).

Local farmers in Chipping and nearby Little Bowland reported experiences during the late 1700s and early 1800s to one Thomas Weld from Leagram Hall, who collected their accounts. There were frequent references to sightings of small beings appearing on the white rock in and around Waddington Fell (scene of the modern day incident involving a car crossing the moors, see p.92). Described as larger than rabbits and appearing and disappearing very suddenly all travellers in this area knew to look out for their presence.

The boggarts were also seen in Grindleton in 1820 by the verger of the local church. He had stopped to light his pipe in West Clough Wood when he heard shuffling feet and a tinkling noise in the air. Looking around he saw a small group of beings about 2 feet tall who seemed curious as to his presence and as if he had intruded on their own private universe.

Such was the verger's local repute that nobody doubted this story. It was confirmed by other visitors to the woods. However, the sightings of these imp-like creatures were not always so benign. They were said to plague local farmers by appearing in the midst of their fields and deliberately terrorizing their cattle, causing stampedes. They also tended to move objects about the farmhouse and cause clanging noises as rocks were thrown at the wall. These rock tossing and banging effects are still reported – although today they form the basis for modern hauntings or poltergeist attacks. The boggarts have been replaced as the presumed cause by phantoms – or in some cases even by aliens creating havoc.

These may merely be changing interpretations of the same effect, which at heart seems to reflect an energy field that can move small things, cause noises in the air and impede electrical systems. The effects remain pretty constant across the centuries, but for yesterday's boggart read today's ET.

Perhaps the most persistent modern version of the boggart's attack comes from Foulridge, an evocatively named village located on the eastern side of Pendle Hill. We have already come across various odd energy phenomena reported in this same area, from the car stop at Nelson to the earth-centred energy balls that emerged from the ground at Earby. But Foulridge has a long tradition of supernatural apparitions. And it centres on the appropriately named Hobstones Farm, hob, as you may recall, being an old name for evil or demon. The elves (or hobgoblins) were once seen dancing on the local stones. It was also the site of a major battle during the English Civil War and cavalier spectres have been reported in the area ever since.

One such incident, described to me by local ghost hunter Terence Whitaker, concerns a troop of Roundheads, riding on horseback and carrying pikes, that have been seen to march slowly towards Colne Edge and disappear like a TV picture being switched off. This seems much like the time-slip 'action replays' of the Second World War bomber planes reported elsewhere in the Pennines (see p.29–30), as if the emotional ferocity of this battle has been trapped in time by the surging energy that seems to fill the rocks around here.

During the 1970s when the Berry family took over Hobstones Farm they started to suffer from a plethora of supernatural events. These have included many poltergeist effects, such as eggs being smashed in an ordered pattern whilst still in their cartons, and the old familiar trick that dates back to the days of the boggart – showers of stones cascading from the sky against the farmhouse wall.

In 1984 a local BBC TV documentary crew visited the farm to make a news feature. They found themselves victims of these strange forces. All their shots filmed outside the building came out fine, but the cameras simply did not function whilst inside the concentration of energy at this spot.

Very similar electrical disturbances have been recorded elsewhere in north-east Lancashire. We saw how there have been camera malfunctions at Chingle Hall, in Goosnargh (see p.83–5) and the attempt to photograph a close-up hovering UFO in Rossendale that mysteriously failed (see p.128). And, of course, the interference on electrical systems of cars such as that reported on Waddington Fell and at Nelson (see p.35–6) fits the same pattern, even if it is ascribed in the modern world to extraterrestrial not goblin activity.

The remarkable car stop case over Pendle Hill in March 1977 is a recent manifestation of these energy forces in its 'alien' guise, but that incident is only the most celebrated to occur during a major flap of activity. It ended a short wave with a sudden outburst of energy in the skies. But the events that led up to that night provide the context to show how these forces ebb and flow.

The build-up activity was first noted on 15 February, three weeks before the 'big one'. A triangular glow of yellow/blue light was seen above Pendle Hill from the small town of Barnoldswick. Within a week this had spread to almost nightly 'light shows' (such as yellow glows forming over the rocks outside Burnley during the early hours of 22 February).

The phenomena were not confined to Pendle Hill. They had a zone of influence that included the adjacent hot spot in West Yorkshire. Indeed on 23 February at a standing stone near Ilkley surges of electricity were seen rising from the ground and leaking into the atmosphere, much like those more recently reported at Earby (see p.33). This is a graphic example of the earth energy transferring from the rocks into the air and, I suspect, fuelling the many strange things that are then seen and reported during these flaps.

More glowing triangles appeared above the moors between Rawtenstall and Burnley on 26 and 28 February, and Oswaldtwistle was the scene of a similar event on the night of 1 March as the pace of this flap of atmospheric emissions increased.

The strangeness of the events markedly began to rise, too, as the wave of activity escalated. On the night of 4 March, for example, just south of Burnley a blue glow appeared and a line of red lights winked in formation above it making a pattern that resembled a watch on a chain (much like the daylight case in North Yorkshire discussed on p.121). This bizarre form began to bob up and down like a yo-yo before fading out of sight. Similar reports have at times been made from in and around the dry ski slope at Rawtenstall.

Another ten sightings followed during the next three nights of the 1977 flap until a six-hour period on the night of 8/9 March that culminated with an extraordinary cloud cigar that formed over Pendle Hill. This was the big event that caused such terror and physical ill effects to the two men in a car at Nelson. That peak night began with multiple red and white lights like fireworks crossing the sky near Helmshore. By late evening on 8 March the by now recurrent manifestation of a triangle had reappeared in the sky over Oswaldtwistle and was seen by numerous witnesses. One man even shone a torch at it and claims that it noticeably brightened up when he did so. By 9 p.m. the triangle was a dazzling spectacle in the sky over Barnoldswick, where a coach party on a trip out witnessed it. Small lights circled the main object like 'bees swarming round a hive'.

Half an hour before the car stop event at Nelson, at about 2.45 a.m. on 9 March, seven late-night shift workers at Oswaldtwistle saw a reddish arrowhead flash across the sky from the direction of Pendle Hill – the position from which, very soon, the massive glowing cigar seething with electrostatic energy would descend from the mists.

The phenomenal car-stop event itself brought this dramatic flurry of activity to a halt. There had been over twenty sightings within a 5 mile radius of Pendle Hill during the three weeks prior to this incident and half of these had occurred within four days up to 9 March. After the car stop there were just two sightings in the same area during the next month.

To me this is prime evidence for an energy phenomenon in the local atmosphere apparently leaking skywards from the ground. It filtered out slowly over several weeks, creating these aerial manifestations and then exhausted itself with the 'big bang' and one very powerful car stop at Nelson.

Remember the analogy that I drew with volcanoes and earthquakes? Scientists monitor build-ups of activity here too, sometimes involving energy leaks from the ground. According to some geologists it might be possible to predict a major tectonic event, when the bottled energy finally explodes, by studying animal and human responses to the leaking energy that slowly precedes it.[91] Much the same thing may occur in window areas during flaps. If we can better understand the way these waves of activity develop then we may perhaps learn lessons that can be applied to seemingly uncontrollable geophysical phenomena. It would be irony indeed if we learned how to curb the fury of the earth by studying the forces that have long been ascribed to the works of the devil.

Of course, these hobgoblin-led phenomena are still occurring. Here is a more recent example from this same area that reflects the pattern. I am grateful to Roger Markham who put the witness in touch (after he first contacted the magazine *Lancashire Life*) and local investigator Rory Lushman who helped me to look into the matter.

The Roberts* family moved to a house on Longridge Fell north of Goosnargh early in 2000. They claimed that they were quickly under siege from strange forces, much as the beleaguered residents of the farmhouse in Chipping had been in the early 1800s or those at Hobstones Farm in the 1970s. The real cause of concern here was a noise, described as a 'buzzing/crackling like very loud electric sparking'. It had often been heard directly over the roof in the dead of night during the weeks that they had lived on the Fell. At times it seemed as if something was touching the roof (much like the old tales of stone-throwing boggarts).

On 13 June 2000 Mr Roberts returned home at about 11 p.m. to find his wife complaining that the noise had scared her. Even the family dog was apparently perturbed. But as Mr Roberts had seen nothing when he drove up to the house they decided to put up with it once again. Going to bed they could now hear an even louder sound – this time resembling a motor. Thinking that youths might be riding motorbikes on the fields Mr Roberts went to take a look through the upper window and saw that a motor was indeed the cause of this new noise – coming from the neighbouring farm where a combine harvester was being used.

However, as he looked out, he noticed that the original buzzing noise was still there, and that it was coming from a glowing object hanging low in the sky. It was shaped like a spinning top with a circle of electric blue glows from the middle. The near full moon was reflecting from its surface proving, Mr Roberts told us, that this was a three-dimensional object. It was next to a tree, and as he watched it began to descend towards the ground, swaying gently from side to side 'like a leaf does when it falls off a tree'. While it was dropping down a small light was circling the top shape creating the effect of a bee swarming around a hive – the same curious description offered about some of the events that took place during the big wave around Nelson twenty-three years earlier.

Mr Roberts went to call the police from the phone downstairs whilst his wife looked through the window. She could not now see the object (it had either disappeared or landed behind the brow of a hill) but she did see a line of sheep in a field behaving oddly. They had gathered together into a tight group and were 'stampeding' away from where the spinning top had descended – another scene that centuries earlier was blamed on a boggart rather than a UFO.

There also seemed to be unusual power surges in the house. The bedroom light brightened and 'exploded', plunging them suddenly into darkness. The phone which Mr Roberts brought from its base downstairs into the bedroom would not give a dial tone. Returning downstairs to try a second phone, which now working, Mr Roberts discovered that the dog was cowering behind the curtains.

Eventually two police officers did arrive and searched

the fields with a flashlight – finding nothing. The farmer, who was on his machine in a different field and probably would not have been able to see the spinning top from there, reported nothing. But one of the officers told Mr Roberts that there had been so many recent reports of strange lights and noises that he had been converted into a believer.

When I first spoke to Mr Roberts he was clearly distraught. He was sitting up at night with a camcorder waiting for the object to return and needed healthy reassurance from me that his children were not in danger. Even so he started to talk to me about 'getting away' because they had had enough. A few days later he told me the noise had returned in the middle of the night and that this was it as far as the Roberts family was concerned. They had already put the house on the market and were getting out of Longridge Fell, leaving someone else to face these forces from beyond their comprehension.

As yet the sounds have not returned.

Rossendale and Calderdale

These two valleys run together, with Rossendale just in Lancashire and Calderdale in West Yorkshire. In fact Todmorden, with nearby Bacup forming the undoubted hub of this red hot spot, is almost schizophrenic in its allegiance: it is geographically in Yorkshire but has a Lancashire postal address!

If anywhere epitomises the Pennine window these valleys must be it. Made up of small mill towns tottering on steep slopes between Burnley in the north-west and Halifax in the south-east it has developed such a reputation, especially for UFO sightings, that, as we have seen, it has the nickname UFO Alley. It is not merely the level of activity here, which is long term and prodigious (making this area easily most qualified to claim the title of UFO capital of Britain), rather it is the quality of the events reported. It has been estimated that as many as one-fifth of the close encounter cases to be reported in the UK have occurred within this area of around 50 square miles. We shall now look at a sprinkling of these events.

Elsie lives in an old house on the moors above Calderdale. She has frequently experienced the way these hills are alive not with the sound of music but with paranormal phenomena. She traces this back to a childhood accident when she fell over the banisters and suffered concussion at the age of five. From that time she has witnessed a catalogue of strange things despite her doctors having found no apparent permanent injury. Psychics have at times claimed that head traumas suffered as a child acted as the starting point for their abilities. Peter Hurkos, who aided police in the search for missing people by way of his 'visions', said that his ESP started after he fell off a ladder whilst working.[92]

Elsie's visions took the form initially of seeing normal people as she walked about – but who turned out to be hardly normal. In 1940, aged seven, she was walking over the moors near Todmorden when she met a woman from a nearby cottage. They had a friendly conversation, and the woman asked about Elsie's parents. When she arrived home she was scolded for claiming to have chatted to this woman – because the old lady had died a few weeks earlier.

Experiences of this sort became a regular occurrence and Elsie even saw strange faces reflected in window glass or mirrors; such surfaces seemed to act like a crystal ball, offering a screen onto which the mind can project images detected within the subconscious. After sixty years of seeing things in her remote moorland home Elsie says both she and her house somehow act like a 'satellite dish tuning into the past'. She cites examples where a kitten, which research suggests might have died in the house in the care of previous owners, regularly 'appears' on her lap before vanishing. Whilst this is a form of 'vision' and others in the house never see the creature, it is also in some sense 'real' because her pet dog became aware of it, staring when the cat manifested. She told me, 'At first he got quite upset – now he is used to it and just looks up, as if curious, then goes back to whatever he was doing!'

Elsie's story is not unique. A man in Bacup reported glowing curtains of light in his bedroom. A woman in Waterfoot told me how she scared her school chums because she could tell them what they were going to have for their tea! A woman in Todmorden used to play a game of staring at the TV set, then looking away at the window and seeing a flash image appear depicting the next scene or story that the set would display. She was able to practise this technique until she was right more often than she was wrong. All these things began when UFO Alley residents were around the age of five and never went away.

These phenomena seem to be a consequence of both the person and their environment. Elsie described how she frequently heard conversations – everyday chit-chat that might have been spoken by the mill workers who had occupied the cottage during Victorian times. These voice-only 'apparitions' may suggest that the 'ghosts' she sees are video versions of the same 'action replay' effect.

Perhaps this house is somehow acting like a radio set, capturing and replaying these stray signals, and Elsie just happens to witness them. There does seem to be evidence of an energy field that resonates in this isolated building. For years there have been unexplained power drains here. The electricity company has made several attempts to identify why fuses, lights, vacuum cleaners and cookers overload and take power consumption way beyond the norm (Elsie called them in owing to the huge bills they were charging). And glows, both blue/green and white, have formed in the house and garden rising from the ground. The building is constructed from quartz-rich local rock. It is also surrounded by a strong electric field (pylons straddle the hills nearby), so it is hard to escape the conclusion that these are somehow 'charging' this spot with powerful energy, just as we have seen elsewhere in the Pennines.

Perhaps most people would experience just an occasional sensation like a buzzing or tingling or see the odd atmospheric glow, but in Elsie's case her brain may have active centres that are somehow more susceptible to this energy. Possibly her childhood fall led to a stimulation of the 'receptor' neurones in her head that allowed her to 'decode' those incoming signals somehow being channelled through the house. If so, then her analogy of being a 'satellite dish tuned to the past' might be remarkably apt. And, of course, this offers exciting possibilities for scientific research, because these energy fields must be measurable; they can be mapped. We can probably predict where and when these window hot spots are going to burst into life. And we ought to be able to build a machine to emulate what Elsie does in a biological sense – one that can capture, record and play back these moments that seem frozen in time!

✷   Jenny, from Walsden, just south of Todmorden, has had a remarkable catalogue of oddities throughout her early life too. These include balls of light the size of basketballs that played around her cot and the astonishing ability to project images of herself through time and space.

She says that 'feeling' is the key to these experiences. If she has an intense motivation to be with someone then her mind seems able to make that happen. Jenny cannot do this consciously; it all happens at an instinctive level. Whilst most of the time these 'voyages' occur in a dream-like visionary form as she sleeps there was one occasion where a friend in Kent saw her manifest briefly in her bedroom. At the same moment Jenny was 250 miles away in Calderdale 'visualizing' herself in a dream to be in Kent.

Indeed an important clue is Jenny's wonderfully vivid dream life, which has included false awakenings. She also has lucid dreams, during which she knows that she is dreaming and can control the events as they unfold. It is also possible for her to wake herself out of these dreams, then return to them and continue the same narrative. Frequently she has dreams about solving mysteries and visiting some magical heaven-like place.

Jenny has powerful visual creativity, which is so common amongst witnesses who have frequent strange experiences. And like other such people she has an extremely vivid recall of her very early life. This is another major clue about how the brains of the more sensitive witnesses are 'tuned'.

Most people cannot remember anything earlier than the age of 2 or 3, because young children process memories in a different way from adults. But Jenny, in keeping with nearly all repeater witnesses from the Pennines that I have met, has clear memories of events that happened whilst she was only a few weeks old and was still in a pram or cot. ⌐ This suggests that a brain which can facilitate visual creativity is a vital component of what triggers these supernatural events – especially if it is in a location where energy fields are strong and cause paranormal events to occur. Most of us will not be aware of these things, but to susceptible people the window becomes alive with all manner of incredible happenings.

Rossendale is just as rich in apparitions. Bank House in Haslingden, which was built in 1886, has long been associated with spectral activity which peaked in the 1970s when (no surprise here) renovation work began to install modern heating and lighting. These ranged from strange noises and objects disappearing and reappearing elsewhere in the house, to coal dust smells and apparitions. These seem to be 'replays' involving the sighting of people who once lived in this spot going through reruns of mundane activities that they carried out during life.

On the night of 14/15 August 1980, amidst a major wave of weird activity in the twin valleys which included the death of Zigmund Adamski (see p.70), pulsing red UFOs over Todmorden (see p.120), and the famous abduction of PC Alan Godfrey (see p.52), an event occurred at Helmshore, Rossendale that fits the same pattern. Andrew Nightingale and a friend were late-night fishing at Ogden Reservoir. It was pouring with rain, something they relied upon to bring the fish to the surface. Both this – the passage of an atmospheric depression – and the weight of water in the reservoir stressing the rock below seem to me to be likely trigger factors, much like knocking heavily on the wall of a house with engineering equipment. Both things strain the earth. Pennine UFOs are commonly seen near reservoirs and quarries. This is no coincidence.

Suddenly the two men realized that there was a circle (believed to be of nine lights) on the water, glowing red. Assuming that they were reflections from an object hovering above them the men looked up, but were astonished to find nothing there. Looking back they found that the lights had gone, but moments later they reappeared, now pulsing in rhythm and clearly rising from *beneath* the water.

Unsurprisingly the men were terrified and fled, leaving their expensive fishing tackle to the mercy of any thief. As Andrew explained, 'There was no way I was going back there until daylight.' Fortunately, when they did return their gear was still where they had left it and the lights had disappeared.

However, in the meantime an elderly woman in nearby Haslingden had made an independent sighting. She did not know about what the fishermen had witnessed but saw a red glow pouring in through her bedroom window. Sitting up she saw a circle of red lights (she estimated that there were twelve) spinning silently across her field of view, still pulsing in and out. This certainly seems to have been the same phenomenon which the fisherman witnessed less than a mile away 'under' the water, but now drifting towards Burnley.

And so the reports go on. I could fill this book with them, but a few more will suffice.

At Stacksteads on 24 September 1982 at 2.30 a.m. Harold Lord witnessed two white lights coming down the brow of a hill straight towards him. They looked like car headlamps, as they moved on a steady path. The only problem was that they then sailed majestically into the night sky and moved away in a shallow path. A dark mass was seen briefly between the two glows.

At Cribden, north of Rawtenstall, on 10 April 1983

Margaret was returning home on a lonely road below the edge when she saw a pulsing white glow over the hill. She stopped the car and opened the door to see a huge light just above her, making no sound. After a few seconds it accelerated from a standing start to head off over the hills. She gave chase but soon lost it.

There are plenty of multiple-witness cases too. On 10 December 1982 a case came to me after I appeared on the popular BBC radio programme *Woman's Hour*. The witnesses were the Low family, who were driving home from Burnley towards Bacup on the road over Deerplay Moor. Near the village of Weir they observed a strange white glow coming from the south. Pulling to a halt they got out of the car and watched for eight minutes as the thing crossed directly overhead, slowly and silently, at an altitude of just 500 feet. Mr Low also did something interesting. He put a comb on the roof of the car and used this to measure the way the object moved. It clearly did so in what the Lows called a zigzag – that is it wobbled from side to side like a falling leaf (see also p.152). At close proximity they had a good view of it as a two white curved sides encasing a rugby ball shape with a red glowing strip at each end. As it moved away north-westward two bright white lights appeared from the south and passed above it, streaking away like jet aircraft (but again with no sound), almost as if they were flying over and inspecting the big object.

Jenny from Walsden also observed some fascinating light shows. Here is how she described some of them to me. 'For some weeks I had been observing fast moving lights . . . They did not move in straight lines but 'wobbled' from side to side. I also saw them split on several occasions.'

She added that in a period of about six weeks (September to November 1978) she saw at least a dozen as she walked down the hills with her dog. At the time she was being particularly vigilant, as were many young woman in the area, owing to the activities of the serial killer known as the Yorkshire Ripper, who often struck in the Pennine towns between Leeds and Manchester. The most spectacular of these events came on about 28 November when a huge white light drifted silently and then in a 'flash' of soundless energy became two that repelled one another 'like stones from a slingshot'. We have met this exact effect before in other cases and it clearly points to charged particles that have electro-magnetic energy and repel one another like magnetic poles.

X Jenny, of course, also had a major close encounter at Walsden (see p.143–5). She never reported this event to the police. In fact she told nobody until she saw me on TV and got in touch. Her reason was the futility of expecting people to believe and the seeming absurdity of parts of her account. Like many witnesses her mind 'succumbed'. 'I was transfixed,' she told me. 'I do not hear voices but this thing "spoke" to me. It did so in the voice you use when you are thinking. A clear mental image of the words, "Do not be afraid." It was less a voice more a "knowing". I felt the words. In an instant I went from terror to ecstasy. It became a religious experience. For obvious reasons I could not explain this to the police!'

She now entered the Oz Factor. 'I was one with this object. I swear that if anything had got out and said "come with me" I would have followed like a lamb. I felt "divorced from myself".' At the same time her mind felt very strange. 'All my experiences from childhood were flashing through my head with incredible speed. Like I was a computer and my memory banks were being drained.'

This is a remarkably similar description to the 'life review' claimed by some who go through a near-death experience (NDE). They also claim to see their life flash before them in a rapid sequence of slides.[93]. In fact NDEs and close encounters seem oddly linked. Both involve seeing misty glows, sensing the presence of an intelligence, getting a religiously ecstatic sensation and a similar long term aftermath. NDE witnesses usually believe themselves to be in heaven but recognize that they must return to the pain and suffering of earth and so feel real sadness. Jenny also 'began to feel very sad'. She said that when the event ended, 'if someone had given me the choice I would have gone with it without question. But it conveyed to me the sense that it had to go and I had to stay . . . I broke down on that hillside and wept.'

The parallels here between UFO accounts and the typical NDE undergone by many people who almost drown or have a car crash are too close for me to reject. Indeed I have come across other encounters in the Pennines where the 'life review' or 'slide show' of images is screened to a witness during a UFO encounter, but it is usually 'rationalized' by UFOlogists as some message being conveyed by aliens![94] I doubt whether Jenny nearly died on the moor that night. So this is not an NDE disguised as a UFO encounter. I equally doubt whether people who do suffer life threatening trauma and report an NDE have instead really been kidnapped by aliens. So what is going on here?

I suspect that both are personal interpretations of a common mind experience that is simply difficult for us to categorize. We can perhaps best envisage it as some kind of energy that somehow touches the visionary centres of the brain, especially that of a sensitive, visually creative person, and stimulates the mind to experience a range of phenomena. Physical sensations are described by each person much as they occur but meaning is interpreted differently – not only by the witness but by researchers who hijack the evidence to make it fit some theory of their own (be it a belief in alien abduction or in life after death). All we can be reasonably sure about is that these things often result in a life-transforming experience. Indeed Jenny's state of consciousness was 'weird', she said, for hours afterwards. She remained in a state of heightened emotion. She felt transformed in a spiritual way. Other UFO witnesses have changed lifestyles dramatically, suddenly supporting ecological and pacifist movements or even taking a major animal welfare stance. NDE specialist Dr Ken Ring told me that exactly the same pattern emerges from people who have these visions and think that they have been to heaven.

The phenomenon in the skies above Rossendale and

Calderdale is an ongoing affair. On 4 February 1988 Angela Farmer*, a laboratory scientist, was driving on the A681 from Bacup to Todmorden when she encountered a strange egg shape over Sharneyford – literally hovering over the county border. It was glowing inside with colour, 'like a swirling liquid or fire embers with constantly changing patterns'. This 'wriggling worm' effect has been reported in several cases of ball lightning – a rare atmospheric plasma whose origins science still debates. It also features in the description of the Nelson car stop so is clearly an important clue about the physical make-up of these phenomena over the Pennines.

In September 1991 a glowing light was seen swooping and diving over the hills near Cliviger. This area, between Todmorden and Burnley, has been the scene of several other close encounters. An ice-blue light was seen there by a motorist at the same time (in November 1980) that Alan Godfrey was being abducted from his police car 4 miles away. It is also close to the spot from where truck driver William Barrett had his missing time experience in January 1980 (see p.52–4).[95]

In February 1995 a dark egg shape hovered low above the wind farm that has been set into the moors on the north side of the Calder Valley from here, at Coal Clough. A triangle with lights at each apex was seen over Rooley Moor in April 1998. And a dancing ball of orange fire was witnessed by several local residents over the moortops at Britannia (between Bacup and Rochdale) on 17 March 2001.

Efforts to co-ordinate a truly scientific investigation into the strange lights that float over this hotbed of activity have long been discussed and have won some low-level interest from the scientific community. But in view of the atmosphere of cynicism, and the belief that this is a silly season story, not in fact a genuine scientific anomaly just crying out to be taken seriously, these efforts will surely falter. It is hoped that this book will kick start the long overdue co-ordinated quest for hard scientific data already code-named 'Project Pennine'. This is within our grasp if we are prepared to stop laughing and instead to start searching for answers.

Wharfedale

East of UFO Alley lies another active Pennine region. This Yorkshire valley is north-west of Leeds and bisected by the River Wharfe. On the way it passes through the small towns of Ilkley and Otley. The countryside is deceptive, with bare rocks, rolling hills, steep valleys and frothing streams. South of the Wharfe, in this small oasis of para- normal activity, lies Ilkley Moor. Popular in song and regu- larly used by walkers and picnickers it is the home to the Pennine sprites, small troll-like beings that have been reported for centuries and are remarkably still, seen even in modern times. Nowhere else in the Pennines is there quite such a continuity of presence of one kind of supernatural being. But Wharefdale is also now a hot spot for UFO activ- ity – perhaps only second to UFO Alley for levels of light phenomena. And this culminated in one remarkable case where the trolls and the UFOs turned up together on Ilkley Moor!

Wharfedale is the home of fairy stone markings – carv- ings etched into rock, displaying curved patterns (not unlike crop circle designs in some respects). These have long been considered markers to the fairy realm, or as we might call it today, another dimension – the doorway to the Pennine window, in fact.

Just south of Ilkley is a once small village, now an outer Bradford suburb, called Cottingley. In fairy lore there can be few more famous spots. The story that made Cottingley renowned was reported on page 38–9. But what remains clear is that the girls who took hoaxed fairy photos there believed they had really seen fairies in the dell. Nor are they alone in this. There have been reports from locals that this area is magical and that small creatures are seen from time to time flitting in and out of the bushes. I recall spending an afternoon with one man who was eager to show the sprites that he captured on film by the stream. His photographs did show images that, if you let your imagination wander, could be taken for supernatural beings between the trees. But there was no question in my mind what they were. The way the sunlight dappled through myriad leaves created a mosaic of light and shade and so took on form and structure.

The human mind is remarkably adept at seeking order within chaos. This is why children look at clouds and see elephants and clowns in their endless variety. So too, I suspect, with the fairies in the dell. We expect to find them and our eyes home in on coincidental forms that appear in the light and shade, allowing our brains to employ pattern recognition and ascribe to disorder the presence of a fairy.

My belief is that this works very much like the infamous 'face on Mars' image, where photographs taken by the landing mission in 1976 showed what looked like a human face over a mile across. The effect of this illusion was very powerful, even when one knew it *was* illusion. An advanced orbiting camera in 1999 took new sharp images of the face and revealed beyond doubt that it was a collection of rocks and craters with sunlight playing on them to resemble a face. New photographs in even starker focus in May 2001 proved this beyond any doubt. Of course, the fact that natural phenomena can cause people to think they have seen fairies is not proof that there never were any real fairies. The belief in these other worldly beings is intense and long lasting and if they do exist anywhere then Wharefedale is probably a good place to look.

To the north of Cottingley sits Ilkley Moor, with more spectacular stone markings as signs of a portal into this other realm. Names like the Fairy Parlour are found associated with these ancient carvings. There is also a longstanding lore connecting this area to goblins, small troll-like beings that are somewhat aggressive members of fairyland. Victorian writer Halliwell Sutcliffe described how there were numerous tales of walkers who met goblins inside the disused mine shafts that cover these dales.[96]

In one case a man hunting birds' eggs above an old lead mine fell into a pit by accident and broke a leg. Trapped at the base of the shaft he was accosted by a number of small beings that were hard to see in the gloom but that kept whispering in his ear the news that he might as well submit to death! But just as he felt himself slipping into unconsciousness a glowing light appeared and was transformed into a tall silvery figure that seemed to fill him with renewed energy and subjugate the trolls. Invigorated, the stricken man was able to call for help again and was overheard by a shepherd who brought help.

There are other tales of this 'silver spirit of the mines', as it is known around Ilkley. It was believed to be a benevolent entity of whom the trolls were afraid and lived inside the rocks, especially within old crevices and mine shafts. Most often, when seen, the silver spirit was reported as just a glowing light coming from the ground – remarkably like some of the earthlight discharges we have seen reported in modern times. Are these old tales encounters with this same energy leaking from electrically charged rocks that were transformed into apparitions by imagination or hallucinations? Or was the 'spirit' a shape read into the glow much as people see fairies in the dappled shade of today's tree branches? Mine workings, of course, are often found at seismically active locations where earth movements have revealed the mineral-rich strata – another hint that this might be the right way to look at these stories.

Either way there is a belief in a 'two-tier' structure to the beings that inhabit these rocks. The smaller beings (usually 2–3 feet tall) are goblins which act in mischievous rather than downright evil way. The tall, angelic humans display god-like compassion and act as supernatural rescuers in cases like that above. These 'tall ones' seem very similar to the 'wise being of light' that is often reported by people close to death who have an NDE and are guided back to life.[97] As we have seen, NDEs and alien contacts share many similarities. But there is an even more remarkable link here with UFO abduction cases.

165

In alien encounters basically two types of entity are reported the world over: small dwarf-like beings with large heads, often called 'greys', who are 3 feet tall and have a disregard for human welfare, engaging in experiments and causing distress but not being specifically evil; and (not infrequently even within the same UFO) another type called Nordics, who are tall, blond, much more human and usually capable of both magical acts and compassion.[98] When the two types of being are seen together it is always the tall ones who have the upper hand – as in Wharfedale lore where the silver spirit held sway over the trolls. In fact this goblin/grey-wise spirit/Nordic parallel is so apparent in these cases that it is hard to imagine that there is no connection.

But what connection could there be? Two possibilities occur. Perhaps these two types of being reflect some inner core to our 'soul' or deepest beliefs – a twin archetype of good versus evil that seems to be at the heart of most of our sense of spirit. Maybe the aliens of today prove this mythology to be alive and well but dressed up in a new guise suited to our technological age (and so not recognized by us as being mythology of the deepest, most meaningful kind!).

The other possibility of course is that there really are beings of these two types existing in some parallel reality that can come temporarily into our own world through window area hot spots such as Wharfedale. Perhaps the ancients were right all along to mark stones and celebrate these areas as special. Throughout history we have met these entities and interpreted them according to the culture that prevailed. So yesterday's goblins are seen as today's little aliens because that is how our society thinks. But in reality these beings may actually be something else entirely, whose true nature we have simply never understood.

✶ According to folklorist Dr David Clarke there have been some intriguing time-slip encounters on Ilkley Moor too. Local writer Nicholas Size reported how at the Cow and Calf rocks (two massive outcrops on Ilkley Moor where dazzling UFOs were seen hovering in September 1982) he had experienced visions of the area as it must have looked when fairy carvings were first etched into the rock face. He travelled back, perhaps in mind or vision, to the days when this bridge between worlds was part of everyday life.

Size reported that he was paralysed during the encounter and also in a trance-like state where time was suspended. This seems like the Oz Factor once more facilitating a supernatural event. Not only did Size witness a ritual sacrifice as bearded men in animal skins showed their reverence for the moor but he saw the Cow and Calf as one single massive structure, not two as now. Geologists suggest that thousands of years ago it may well have had this form and that the connecting rock face may have been broken up across the centuries to construct the base of early roads in the area.[99] **J**

Overlooking the Cow and Calf is Fairy Kirk or Fairy's House, so named because in Saxon times a planned church was never built when poltergeist activity (ascribed to the elemental beings so prevalent in this area) made construction impossible. The activity was of a form familiar in the Pennines – a rock-throwing assailant that terrified the workers and construction materials being moved by unseen forces. Five centuries later the old quarries here were replaced by a favoured spa, where spring water was used as the basis for a healing baths. These White Wells were used right into the twentieth century and a tearoom took over to serve hikers. Indeed part of the bath still remains unused and the spring water gurgles.

There were also reports of goblins seen around White Wells. In 1878 one summer's morning William Butterworth, caretaker of the spring baths, attempted to open the building but found his key revolving in a circle and the door wedged shut. Some force was holding him back from entry. Eventually ramming his way in he was stunned to find a number of beings under 2 feet tall and clad in green, frolicking in the water. A sound like a million bees buzzing at once filled the room. Upon hearing his exclamation the entities scurried away out of sight behind rocks.

As we have seen this humming/buzzing noise emerging from rocks has been reported in the Pennines much more recently. I think it results from the earth energies that in other ways cause the lights in the sky to be visible. It is literally the engine of the Pennine window being heard at work. This noise has even been reported in modern times from the moors near White Wells.

Researcher David Barclay described his own experience near the Swastika Stone in summer 1984: 'Suddenly the air was filled by a sound suggestive of an enormous number of bees in full flight . . . It seemed to come from all around us.' Barclay said it swamped every other nearby noise but 'there was not a bee to be seen'. The noise stopped just as suddenly and completely as it had begun.[100]

Lights in the sky have unsurprisingly been regular visitors to this area and are particularly active during waves and flaps that form the rhythmic cycle of the window. That was especially the case in November 1980 when Britain experienced a major burst of activity that saw the Pennines alive with close encounters, the best known being the abduction of Alan Godfrey at Todmorden on 28 November (see p.51–2).

Five days earlier it was Wharfedale's turn to take centre stage. On 23 November at 1 a.m. 22-year-old Nigel Mortimer awoke 'for no apparent reason'. He felt 'an urge to look through his bedroom window'. Nigel lived in Otley and his room faced north. He saw a bright white ball moving in the direction of Menwith Hill. Admiring it as what he took to be a bright meteor, he was surprised when it stopped dead. As he watched the oval mass it was seen to be a bluish colour and surrounded by a reddish mist or vapour, reminiscent of other local cases. Another familiar feature of this case was that the object had stopped over Lindley Wood Reservoir, one of the favoured haunts of these light phenomena.

Just as with Jenny at Walsden (see p.159–161) Nigel Mortimer reported to me how the experience created an extreme emotional response. He felt elated, but as it shot away, he said 'I felt sad, lonely and empty – as if I had lost a friend' – almost exactly the words that Jenny used. Although Nigel went on to become deeply interested in these things and set up his own UFO investigation team, Connect, it was this experience that changed his life. And we do not need to depend on merely his testimony for what he saw – as two others saw things that night. At 1.30 a.m. a woman at Burley-in-Wharfedale reported seeing an oval with 'windows' on the edge moving in a silent passage towards Menwith Hill. And a 46-year-old postal worker heading for an early-morning start sorting the mail at Otley. He was passing Otley Chevin (a hill that has spectacular views over the Wharfe valley) when he saw an object moving from Weston towards Burley. He reported the matter to Otley police on arrival at work. His description matches the typical Pennine glows – especially those seen in UFO Alley.

The Otley postman described what he saw as 'a bright orange sphere that crackled as if surrounded by lightning. Inside the orange ball there was a core mass of grey-green colour'. His sketch indicates a multi-layered oval with moving rings of energy around it. These accounts do suggest an electrically charged atmospheric energy.

It was not merely useful that there were back-up witnesses to Nigel Mortimer's own experience, it was essential. For after Nigel saw his UFO at Otley he was overcome with an intense tiredness, as if all energy had been sucked from his body. His mind also seemed to be letting the event 'drain out' like water from a sink. His memory of the event was literally disappearing. Fearful that he was forgetting key details of this momentous incident Nigel made some notes and left them in the room. But still worried by the way his mind was fast emulating a sieve he also took the precaution of placing an ornament beside his bed so that when he got up in the morning he would practically fall over it. That would (painfully!) jog his mind. It was lucky he did this. When he awoke he had totally forgotten the experience and only regained a vague awareness when he struck the ornament and snatched full memory back from oblivion only when he read his notes.

The most extraordinary Ilkley Moor encounter happened just a stiff hike up the slopes from White Wells. It can only be described as 'a goblin in a spaceship' – in fact a classic modernization of the story of these beings in a space-age supernatural adventure.

It was reported to me by Philip Spencer*, a former policeman who found my address from a book in the library forty-eight hours after the event. Later I was able to meet him and with my colleagues Peter Hough and Arthur Tomlinson (who both did great work on this case) have long pondered this amazing tale. The witness has shunned media interviews, is not interested in making money and assigned copyright in his evidence to Peter, but he has always been willing to answer any questions we have fired at him.

Around dawn on 1 December 1987 he was walking (as he often did) over the moors from Ilkley to the village of East Morton. It was just 7.15 a.m. and dark. Suddenly he heard a humming/buzzing noise, as has been heard on the moors before, and spotted an imp-like creature – small, squat, bluish-green and not at all human, stooping on a rock and seeming to gesture at him. Instinctively Philip took one photograph, before it scurried away behind an outcrop. He chased it, arriving just in time to see a disc-like object rising upward. He was too stunned to take a second photograph (one worrying aspect of his otherwise credible testimony).

Naturally shocked, Spencer abandoned his plan to visit a relative and returned to civilization, using up a few shots on the film by taking pictures of bridges and bus stops as he passed them (Peter and I examined all the film and it is consistent with this story). He then decided to get the film developed uncompleted and took a bus to Keighley where he knew there was a shop that processed as you waited. Convinced he was not going mad and that he did have a stunning photo of the little green man he found my address and the research was soon underway.[101]

This is a complex and baffling case, full of details. Six months of investigation followed, involving three independent photographic analyses (one carried out by Kodak), a study of Spencer by clinical psychologist Dr Jim Singleton and the investigation of physical evidence by university scientists. This evidence involved a compass that had reversed polarity (which UMIST engineer Dr Spooner suggested could happen but would require the source of an EM field such as might be created by a hospital scanner).

When Spencer had reached Ilkley town he had found that two hours of time had disappeared. Under regression hypnosis he related an abduction account of being taken inside the UFO and shown a rapid series of images like a movie or slide show (a familiar motif, as we have seen). This revealed that the photograph (clearly taken in daylight and not pre-dawn) was shot at the 'end' of the sighting, not the start as consciously believed (and so at about 9.30 a.m.); the 'memory jump' thus occurred before then.

Tests on the photograph can only reveal that it is a real object on the moors. It is between 4 and 5 feet tall – but, of course, it is impossible to know whether it is a model, a child dressed up in a suit., an alien or a goblin. All we can do is trust the witness, puzzle over this extraordinary photograph, be properly cautious as to other explanations but ponder the link with the White Wells goblins seen 109 years before.

West Yorkshire

This large county has a dense population (especially in the Leeds-Bradford metropolitan area). However, it is on the less peopled north-west corner of the county that attention should focus in particular – the part that borders the Calder Valley to the west and Ilkley to the north. Perhaps not surprisingly, this is where the most activity has been generated.

Holmfirth is a pretty village a few miles south of

Huddersfield and surrounded by rolling hills and rather less harsh Pennine landscapes than elsewhere. It is famed as being the location for the filming of the world's longest-running situation comedy, the BBC's *Last of the Summer Wine* which for thirty years has brought us simple tales of Pennine hill folk and their deliberately eccentric adventures.

Scholes is a tiny hamlet a mile outside the village which was the scene of a series of weird events witnessed by Audrey Hanson*. They began as early as 1909 when the room in which she was then playing as a child was suddenly filled with an intense glow that seemed to ooze from the walls as though they were 'painted in glow worms'. This left a magical atmosphere that only subsided when the glow disappeared. During its presence time seemed to stand still and there was a faint humming/whining. It was almost as if Audrey were 'plugged in to another dimension' she said.

On another occasion whilst relaxing by a stream, she suddenly found herself 'transported' to the same place but in a different time. The trees and riverbank were the same, but there were people standing there that she seemed to recognize but could not name. Oddly they were wearing futuristic clothes – completely strange for this period (during the First World War). It was many years before Audrey saw people actually wearing similar apparel. She then knew that she had witnessed a group of people dating from the 1970s – sixty years into the future. They had vanished 'in a blink' as she turned around for a moment.

Audrey also had a sighting of what we now call a UFO to the east of Leeds. Whilst leaving the railway station one winter's day in 1942 she saw an orange/red ball float from the sky low over a cricket pitch. She watched it edge slowly in her direction, and felt a sensation like a tickling – perhaps a result of the electrostatic field. The object shot off towards Garforth and was apparently seen at the same time by a friend of Audrey's who lived in the nearby village of Barwick in Elmet.

They say that buying and selling a house is one of the most stressful activities in which a human being can engage, and that was certainly true for Mrs Belmont*, who told me about what happened to her during the late November 1980 wave that brought the Pennine window vividly to life. Of course, she had no idea that this wave was occurring and her mind was on selling her home near Ingrow on the road to Haworth, home of the famous Brontë family and today a major tourist lure with a perfectly preserved steam branch railway threading the narrow Worth Valley.

Having shown some prospective buyers around her home that evening the three of them stood in the garden discussing the sale when the sky above them noticeably darkened. Bemused the witnesses all looked up to see an enormous black 'cloud' that obliterated the stars. Before there was much opportunity to work out what it was, the truth became evident. They were looking at the flat base of a huge object hovering silently overhead.

As all three watched, a sequence of lights appeared – 'like Christmas illuminations being switched on'. Mrs Belmont gazed in awe as the thing drifted away. 'It was huge,' she noted, 'and moving extremely slowly, taking ages to move away.' When it was some distance from her it accelerated rapidly and vanished in seconds. But sadly, this unexpected event had an unfortunate consequence. Her would-be house buyers fled into their car, muttering something about the area being 'spooked'. They were never heard from again!

This phenomenon could have been an electrically charged cloud. The 'lights' might have been internal energy of the kind seen elsewhere in the Pennines. But there is an added twist. During the 1980s the steam railway company was constructing a station at Ingrow, – moving another building stone by stone from the closed station at Foulridge.

Another case, from a couple of miles north of here, near the village of Glusburn, illustrates the same range of interwoven phenomena. In fact it neatly ties together some of the events reported in this part of the book and has more than a passing resemblance to the previous case. It was the early evening of 7 September 1989. The Ayrton family (mother, daughter and son) were returning from a football match in which their boy had been playing. Suddenly they noticed a yellow glow over a nearby mill and debated what this might be. They rejected various options such as the sun (long set) or a meteor (it was not moving except for a slight 'rising'), but they were keen to get home to watch *M*A*S*H* on TV. As the daughter put it; 'Before we had time to take in what was happening the light – whilst still rising upwards – split into two . . . Mum told us we were going home – now!'

However, after marvelling at the way the object had acted like a cell dividing (a running theme in Pennine light cases, as you will have seen) something else happened. Suddenly 'the thing was over our heads. As we looked up we saw a large mass – but we could not draw the shape if we were asked – with lots of bright, different-coloured lights underneath.' Mrs Ayrton called them (as have others) disco lights. As it passed over them there was a faint humming/whining sound and they briefly looked at each other and then turned back. In seconds it had completely vanished. They scoured the sky towards Keighley and Haworth, where it had been headed, but the sky was inexplicably empty.

Two months later, by chance, a possible solution to the mystery emerged. They consulted a relative who had been in the RAF. He realized that he had already been asked by someone else about an object they saw on the same night and so arranged for the witnesses to swap stories. That woman had been half a mile south-east of where the Ayrtons had been walking. She saw exactly what they did but then witnessed the object flip on its edge in an amazing motion before it reached her position and it sped silently away northwards. The Ayrtons, unaware that in a matter of moments the object they had been watching had now changed course dramatically, had been looking for it as before to their south. In fact as they scoured the 'empty' sky it was making off at speed behind their backs!

This same area also provides one of Britain's most well evidenced cases of an alleged past life. Nicola Peart was born in Keighley during the late 1970s. In 1983 she was bought a toy dog as many youngsters are at that age. She announced that she would call it 'Muff' – the name of her dog when she was last alive and a boy. Baffled, her parents asked what on earth she was talking about and Nicola described her life 'when Mrs Benson was my mummy' and how they lived in 'an old stone house at Haworth'. Her father had worked on the railway and was always coming home dirty. She (or rather the boy she was remembering) had been killed when he strayed onto the railway line and was struck by a steam train.

Unsurprisingly, the Pearts thought this was imagination. After all the 5-year-old girl lived in one of the few areas where steam trains still ran on a daily basis. Keighley was the terminus of the branch line in fact. Moreover, a few years before her birth the movie *The Railway Children* had been filmed on the line. It was set around the time that Nicola seemed to be remembering and it had vivid images of a young child trying to prevent a train accident by standing on the line.

However, a shock awaited the family when they went with Nicola to Haworth – where she had never been before (at least not in this life). Although they got lost, she led them straight to an old stone house that she said was her last home. Checks revealed that a family called Benson had indeed lived here. The father was a railway man and they had a son born in 1875 who had died as a child (cause not listed).[102]

✳ Possibly the focal point of activity in West Yorkshire is Hellfire Corner – a crossroads beside woodland in the settlement of Wyke. Situated in the triangle between Bradford, Brighouse and Halifax, Wyke Woods have become the centre of attention for West Yorkshire researchers.

Nigel Mortimer traced the use of the name back to the 1940s when a fatal motor accident occurred and the driver who ran his car into a wall claimed a bizarre cause. He said that he was distracted by the sudden appearance of a strange glow climbing into the sky from the wood. Folklore researcher Dr David Clarke says, however, that the name had been unofficially applied by locals before then – in fact probably predating the local roads. It has simply gathered a reputation over the years for being a place where frightening things were seen to happen. Some paranormal researchers allege that this is because of the leys – invisible lines of energy within the earth's biosphere. At places where they intersect they reinforce either a positive or a negative flow of energy which can then manifest as good or evil phenomena at the intersection. If positive leys cross then the area might become renowned for possessing a 'healing' energy – perhaps like White Wells spring. But if negative forces interact then it is believed to instil depression and may provoke ill health and accidents.[103]

There is an interesting parallel here with the ideas that we are developing in this book about earth energies. We have noticed how the glowing lights created at hot spots within the Pennines often appear to split and repel one another. A logical reason for this might be that when a charged energy field divides into positively and negatively ionized particles these act like the opposite poles of a magnet. It may not be too far from oppositely charged 'earth energies' to friendly and unfriendly 'ley' crossovers charging a window area hot spot for good or ill.

Paul Bennett, an earth mystery researcher who has also focused on this location, found children at Wyke who feared playing in Judy Woods, closest to the crossroads, because of white smoky glows that they had seen rising up from the ground between trees. They interpreted these things as ghosts and considered the woods to be haunted, but we might view them rather more dispassionately.

It is worth looking at the genesis of a flap of activity that focused on Wyke Woods in 1981. It was well studied at the time and provides useful information. Of course, this was not the only area of the Pennines which was active at the same moment; there were things going on in other hot spots too. At Weir, within UFO Alley, on 15 October (during the Wyke Woods flap) farmers reported seeing several lights dancing over power lines and trailing sparks to the ground. At Howden Moor reservoir in the High Peak of Derbyshire a buzzing light was seen low over the surface.

Although there were sightings at Wyke during the summer (for instance of a floating moon that drifted, grew in brightness and silently exploded over Low Moor) the real starting point for the flap was in October 1981. For several days police received reports of streaks of light like fireworks or silent sheet lightning. Indeed the police wrote these stories off as just that, although to half a dozen different people who saw them they were something stranger.

Paul Bennett summarized the reports as follows: 'What seems to happen is that . . . the entire sky gets lit up, only for a second or two, but definitely bright enough to read by. Then the burst instantly dies and perhaps a few minutes later another "flash" will occur.'

It is easy to see why this seemed like sheet lightning. But the authorities would be unaware that researchers have seen this effect as a very common trigger to numerous waves in the Pennines. The same glows occurred in August 1978 in the villages around Menwith Hill and were followed by an escalating wave of lights in the sky. The police investigated but gave up, just as at Wyke Woods three years later.

The same thing happened in 1982 in Todmorden, as we have seen (see p.76). Police received almost 100 calls from people in the Calder Valley about strange flashes of light illuminating the night sky. Police even went so far as to warn locals not to go 'skywatching' – although this was probably just a wise precaution to avoid the dangers of wandering the moors in the dark. In Wyke Woods in October 1981 there was no sudden burst of energy to end the light show, as occurred in Todmorden. It escalated over the month as if the energy leaked more slowly skywards.

On 18 October Keith Theakstone observed three white lights and then 'a whole string of them' dancing about the sky like marionettes. They vanished in a silent blinding flash of light. Two nights later Paul Frost saw a large ball of light bowling along the ground at Low Moor and surrounded by a shower of electrical sparks. A faint humming noise was heard. On 21 October, hairdresser Raffaele Nobile and his mother saw what she termed 'shining marbles, which glistened as they moved – white, yellow, pink but most numerous was red'. They seemed to drift and wobble and then suddenly dart away at tremendous speeds. Her son reported a humming/buzzing as a large glowing light did what by now we might predict and split into three parts. Two of these shot away as if repelling one another. The third sank to the ground inside Wyke Woods. Scientists and astronomers in Yorkshire were sceptical but amateur astronomer David Roberts saw two of the 'fireballs' for himself on 30 October. They did the splits and sent each other rocketing in opposite directions. He said he was now 'convinced something weird and exciting was happening'.

There was no earthquake (as in Todmorden) to end the Wyke Woods flap. But something dramatic did occur. The concentration of energy at Hellfire Corner seems to have led to tragedy. On 1 November (after which there were no further reports of lights in the sky for weeks) there was another accident. A bus crashed after the driver lost control, and he was seriously injured. According to Nigel Mortimer he reported seeing another smoky white light near the woods.

But it is worth ending with one of the most impressive cases from the area around Wyke reported during yet another flap of sightings (in July 1977). Mrs Fowler* was walking down a sloping meadow, heading for a summer's evening with her horse in an adjacent field. It was a beautiful day. Suddenly 'for no apparent reason' – a comment we hear so often – 'I glanced away from Hunsworth Hill towards the north-west'. As she did so she 'froze to the spot with fear because there was a flying saucer hovering just 1 foot above the ground'.

From only a few hundred feet away Mrs Fowler had an excellent view of the object that was shielded from the road by a dip and floating next to a rocky outcrop. The most noticeable thing was a red cone of flame 'like fiery lightning' coming from the flat base into the ground, 'earthing' itself. Above this was a silvery hat shape with what looked like white lights or windows in a circle round the middle. She stared at it for some minutes and it began to 'wobble' like a spinning top and then to rotate fairly slowly. Within seconds and with a silent flash it shot straight up and almost vanished like magic, rather than flying away.

Mrs Fowler was inclined to describe this as a 'craft' that was taking off with a burst of flame. Indeed, she said, 'I was quite disturbed by this experience because in a flash it literally altered my whole conception of the universe.' But we might wonder if the flame was a discharge from the ground, creating a rotating mass of energy that took on a solid form attracting particles into its electrostatic field. I suspect that quite often energy phenomena are being perceived as structured craft simply because this is how humans expect to see these things. If you expect to see a UFO the chances are that this is what you will observe. But strip away expectation and we have another fascinating example of an electrically charged energy that is emerging *from* the ground.

South Lancashire

This part of the window is a ribbon of small industrial towns such as Bury and Rochdale that still treasure their Lancashire heritage, but are gradually being swallowed by the city of Manchester – whose boundaries have now almost merged with these towns. Interestingly, this is crucial. Whilst you might expect increased population density to lead to a rise in the number of reported phenomena, the inverse is actually true. There are ten times as many recorded cases from UFO Alley than here.

Why is this? More events tend to happen in quieter, rural locations, than they do in places where the bustle of modern life is dominant. To some extent this may simply be because increased light pollution from houses, cars and street lights makes it harder to get in touch with the hills. You are shrouded within your own environment and not an open part of the Pennines as elsewhere. I also suspect that witnesses are less in tune with nature or cannot enter an altered state of consciousness – the sort of calm and quiet that induces necessary reverie – given all the distractions afforded by city living these days. But there are pockets of activity here, most specifically in the corridor between Bury, Rochdale and Heywood, where plenty of odd things have still been reported.

One intriguing local legend tells of a farmer in what was then a rural area around Bury who in the 1840s went on a spree of daring robberies. Ironically, Bury is perhaps famous as the home of Robert Peel, founder of the first modern police force (or 'Peelers' as they were called). And justice put paid to this local crime wave, with the farmer being shot whilst escaping the law. Ever since there have been tales of his vengeful ghost haunting the area of Prestwich, which by Victorian times had become a favoured residential area for merchants from Manchester. One place where the farmer's spectre was seen is the Same Yet Inn. Strange events were sporadically reported right up until the 1990s, involving typical poltergeist activity.

Amongst the things described by occupants of the inn were bottles literally flying off the shelves and the tills opening and closing. But the strangest thing of all occurred in early 1994 when a shadowy mark, which seemed to be a drying or condensation stain, appeared on one inside wall of the building. This, some locals said, looked like the phantom robber. Of course, most people laughed off this story. But in March 1994 they were not laughing quite so loudly. An unexplained fire occurred overnight which did extensive damage, but thankfully nobody was injured. However, the fire brigade was puzzled as to how the heat subsided so rapidly. By the morning the walls were not even warm to the touch. Even stranger, only one wall escaped destruction by the flames, the one with the shadowy damp patch!

Another incident occurred very near to the Same Yet in September 1976. Mary Cotton* told me the following: 'I was driving from Prestwich to Bury with my young daughter in the front seat. I was not thinking of anything spooky. Then, out of nowhere, something hit us. A car rammed us from the side and almost immediately I must have become unconscious. But there was something else – something totally bizarre. I felt a slight jerk as if I had been pushed through the roof of the car and now I was floating in the air watching the scene unfold with curiosity.'

Mary went on to say that she felt no fear but was distressed about her daughter. 'She had been thrown from the front seat into the rear of the car and looked in very bad shape. But I knew she wasn't dead. As for me I felt no pain. I was just a mind on its own looking down at the flesh and bone below, which after a few moments I realized was me – or rather my body – crushed against the wheel and obviously dead to the world.'

From her position hovering unseen about 10 feet above the car Mary had a panoramic view of what happened next. 'Two men arrived and I could see them struggling with the door, which seemed to be wedged. Eventually they got it free and started to pull at the body. It was like watching them move a doll. But then as they pulled 'me' outside I suddenly shifted position again and was inside that doll looking up at the men and moaning with pain.'

Thankfully, although her daughter was very badly injured, both victims survived this accident, but the out-of-body experience left a vivid impression.

Another strange ghostly happening, this time with physical evidence, took place 5 miles to the west at Butterflies Nightclub just outside Oldham. The story of this building is interesting. It had been in use for over a century but was converted from an old Victorian property to its more modern role by extensive renovation work. As we have seen before there seems to be a connection between building work and supernatural activity. But this time that connection operated in reverse. For it was *during* the work, in 1936, that a supernatural imprint may have been left when one of the labourers, George Lloyd, was killed after a heavy beam crashed on to him.

Since that tragedy there have been reports by workers and customers of a strange sensation, as if someone were watching them, and other paranormal events that resemble low-key poltergeist activity in the building. Then came a remarkable episode in the early hours of 27 October 1991.

The club had had a busy Saturday night on the 26th and the tired manager, Cameron Walsh-Balshaw had decided after work ended at around 3 a.m. to go for a cup of tea with his assistant John Reid, who lived locally. He had to drive all the way to South Yorkshire and wanted to freshen up before the long drive across the Pennines on a cold and dark night. Just as he was about to leave for the drive home there was a call from the police. The alarm system at Butterflies had gone off. This happened sometimes, as the system was sensitive. Reid usually went to meet the police and find that it was a false alarm. But since money was locked in the building it had to be checked. When the two men met the police at the club, nothing seemed amiss; everywhere was secure, the money was still in the locked room and there was no sign of a break-in.

To be sure that all was well they ran the security film through. The camera used infra-red beams to illuminate dimly the corridor leading to the cash office, out of sight behind a wall. If anything moved through two successive beams in the corridor the alarm was triggered. Something as insubstantial as a cloud of smoke had tripped the system before. But the camera (which for insurance purposes always used new tape to ensure quality) would confirm if this was just another glitch.

It did no such thing. When replayed there was a stunned

silence as the men watched for several seconds the image of a floating white form, vaguely resembling a man's torso in a sleeveless shirt, coming along the corridor towards the camera, then turning into the office. But it did not open the door. The shape passed *through* the wall as if it was not there! As the police log confirmed, the time that this floating mass appeared on the tape (4.32 a.m.) was precisely when the alarm had been triggered.

This seems to be an extraordinary example of a haunting, or indeed a typical Pennine energy emission floating inside a building like so many reported in this book. It crossed the boundaries between reality. It was seemingly not real in that it behaved like a video replay, but it was substantial enough to trip a computer-controlled alarm.[104]

Of course, there have also been plenty of UFO sightings in this area, but one problem is that the main routes into Manchester Airport pass nearby and misperceived aircraft are common. One odd case occurred on 2 April 1976 when Detective Sergeant (later inspector) Norman Collinson was returning from night duty at 1.50 a.m. He was on the M66 motorway approaching the turn-off to Heywood beside what today is the East Lancashire Railway. He was so intrigued by a brilliant white disc he saw (a quarter the size of the full moon) that he turned off and gave pursuit.

Climbing east towards Heywood he stopped as the object hovered above his car, low down and made 'movements' from side to side. He then gave chase once more as it accelerated away, stopping once more to observe it and trying to identify it as a military helicopter. But suddenly the disc unexpectedly shot from a standing start to a phenomenal speed and disappeared in about a second and without sound towards the hills. So impressed was Norman by this experience that he joined our UFO investigation team and stayed with us for seven years, until it became clear that his rising status in the Fraud Squad was not altogether compatible with the way the public views people who see strange lights in the sky.

Another unresolved event in this area that took place at

Rochdale on 23 January 1982. 'I never believed in UFOs', witness Jeff Garfield told us. 'But after I saw what I saw it changed my life.' A down-to-earth rugby player and council pipelayer he was driving in his car at about 6.30 p.m. when he saw a bright star that 'suddenly went out'. Puzzled he slowed the car to a crawl and looking up saw that a huge dark mass was drifting over the top.

His son was with him and despite the presence of other traffic he stopped the car so that they could get out to watch. The thing was huge – 'the size of a rugby ball at arm's length and moving so slowly it was amazing'. There was no sound at all. He added, 'I just do not understand why the whole town did not see it. They should have done. You could not miss it.' As it passed directly overhead they could see it was shaped like a whale and had small white lights studded in the base (at least a dozen). It took four minutes to move away eastwards.

We found this a fascinating case to investigate because the main witness was so utterly sure of what he had seen. He was very convincing, and he was describing something that was apparently real (given that his son saw it as well). But we had to face the real dilemma – how could it have been real when nobody else of the thousands in Rochdale that night saw its passage? It is this sort of paradox that is at the heart of the paranormal, especially in the Pennines.

A possible clue is that Jeff Garfield had a track record of seeing incredible things. As a child he had observed weird things in his bedroom, including angelic entities. Nobody else could apparently see them and so he taught himself to accept that they were 'just hallucinations' but 'they seemed so real'. Perhaps this indicates that Jeff was a visually creative person, the kind that seems so often to experience these close encounters.

As he said, the incident had a profound effect on his life. He took an interest in topics such as conservation and nuclear disarmament. His workmates were stunned by his sudden desire to move all the worms out of harm's way before their machinery dug up the ground. As for what he saw, he remarked: 'I don't care if the top scientist on earth said what I saw was a jumbo jet I wouldn't believe them. No way. No moving thing on earth can move that slowly.'

North Derbyshire

After the relative quiet of the northern Manchester dormitory towns the Pennine window explodes into life again when we reach this area to the south and east of the city. It is right up there with UFO Alley and Ilkley/Wharfedale as the hottest of hot spots.

This is perhaps the most scenic of all Pennine regions, with the start of the the Pennine Way – and the deep valley gorges found around Edale in particular. There are some spectacular caves, such as the Blue John mines and Speedwell Caverns around Castelton. This region is also steeped in folklore. Devil names abound everwhere, although some, such the mount once called Devil's Arse near Speedwell, have been altered to please modern tastes! Although even here in 2001 the tourist potential of reviving this name was officially recognized.

The small town of Glossop is now popular with commuters from Manchester, being surrounded by moors on three sides. If you were to study what makes the Pennines truly weird then there could be no better place to start because within a 10 mile radius of the reservoir-filled Longendale Valley that stretches off eastwards towards Sheffield strange phenomena are literally everywhere. Indeed local researchers dub this 'the Haunted Valley'. Anomaly hunter Debbie Fair has even set up a unique webcam that offers computer users live internet shots of the barren hills surrounding Glossop so that they can 'skywatch' from their armchair!

Since this area has been exceptionally well covered by Dr David Clarke in an earlier book in this series, I will only cover a few highlights (although it is hard to know where to start even with these) and refer you to that book for much more.[105]

Probably the most famous of many spooky tales connected with the High Peak is that of Dickey's skull. Since the sixteenth century this real skull has resided in a farmhouse between Chapel-en-le-Frith and Whaley Bridge because it was 'cursed' by its former owner. After returning in ghostly form following his murder, 'Dickey' is supposed to have said that if this severed head was ever removed then doom would result. But although long assumed to be male, the skull was actually proved by modern lab tests to be that of a woman. It is believed to be a landowner whose head was severed during a fight with her sister amidst a bitter family feud about 350 years ago.

Attempts to buck the curse have been made – less frequently as time has gone by, since the early ones reputedly met with disaster. In the late 1700s the skull was even once thrown into the picturesque Combs Reservoir. All the fish died of a mystery illness soon after and, naturally, Dickey's skull took the blame. It was quickly retrieved and returned to the farm.

Claims were also made of strange floating lights seen over the land and of frightening noises – often interpreted in legend as 'Dickey's laughter' – which were witnessed by passing horses and coaches.

In 1862 Dickey even brought the London and North Western Railway to heel! The company was forging a line through the Pennines from Stockport towards Buxton and attempted to build a bridge across the haunted farmland. Scoffing at claims that Dickey would not like this disturbance the navvies worked feverishly but the curse struck. The soft land, which had been surveyed as perfectly safe, kept inexplicably collapsing. Tools moved about from one place to another as if unseen hands were responsible. There were 'shakings' of the ground and strange booming noises in the air. Of course, from our knowledge of how building work seems to upset the delicate balance found in these window hot spots we might well have predicted that trying to build a railway here was not a smart plan! Hardened track gangs had soon had enough and refused to disturb the ghost. The company had to alter their route. Today the railway runs between Whaley and Chapel in a long circuit through some of the best scenery in north Derbyshire as it skirts Combs Reservoir. The crossing that was built is Dickey's Bridge.

Mines and caves dot the peaks and have long been associated with the supernatural, ranging from traditional ghosts seen in the Blue John Mines (one noted for announcing his presence by whistling as you walk towards a corner in the dark) to black dogs which are said to dwell in caves and are often seen only as fire-coloured eyes with a dark, ominous shape behind them. And the mines are also haunted by strange noises that escape from the rocks.

Another legend, especially in and around Castleton, concerns the Fiery Drake – a floating ball of orange fire that is said to drift along the shafts underground. Workers associate its presence with coming disaster – possibly at least partly because its appearance caused them to flee and when doing this in darkness they sometimes had an accident.

Then there is the wicked hairpin bend on the Woodhead road out of Glossop. This falls on lonely moors near the ribbon of reservoirs that now stretch along the Longendale Valley. Dazzling blue glows have been reported by local people, park rangers, walkers and drivers passing through, and scare the wits out of the uninitiated. But they are not a modern phenomenon. The bend has gained the name Devil's Elbow because of the frequent tales of strange lights right back into the mists of time. Indeed the legend that dates the origin of this name has alleged that two lovers made a deal with the devil to cement their relationship. But denying this Faustian pact they dared the pass, only to be snared by Satan. The description (from a 1906 account) of what happened next seems eerily familiar. As the devil appeared to 'freeze' them in their tracks a strange light manifested in the sky and scared even the devil. Unable to strike them dead, Satan could only watch as the fairy glow swallowed up the young couple to preserve them from evil. This sounds like the blue glows that are still seen to emerge from rocks here.[106]

Indeed, many of the stories are recognizable to us even behind the myths that clothe them. Whilst we hear of strange buzzing sounds coming from the ground, of floating lights that we assume to be UFOs and of phantom animals with glowing eyes that roam Ollersett Moor and which we call alien big cats, none of this is new. All we are doing is updating legends into the twenty-first century. It seems likely that our children's children will tell similar folk tales long after today's 'reality' is left uncertain by the passage of time.

As a typical example, here is an account from the parish records of an early recorded incident. To the people of the day it was a supernatural wonder, but it was just another Pennine light. At 9 p.m. on 30 March 1716 locals at Chapel-en-le-Frith saw a glow rising up from the ground which illuminated the northern sky. It was so bright that 'you could have read a book at that time of night'. The earth energy streaming skywards was said to look like 'long picks of a large bigness, some black, some the colour of the rainbow, some a whitish colour'. According to eye witnesses these discharges 'broke into flashes like lightning or smoke . . . as fast as you could clap your hands'.

On 28 January 1989 the Charlesworth family from New Mills reported a sighting to me via the Jodrell Bank science centre. I was immediately able to initiate an investigation and rule out aircraft or helicopters as the cause. The only other possible solution (the moon shining through clouds) was refuted from astronomical data (the family saw the moon elsewhere in the sky). A few days later Roy Sandbach and I went to their house, which affords a spectacular view over the hills south towards Chinley and Chapel-en-le-Frith. What Barbara and her two children, James and Sarah, witnessed that night would have been familiar to the folk at Chapel 273 years earlier.

James and Sarah were in the kitchen having a midnight

drink with only a light over the table illuminating them. Their mother came in to get some water to fill a hot-water bottle before retiring to bed, and saw a strange thing in the sky over the hill to the south-east. All three then went to the window to watch for about three minutes – turning off the room light as they discussed possibilities and to eliminate any prospect of a light reflection. 'It was so bright I could see it even with the room light on,' Barbara told us. 'My first thought was "what's that?" and I called out. There were three rows of lights, like floodlights, that were not moving. The whole thing was just above the hill maybe a mile away. It was lighting up the valley below.'

James said; 'At first glance it was like a broad light – like a car headlight. But we were later able to compare this with a car on the hillside and it was nothing like it. This glow was far more remarkable. When I got to the window there were beams coming out of it in several directions.'

Sarah noted: 'It was half the size of the full moon but the rays of light that were coming out were much bigger. One light ray went out, then another came on and moved out. This created an effect like it was rotating but I am not sure that it actually was.'

'The beams were ten times the size of the floodlights,' Barabara explained. 'They kept streaming out and wavering, as if moving about a bit. We watched it for at least forty-five seconds and then it just went out. All of a sudden it was not there any more.'

Sarah confirmed,' We stayed up watching the sky for ages afterwards. If it had been only the one of us that had seen it we might have wondered. But all three of us saw it so we knew it was real.'

During their skywatch they saw (and clearly heard) a mountain rescue helicopter, a common presence in this area. This again allowed comparison but the dim lights of this craft were dismal alongside this strange sight, where feelers of light were somehow being projected skywards from one central glow.

The Charlesworths were looking south towards Chapel;

189

the people of Chapel in 1716 were looking north towards them! In between was the edge just outside Chinley. Nearly three centuries apart and in two different cultures families observed a very similar light show over this hill – much like those we have seen in other parts of the Pennines when this window chooses to put the supernatural on display.

BOLs, or Balls of Light – are much the most common phenomenon to be reported these days in the High Peak. Here are just a few examples.

On 22 February 1993 four people were driving near Devil's Elbow, including a security guard and a nurse. They told NARO: 'At 8.40 p.m. we spotted a strange white glow in the north-west towards Mossley. It was an extremely bright bluish white light that pulsated deeply. As we watched it moved slowly eastwards and then hovered over Crowden reservoir. We lost sight of it over Bleaklow. We stopped to consult the map but there was nothing there – no roads or farmhouses.'

This may well be the Devil's Elbow light, as there have been many similar reports made to the youth hostel at Crowden and to the mountain rescue team (by folk thinking the light is a distress flare). But there is another possibility – just to show that we always need to seek sensible answers. To the north of Crowden there *is* a pulsing light, the beacon on the Holme Moss TV transmitter mast. When seen through mist this can look eerie. When driving on this twisting road it can appear and disappear as intervening topography alters. And when in a moving car in the dark it is common to think the light is moving when in reality it is your motion around unseen bends that creates the illusion. But of course, Holme Moss is a modern light. It could not have led to sightings centuries ago.

On 27 August 1984 two science technicians from Sheffield were hiking over the splendour that is the Vale of Edale. When they were near Nether Edge at around 11 a.m. that sunny morning they saw 'a spherical shining ball moving down the hill'. They were able to watch it very closely for several minutes and discuss what it might be. They considered options such as a piece of plastic caught in an updraft and reflecting the sun. But this idea was soon dispelled because the light approached a barbed wire fence over a dry-stone wall, and did not get caught in the wire. 'It proceeded down the valley,' the witnesses reported. 'After moving through the field it appeared to pass through the fence' – doing so uninterrupted.

The dazzling ball was only a few inches in diameter but clearly self-propelled and floating – yet also 'controlled'. Indeed it climbed up to a height of 20 or 30 feet to rise over a group of trees, hovered there as if observing the terrain ahead and followed the course of the Hope to Edale road as it disappeared upwards. It was last seen climbing at speed until it became lost into the clouds. Checks later revealed that it could not have been a toy balloon as it was moving against the wind.

Similar reports abound in the High Peak. For instance, in April 1983 two doctors on a walking holiday at Torside, north of Glossop, spotted a silver-blue ball as they traversed the Pennine Way. This was on another clear day, at 1 p.m., allowing them to witness the object in perfect detail as it was drifting across Sykes Moor before rising suddenly and rapidly into the clouds.[107]

These BOLs are a very real and frequently observed phenomenon in this area.

South Yorkshire

The Pennine window is largely bounded by three of Britain's major cities, with Sheffield forming the south-eastern edge of the triangle, which also includes Manchester and Leeds. Whilst this spacious and hilly city is close to the heart of the Pennines, and many western suburbs blend into the moors – there can be little doubt where the true centre of activity is to be found. You need only look a few miles either side of the small settlement of Stocksbridge. This is one of the most haunted locations within the entire Pennine hills.

Immediately south of Stocksbridge there are craggy cliffs and active locations such as Wharncliffe and Worrall. To the west, as the often snowbound passes take traffic over the Pennines, there are steep valleys and numerous reservoirs such as Ladybower. This is real supernatural country.

As we have already seen, time anomalies are the flavour of this part of the window. There are ghost planes and spectral aviators that came to grief on the moors (see p.29–30). The use of the reservoir to practise the 'dambuster' raids on the Ruhr Valley has gone down in modern folklore and left its mark. I myself was witness to one of these flights of the phantom bomber in the summer of 1999 when I heard what I took to be a low-flying heavy military aircraft pass over my home and head north-eastwards towards Sheffield. I was mildly curious, but not curious enough to assume it was anything other than an ordinary plane (as do at times pass over). I kicked myself later when reports came in, including from an off duty pilot in Chapel-en-le-Frith, saying that they had heard this same drone but (being outside) could plainly see that no bomber was causing it! We had heard a ghost plane on its eerie flight.

However, much more than ghost Lancaster bombers are to be found in this part of the Pennines. Here is a fascinating story told to me by Jane Hayes* from Stocksbridge. As a courting teenager in 1948 she, her boyfriend, a work mate and that girl's boyfriend would often camp in the local woods. Wharncliffe Crags were especially popular. But one weekend they made the mistake of visiting a small wood south-west of Stocksbridge known locally as 'Spooky Woods'. They soon discovered why it had attracted this curious appellation.

'On this particular Sunday,' Jane reports, 'we four had eaten our meal, chased one another around the rocks and fir trees and after throwing soil onto the wood fire we sang a few songs and retired to our tent . . . All at once we heard a noise which sounded like a horse galloping. It was coming from the distance and growing nearer and nearer until it was so loud it was like a heartbeat throbbing. We all looked at one another and were petrified. This thing was coming straight at us! I really expected to be trampled to death. But just as it reached the tent it stopped. It did not turn around or go back. It disappeared instantly. We plucked up the courage to go out and look. But there were no hoof marks in the soft earth. It was impossible. My friend's boyfriend yelled, 'Let's get out of here' and we ran to the nearest farmhouse. We have often talked about it since. It was completely real. We heard the sound of a horse that wasn't there.'

Or, more likely, they heard the replayed sound of a horse that once *had* been there.

Nor was this the only strange thing in these Stocksbridge woods. Jane later discovered from local farmers that they had often seen lights but when they went to investigate there was nothing there. This was how the woodland gained its reputation. In about 1958 Jane herself and her young son witnessed an enormous circle of lights the size of the moon that hovered over the reservoir at the back of the woods before simply winking out. They were never able to explain what it was.

Stocksbridge woodland has certainly earned this bizarre reputation. It has been riddled with many other frightening episodes that seem to reflect both out-of-time sounds and visions as well as vanishing lights. These have been independently reported by people who had no idea about earlier accounts.[108] Larry Mayer was one witness to experience the odd sights and sounds in these woods. This is the story told to us at NARO.

One day in the late 1930s he had been playing in the trees when he heard a sound like a choir singing. Looking up to find the source of this music he could see nothing except a dark hole that formed in the air and blotted out the sky. Then the sound just disappeared.

But this was far from the end of Larry's adventures. On 19 September 1987, after moving away from the Sheffield area to live in Manchester, he returned to Stocksbridge for a family wedding. As he turned onto the main road over the

Pennines he drove past the woodland in front of Langsett Hill and saw something strange in a clearing, which he described as rows of lights in a circle. He could not know he was reporting what Jane Hayes had described here thirty years before.

Larry now realized that the road around him was eerily quiet. He felt a strange sense of calm over the area – just as we have noted at the onset to these 'time-slips'. So he stopped off the road to consider whether to walk back and look inside the clearing, but he chose to drive on. A few minutes later, as he crossed the Woodhead Pass, he came upon an accident. A car was overturned and police and other emergency services were just arriving to assist. Had he not been delayed by the lights in the wood he could have been caught up in this smash. Driving past the rescue Larry reached home forty minutes later to discover to his shock that it was incredibly late. He travelled this road often and knew to within a few minutes how long it should take to make the Pennine crossing. But that evening over an hour disappeared somewhere near the Stocksbridge woods.[109]

Completely unknown to Larry, odd things had been going on in the village during the previous few weeks, connected with the building of a by-pass following the Don valley. Security guards Steven Brookes and David Goldthorpe were guarding the earthworks and witnessed a group of small figures dancing in a circle underneath electricity pylons that then straddled the building site! Assuming at first that they were trespassing children they closed in. But the figures completely vanished, leaving no footprints in the muddy work site – impossible given the number of 'kids' they had seen. Making enquiries, the two guards soon discovered that workers housed in a number of caravans had heard the sounds of 'children' at this spot in the dead of night during previous days, but on going out to warn them off they had found nothing. These people were all unaware of the range of local tales from other people about 'replayed' sights and sounds.

Days later, on 7 September, just before Larry Mayer saw his circle of lights, another incident occurred on the major road scheme. The same two security guards saw what looked like a man on the overbridge beside the building site. They shone their car headlights to illuminate the scene but the beams passed right through the shadowy figure and it promptly vanished! They rushed to the local vicar for pre-dawn reassurance and the police were called in. Exactly seven days before Larry Mayer had his frightening experience – on the night of 12 September – officers Andrew Bentley and Michael Keen staked out the site and were terrified when the shadowy form of a man reappeared near their car, accompanied by an eerie sensation that made their skin crawl. The figure came right up to them before vanishing. It was wearing clothing from the Victorian age, including a cravat and frock coat.

Just north of here the old Woodhead railway reaches Penistone and a line cuts through old pit shafts heading for Barnsley. At Silkstone, only 3 miles north of Stocksbridge, yet another strange incident was recorded. On 25 October 1997 Daniel Geraghty and Daniel Takeer were returning from a fishing trip when they heard footsteps on the hill between there and Stocksbridge. Then there was a noise like rustling leaves and looking back the youths spotted what they called 'a little girl dressed in funny, old-fashioned clothes and surrounded by a white mist' – the classic signs of a typical time-slip vision.[110]

The two terrified witnesses walked on, having to pass within feet of the figure, who seemed to watch them as they went by. On arrival home they told Ken Geraghty, who helped create an artist's impression of the girl that they had seen. This story and the sketch appeared in the local paper and brought forth a stunning response. On 10 November, a 68-year-old woman cautiously came forward to admit that she recognized the sketch from old family albums. It looked very much like her aunt, who had died when aged just eleven, when she was accidentally shot by a local farm worker whilst cleaning a gun. As soon as the boys saw a photograph taken three years before Emily was killed they said it was the girl. Daniel even noted that they had seen a black neck choker, which the girl had been fond of wearing. Her niece confirmed that just before the tragedy Emily had been known to play on the same track where the apparition was seen in 1997. But the girl had died eighty-nine years earlier in 1908!

I will close with one further case, this time in Nether Edge. It involves the Browitt family who had a most unusual haunting over a period during 1986. David, a decorator, was often doing repair work around the house. His wife Beryl also had an impressive track record of strange experiences, including lucid dreams, where she could control the content, and out-of-body visions, where she floated free of her physical self. There were also frequent minor poltergeist events around the house, such as objects moving of their own volition.

But the most intriguing phenomenon was a floating amorphous shape, which was seen on a number of occasions, especially in the main bedroom. It resembled smoke or vapour but seemed to be composed of fine particles that came together into a cloud that was roughly shaped like a person. This drifted about the room, sparkling like thousands of fireflies, then just as quickly as it had appeared it would vanish. They soon regarded it as a form of haunting.

Beryl usually kept clear when this misty shape appeared, but on one occasion saw it too late and had walked through it before she had time to stop. It did not in any way impede her passage. However, it did give a cold sensation to the exposed skin and left an interesting legacy. It seems to have charged up the atmosphere with static electricity. The fine hairs on the end of her arm were made to stand up as if they had been energized. And residual electrical problems were caused around the house for a few days – equipment such as TV sets not working properly when she was nearby.

What may well have happened here is that there was an electrostatic force field associated with this 'apparition'. Beryl, being susceptible in some way, was literally 'charged' by her passage through this field just as one can rub a silk tie to cause a balloon to stick to the body through electrostatic energy.

The 'apparition' might well have been nothing more than fine particles of dust from around the house attracted to this electrostatic field in exactly the same way. So when the field was active because the window had been triggered a cloud of particles would gather together and gradually dissipate as the energy subsided. The 'shape' seen behind the cloud probably owed more to imagination than reality. All that was visible was an electrical mist, pretty much as Beryl Browitt described it.

Indeed, I suspect this may happen often in windows, and not only inside buildings where it can become a common source of many a 'ghostly' tale (for instance the floating mass that triggered the security camera in the Oldham nightclub) – (see p.182–3). I think it is very likely that many UFOs seen in and around window areas are similarly insubstantial. Witnesses describe order and form but mostly see glowing energy fields and clouds of dust temporarily bonded together by the attractive forces generated. In the Pennines many of these paranormal events may literally be made out of dust.

South Pennines

We have reached the southern end of our tour of this diverse region. Bounded to the north by the Cheshire towns of Macclesfield and Congleton, it spreads eastwards into part of the Peak District National Park. Here the Pennines combine with river valleys, especially around Dovedale, to cut limestone gorges. At the southern end is Staffordshire, with Britain's best-known theme park Alton Towers built around wooded gardens in undulating hills. The Pennines peter out south and east of the Pottery towns around Stoke-on-Trent, descending into the low fault-riddled terrain known as Cannock Chase between Uttoxeter and Walsall.

Much of this area has a low population density and there have been some spectacular cases reported here. In fact some of the most thoroughly attested encounters have been recorded in this area and it also probably has some of the best-known folk legends in the Pennines.

On 16 May 1993 a group of young people under the care of a senior supervisor had been on a day trip from a children's home viewing the Pennine outpost of Alderley Edge. This western extremity near Macclesfield offers fine walks and superb views across the Cheshire Plains. It is steeped in supernatural lore. The writer Alan Garner has set many spooky tales round here, discussing ghosts, curses and time slips.[111] These are escapist fiction but rooted in the paranormal that abounds here.

It is believed by many researchers that Alderley is a major energy crossover, rather like Hellfire Corner (see p.175–6). The lines of earth energy are considered so strong that people can feel their power – on this occasion working for good. It is very much like a natural feng shui of the landscape (indeed this now topical Chinese belief originated from an almost identical concept where unseen 'dragon' lines charged the earth with power). Pagan ceremonies and witchcraft rituals have long been practised at Alderley because the lure of this powerful spot is so strong.

At the Edge there is a very old association with Merlin. You can find it marked locally through place and building names like The Wizard. This all depends upon the key belief, spawned by long-lost stories many centuries old and widely believed even in these days, that King Arthur, his knights and Merlin the court wizard are all in a state of suspended animation waiting in another dimension that is hidden beneath a window in the rocks. They are waiting for the moment when the kingdom faces its greatest peril. Then they will rise from the netherworld to save Britain from tragedy. Quaint as this may seem, local folklorist Doug Pickford reports that in 1940, when Britain stood alone against the seemingly invincible Nazi invasion, academics from Manchester University were sufficiently minded to meet at Alderley to try to coax the spirit of Arthur to emerge![112] The knights did not literally rise – although perhaps symbolically they did. For Britain was spared what seemed to most outsiders quite certain defeat thanks to the wizards of the air force in their flying dragons (the Spitfires) – not to mention the failings of Hitler and no little dose of miraculous fortune.

The party of children drove from Alderley to Mow Cop, a rocky outcrop near Kidsgrove and one of the last throws of the Pennines, known since druid times for its healing waters. At nearly 1 a.m. they saw a huge white light plunge out of clouds and silently pass above them before spurting off northwards climbing again. Had Merlin and the white knights emerged from their slumber?

Not surprisingly frightened, the team called the radio telescope at nearby Jodrell Bank (writer Alan Garner by coincidence long having lived in an adjacent field)[113]. Jodrell called me next day and the answer was found. A holiday flight from Glasgow to Ibiza hit trouble over the Pennines. At Mow Cop it made an emergency turn and descended rapidly to fly into Manchester, but the turbulence rising from the hills at this low height was a problem and the landing was abandoned. The jet climbed back up, returned to Glasgow and made a safe landing there. No doubt passengers had no idea of the UFO scare they had created on route.

In between Alderley Edge and the main Pennine ridges to the east is the small village of Prestbury. Doug Pickford told me that this is on dragon lines from Alderley and has been a place of reverence for centuries. A dragon is believed to sleep under the earth here. Even now some locals use the age-old term 'the village of the dead' to refer to the village. He had received stories about hauntings associated with Butley Hall, just outside the village. These were connected with a servant family and the tragic death of a young child. This information intrigued me, because I also had several stories of modern apparitions coming from the same place.

Gladys Rogers*, for instance, described how she

witnessed golden balls of light coming out of the ground between Prestbury and Bollington. These culminated in one incident in October 1976 when she felt a sudden 'awareness' that something was in a neighbour's garden. Going to take a look she was confronted with a 'large floating shape like a man but glowing all silver. I could see no face and the head seemed out of proportion to the body – much smaller.' She described how as she watched this spectral form drift across the ground, seemingly floating above it, 'I could feel what was almost like an electric charge coming out of it. Energy was lighting up the ground.' It vanished with a flash.

However, the most intriguing case that we followed up came from the landlord of the Ash Tree Inn at Butley in the mid 1980s. He was called Phoenix, in of itself a delightfully mythological name. A phoenix, of course, is a free spirit bird that is reborn to new life from the fire and ashes. The inn is on an old site at the crossroads where traffic would go east to Bollington, south to Macclesfield and west towards Alderley. The Phoenix family took over the inn during the mid 1960s and immediately became aware of strange things going on here. In particular they heard footsteps tramping about in the dead of night. At first they thought it was their young daughter unable to sleep, but she was always asleep. After a while they simply accepted 'the ghost' and found the noises had apparently often been heard by others. Once they learned to live with their supernatural lodger things calmed down.

However, there were then sporadic poltergeist outbreaks, where objects would move about of their own volition. The most curious of these was an old toby jug placed on a table near what locals call 'the creepy spot' (so named because total strangers would move away saying they could feel a strange tingling electricity that made their skin crawl – much like Gladys Rogers, in fact). The toby jug placed near here would regularly move by several feet during the night. At first they assumed somebody was doing it on purpose. Then they accepted it as 'the ghost'. It carried on doing this with regularity until they moved to live in a house at nearby Bollington (rather than living on premises) and took the toby jug with them. It never moved again.

Whilst the Phoenix family learned to live with their unseen guest, his brother did not. He moved into the inn with his wife for two weeks to let Mr Phoenix go on holiday. During the stay the weird activity went haywire. Not only were the footsteps heard incessantly and objects moved about the room, but on several occasions the poor couple were pushed to the ground by invisible forces and the terrified woman was once pinned against a wall by an unseen presence. They spent the last night before the Phoenixes' return wide awake with the light on, vowing never to return to the Ash Tree.

These experiences (which occurred throughout the 1970s and 1980s) led to a more modern kind of apparition. And this particular sighting of a UFO must go down as one of the most impressive on record. At 8 a.m. on 16 September 1981, Mr Phoenix was taking his dog for a morning constitutional on the grass verge opposite the pub. Suddenly, approaching from the Prestbury direction, came a most extraordinary object. It was a clear, sharp morning, and the object was very low and therefore unmistakable. In shape it resembled a jelly mould or beer glass cut in half, an effect enhanced by the hexagonal windows around the circular form. There was a flat base and more strange than this a small arm protruding from the side that rotated in a circle around the object as if it were some kind of probe on a pole.

Mr Phoenix watched in amazement as the thing hugged some electricity power lines, crossed directly over his head (revealing it to be the size of a house and yet utterly silent) and then hovered over pylons on the slopes rising towards Bollington. In this period of a minute or two a cyclist had ridden along the road and nearly fell off his bike in astonishment (Mr Phoenix later made the effort to watch for him passing again so that he could contact him and reassure himself this event had happened).

The two men now felt odd – as if they were being

watched – as the object reversed its course and started to drift back westwards towards Alderley. Mr Phoenix rushed back indoors and Mrs Phoneix confirmed that her husband had come in ashen-faced with shock. The story was reported to an airline pilot (this is a prosperous area and many pilots live locally). He was sufficiently intrigued to call contacts at Manchester Airport later that day, who eliminated any aircraft or weather balloons as the cause. Exactly what this thing was I do not know. But it seems to have had an affinity for the power lines and reversed course over the inn. Indeed it might be said to have drifted along the 'dragon lines' that Doug Pickford says may intersect this area. And the existence of the 'creepy spot' inside the inn might support the suggestion that the presence of earth energy can even be felt here from time to time.[114]

Are the same forces responsible for the footsteps (the haunting), as a form of time recording, and do they also provide the energies that move objects around? Perhaps Butley is at the focus of forces that manifest on a grander scale all over the Pennines and power so many supernatural happenings.

Intriguing as this close encounter is, even odder things have occurred in the far south of the Pennines – Uttoxeter and Cannock Chase in Staffordshire. Here two related yet independent cases happened which may be perfect examples of the mysterious energy that fuels the Pennine window. On 22 September 1987 the Gunters* and their 21-year-old son Dominic and his teenage friend, Stephen, were heading into Uttoxeter, passing Baggots Forest and the village of Abbots Bromley. From these four excellent witnesses we know that the time of the event was 10.18 p.m. precisely.

They were passing through a dip in the chase with the road rising ahead of them when an object appeared in the east and shot at great speed directly in front. It was low and huge 'covering an enormous expanse of sky' and Mr Gunter said, 'We felt like toy soldiers in a scene out of a Steven Spielberg movie.'

The massive object was now hovering 20 feet over them and they referred to the 'mesmeric' effect this had on reality. 'I couldn't believe my eyes,' Mrs Gunter said. It was a huge triangle with pulsing white glows and a flux of multi-coloured lights (blue, green, red and gold). 'The colours were very vivid and neon-like,' she added. They pulsed and throbbed, making this whole encounter seem like the 1977 incident at Nelson (see p.35–6), except that at Abbots Bromley there was no effect on the car engine or lights.

As they drove away from underneath it, the object banked slightly. Then in complete silence it climbed vertically and was gone. So stunned was Mr Gunter that he nearly drove into a car coming the other way (the occupants did not come forward). Terms like 'a marvellous, indescribable experience' conveyed the bafflement such a sighting can bring.

An interesting postscript added by Mrs Gunter was that after it had gone 'my whole body felt as if it had been electrified.' We have seen several times before how this sense of being 'charged up' is a common theme in the Pennines.[115] The date of this event, incidentally, was three days after the Stocksbridge wave (see p.191–6).

Less than a year later, on 4 August 1988, there was a second impressive sighting on Cannock Chase on the other side of Blithfield Reservoir and near the village of Little Hayward. The case was a joint investigation between Clive Potter of BUFORA (who had looked into the Abbots Bromley incident) and Susan Dean and Kevin Flannery of the group Skyscan.

Two people, Reg Morgan and Gloria Hall, were driving home from a Gingerbread group meeting that night. It was just after midnight as they traversed this rural road that skirts the chase. Gloria spotted the object first and was stunned into silence. Reg noticed that she had stopped talking and looked up. They both then had a clear view of a circular mass about 30 feet high and as large as a house. It glowed with a deep reddish colour that pulsed in a throbbing manner but was also surrounded by a cloud or mist that went down towards the ground. Indeed the object was so low that this cloud touched the top of a hedge beside the road. The whole phenomenon was mostly just glowing energy – described as 'fluorescent and infra red' – and a strange cloud or mist from out of which a semi-solid object emerged. After about 30 seconds the pulsing mass just disappeared, but it reappeared a few seconds later to the north towards Uttoxeter (with no indication of how it had moved there. It then disappeared. During its presence the two witnesses had both experienced a strange sense of calm and sudden quietness that seems very much like the Oz Factor back at work.

We were called in when the local newspaper reported the story and called me for help. I promised an investigation which Clive Potter and the others duly provided. What particularly aroused our interest was that Reg and Gloria commented that they went back in daylight next day to look at the hedge where the cloud had touched and there were clear signs of damage, with the bushes pushed back as if by some force. The couple had reported it immediately to the police in Great Haywood, but they did not seem keen to take the matter further. The investigators searched the area of a 4 foot tall hedge where branches were uprooted, twisted out of the ground and in some instances denuded of bark as if by a strong force.

Dr Michele Clare, a plant biologist at the university in Sheffield, studied samples. Meteorologist and physicist Dr Terence Meaden also took an interest in the possibility that this was some rare form of atmospheric energy vortex. Indeed one of his colleagues from the Tornado and Storm Research Organisation (TORRO), David Reynolds, lived in the West Midlands and went to visit the site. The conclusions of these studies were that the damage was a physical uprooting, but it was not possible to say what energy had caused it. It was not heat, but there were no adjacent tracks to indicate that any machinery had operated in this spot and the damage was very localized.

Overall, the most likely answer was that this was either

an atmospheric plasma or an earthlight (it occurred in a geologically faulted area). The glow resulted from the misty cloud that surrounded it, as prevailing weather suggested. There may have been sufficient energy within this phenomenon to uproot parts of the hedge. The red glow, incidentally, makes perfect physical sense. A study of such energy ball sightings shows that they are frequently bluish/white when the atmosphere is dry; the electricity releases blue ions from dry air. But when the weather is damp and the atmosphere moist (as it was here) the increased hydrogen leads to an extra reddish colour. It seems unlikely that most witnesses, being naïve of such physics, could consistently describe the right colour for the phenomenon by chance – not unless this is evidence of the genuine properties of the energies involved.[116]

North of Uttoxeter there is an added danger from these floating clouds of energy – they can kidnap you! That possibility will become apparent from some of the events in this area. But first consider a frighening incident on 30 August 1992 when five people were on a weekend trip to the countryside between the Manifold Valley and Dovedale on the Staffordshire/Derbyshire borders. They were staying in a converted barn off the road from Leek towards Ashbourne, in the Milldale region and a few miles south of the Arbor Low stone circle. They were in a very isolated spot at least a mile from other houses.

At 3.30 a.m. one of the party, Mrs Dennison* struggled in the dark down the steps to go to the toilet after failing to find a flashlight. Outside she noticed that it was oddly light. Going to look she soon discovered that the moon was not the cause, as it was only a thin crescent and elsewhere in the sky. Instead the whole of the hillside was being lit by a huge white cloud that was formed of multiple white dots like a myriad fireflies. She stood in awe of this sight (something never seen in their many previous rural trips) as it hovered for about three minutes. Then she woke the others. The object had now moved slightly and was illuminating her way through the barn. But by the time her daughter had woken it was heading eastwards towards Dovedale. Three of the five women saw something (the other two failed to wake up!).

However, the frightening part came when they realized that their dog had become terribly distressed. It was a seasoned traveller and enjoyed staying the night inside the car parked outside the barn, where it slept and acted as guard. But this event seems to have terrified the poor creature and it had literally gone berserk, clawing so badly at the door that it was almost ripped off its hinges.

A little south of here is Mayfield, a village on the county border near the market town of Ashbourne. On 20 December 1988 there was a strange episode there at 7.40 a.m. Phil Marshall* was riding to work on his moped from Ellastone when he spotted a pyramid of light in the sky and began to feel very strange. There was a strange sense of calm and the next thing he knew the object had gone. He was also feeling rather unwell. Once he reached Ashbourne two things became clear. His motorcycle was malfunctioning (but checks by engineers found no fault and it worked fine that night). And it was also rather later than it should have been. At least several minutes had disappeared. Phil had a pounding headache, sore eyes, dizziness and a tingling sensation like pins and needles that gradually subsided. All of these are classic witness symptoms that have been widely reported in the aftermath of such energy encounters.[117]

The village of Mayfield features in an even more recent strange encounter, in which an old stone cottage became the focus of a powerful haunting. So severe were the effects, involving figures walking around and strange noises, that the occupants refused to pay some of the money due for the purchase of the property, saying it was haunted and taking the matter to a well publicized court case in 1999.

This case is reported in more detail by David Clarke in his recent book.[118] I visited the harassed family myself in 1998 and was able to see the trauma that the experiences were creating as they unfolded. There was building work going on, even to the extent of digging up their garden looking for the bones of the 'restless spirit' they thought must be to blame. During this visit I was also shown some footage taken by the family on their camcorder in one of the haunted rooms. Although as evidence of a ghost it was not very exciting, it had another meaning for me. The footage showed a mist rising from the stone and swirling around until it fogged out the camera lens. Just as quickly it disappeared.

This 'spectral smoke' is interestingly like the mists and energy forms that have been reported across the Pennine window and have sometimes been seen to come out of the rocks. It reminded me of the smoky earthlight that I saw for myself rising from the fault-ridden Berwyn Mountains.

In this same part of the Pennine window there was a remarkable close encounter on 16 June 1991 involving Bill, a businessman who was driving home late at night through the Staffordshire moorlands. Because he had consumed a lot of coffee he stopped on the road from Leek (literally for a leak!) by chance next to a neolithic site called the Bridestones, where people have worshipped the power of earth energy for thousands of years.

It was about 1.30 a.m. and yet above the stones there was a bright light, much like that which terrified the holiday-makers in the barn near Arbor Low. Bill decided not to go closer when the ball of light began to shower golden sparks like flecks of electricity down towards the ground. Instead he scurried back to his car but the vehicle was drained of all power. Getting out to see if he could find what was wrong he noticed that the golden cloudy mass was heading straight for him. Simultaneously he felt rooted to the spot, a strange sense of impending unconsciousness and a pain behind his eyes like a knife stabbing his head. Then he blacked out.

Bill recovered, flat out on the ground some distance away, amidst a group of trees. He was weak and completely disorientated as he struggled back to consciousness. He could barely walk and had to crawl on all fours looking for his car, cutting himself in the process. For he was only wearing his trousers; his shirt and shoes were missing – they turned up on the floor next to his car. As he staggered to his feet to get dressed he instinctively brushed the dirt off his clothes and sparks of static electricity shot out. Still disorientated and tripping as he fell towards the car, Bill found that his keys were still in the unlocked vehicle. To his relief it now started first time. He drove off – at great speed! – noting that the clock read 3.05 a.m. – meaning ninety minutes had disappeared from his recall.

Bill declined to go public with his story, certain that it would compromise his successful business life. But he is a personal friend of folklore writer Doug Pickford, who tells me he is certain this is a completely truthful story. It seems a remarkable encounter that fits well with the many other cases of energy balls that make their home within the Pennines.

In almost the same location, in January 1974, another terrifying experience occurred. Jeff, a student teacher, and his fiancée Jane (both aged twenty) were driving near Leek at 9.30 p.m. when a green mass appeared in the sky. It followed them for a short distance before heading south towards Cheddleton. Even though it had disappeared the young couple felt a strange sense of presence, as if they were being watched. Despite being in the middle of nowhere, they stopped, and got out of the car and stood in the middle of the road staring at the sky. They later found this action inexplicable!

Directly overhead was a huge dark mass and from this silent monster came two beams of light. A green one lit up the road and another – blue – illuminated the car. Then they slowly moved together, forming one big circle that swallowed up the car. The terrified couple leapt into the vehicle (the engine was still running) and 'on impulse' shot off over the moors in the direction that the beams were now headed. Moments later, so it seemed, there was a bump and they 'came to' as if waking from a hypnotic trance. The bump turned out to be a cattle grid at Ilam, a village on the edge of Dovedale. Moments later there was another jolt and, with no break in the flow of time, they were now mysteriously in suburban streets. They found a police station and discovered it was Macclesfield – 25 miles away! What was worse, it was 3.30 a.m. Six hours had somehow just disappeared. The police had to send a patrol car to the homes of their distressed families to try to explain what had just happened to their son and daughter.

Not that anyone can really yet explain what did happen, of course! All we can do is try.

Appendix I
A Quick Guide to Hot Spots

Cheshire

Alderley Edge
Supposed ley cross-over point associated with myths and legends about earth power and magical forces hiding in another dimension ready to save the earth.

Macclesfield
Town with numerous stories of haunting and sightings of UFOs over the Pennines to the east, but also where it it easy to misinterpret aircraft heading north into Manchester Airport.

Prestbury
Known as the 'village of the dead'. Famed for hauntings, poltergeist effects, UFOs and a sleeping dragon supposedly buried under the ground.

Derbyshire

Ashbourne
Pretty market town with a spectacular alleged haunting in 1998, a major UFO sighting in 1980 and within an area noted for strange lights.

Chapel-en-le-Frith
Home of the curse of Dickey's skull and a time replay that haunts the church.

Chinley
Where lights emanated from the rocky edge and an alien big cat was seen on Ollersett Moor.

Dovedale
Beautiful gorge only accessible to walkers between Buxton and Ashbourne. Centre of Pennine activity for dislocations through time and space, mysterious lights and alien kidnaps.

Edale
Start of the Pennine Way hikers' trail and at the centre of a region where earthlights are often seen.

Eyam
Haunted village east of Buxton with grim but heroic legends.

Glossop
At the heart of the High Peak hotspot – associated with legends such as the Devil's Elbow to the north and the multiple lights seen in the Longendale Valley eastwards.

Hope
Noted for time-slips and the High Peak ghost aircraft; also south into Ladybower Reservoir.

Winster
Between Buxton and Matlock Bath (known as 'Little Switzerland' owing to pretty gorges), noted for humming sounds emerging from the rocks. Also a flap of lights in the sky between summer 2000 and early 2001 including video footage of a big pink blob taken at Bonsall in October 2000.

Appendix I

Lancashire

Bacup
Town at the east end of the Rossendale Valley and one of the biggest UFO sighting hot spots in the UK, especially focused on quarries and in surrounding villages such as Stacksteads and Weir and moors east to Todmorden.

Boggart Hole Clough
North of Manchester, now a parkland, long associated with the west Pennine goblin or spook called the boggart which for some still practises mischief on passers by.

Bowland
The surrounding forest and fells are the reputed home of rock-throwing boggarts and 'spooks' that interfere with local motor cars.

Foulridge
East of Pendle Hill, where resident boggarts have led to modern day poltergeist activity. At nearby Earby earth-lights have been seen emerging from the ground.

Goosnargh
Village with Chingle Hall nearby – one of the most haunted houses in the UK with various lights, sounds and electrical effects recorded there.

Oldham
Town surrounded by villages where major UFO flaps occurred during the 1970s when police chased the 'phantom helicopter' over the moors. More recently the scene of the classic video recording of a nightclub ghost.

Pendle Hill
For centuries associated with witchcraft and magic; in more modern times its poltergeist attacks have extended to glows

emerging from the mountain and electrical effect laden close encounters.

Rochdale
A hot spot for both poltergiest and light-in-the-sky activity.

Staffordshire

Leek
Around Rudyard Lake, the ancient Bridestones and the remote roads across the Staffordshire Moorlands heading east into the Pennines have numerous sightings of lights and associated time anomalies.

Mow Cop
Rocky outcrop near Kidsgrove and reputed home of healing spring, centre of strange light activity.

Uttoxeter
Cannock Chase to the south is the location for evidential close encounters with energy-rich light phenomena.

Yorkshire, North

Appletreewick
Light phenomena long seen here, once associated with the trolls in nearby mines.

Carleton Moor
Various reports of lights that have been photographed over the rocks.

Cracoe
Light phenomena regularly seen – some proved to be strange optical reflections off the rock surfaces.

Menwith Hill
Secret US base and focal point for numerous lights in the sky above surrounding villages.

Yorkshire, South

Stocksbridge
Hot spot north of Sheffield – home to time-slips, ghosts, and UFO-associated temporal anomalies.

Totley
Earth energy seen rising from ground and time-displaced events including flying dinosaurs.

Yorkshire, West

Cottingley
Dell where fairies have long been seen, scene of famous hoax photographs.

Hebden Bridge
Calder Valley area rich in folklore from Celtic times and both time anomalies and UFOs in modern day. Stone head markings of an alien-like face in and around nearby Mytholmroyd.

Ilkley Moor
Rocky moor long said to be home of goblins and fairies, also healing springs. Many strange lights in the surrounding villages and modern goblin encounters.

Shipley
Sightings of flying dinosaurs in the valley east towards Thackley.

Todmorden
The single most haunted town in the Pennines, centre of alien contact and UFO encounters; also noted for electrical effects and time-slip activity.

Wyke Woods
Strange lights, misty earthlights rising from the ground and reputed ley cross-over at Hellfire Corner said to have generated 'negative' vibes.

Appendix II
Facts and Figures about the Pennine Window

I have said that the Pennine moors represent the biggest window area within the UK. This is a serious claim, especially set against numbers sometimes quoted by the media about hundreds of sightings being made in some suddenly active town. So how can I justify this suggestion?

A concerted effort to log sightings in some hot spot will increase the apparent number of strange things being seen there. This is an artificial tweaking of the system, merely boosting the percentage of events that are recorded. It may not indicate that many more are happening. The number reported is always significantly less than the number being observed; it is human nature. You do not create a window area just by enhancing temporarily the levels of ongoing activity that are made public. But although good records do not exist for comparative purposes in terms of apparitions, time-slips or assorted other phenomena, such a judgement *is* possible with UFOs. Numerous groups exist to record this information and they have been systematically doing so for the past fifty years.

This allows me to publish a cumulative set of statistics compiled from primary sources in the UK. The figures below rely upon the data from twenty-seven organizations that have kept records and have existed for at least three years (this improves the quality of data because it means the groups doing the recording have had some experience). The two largest organizations are the British UFO Research

Association (BUFORA), founded in 1962 but based on several local groups dating back as early as 1952, and NUFON, an alliance of regional groups across two-thirds of the British Isles, founded in 1974.

Here is what this study reveals. (All the figures cover the period 1947 onward; the last year tallied was 2000).

During that period my records (which should, of course, only be considered as a guide) show 10,278 sightings reported in the UK. This is a minimum figure because opinion surveys have long shown that only about one in ten people publicly report sightings for various reasons (most commonly a fear of ridicule). Yet even this total indicates an average number of about 200 sightings per year. When you bear in mind that every country on earth reports strange things, too, then you start to see the extent of the problem.

Of the 10,278 sightings on my records, 3,260 cover the north of England (that is all the counties bounded by a line from Birmingham in the south, to East Anglia and Lincolnshire in the east and to the Scottish and Welsh borders). If we now look at the total reported *only* within the Pennine area (as defined in this book) there are 1,076. That is almost a third of the northern England figure and one-tenth of that for the entire British mainland.

To put that into better perspective, here are comparative percentages for the number of reports shown alongside the area of the country covered and the size of population involved in these areas.

	Total reports:	(% British Mainland)	(% British Total reports)	(% Population)
All	10,278	100	100	100
Northern England	3,260	26	32	22
Pennine Window	1,076	4	10	1

To summarize, this tells us the following. If you take northern England in general it has almost a third of the sightings on record yet it is just a quarter of the area of the mainland and has a population that is about a fifth of the British total.

These figures are not particularly significant, although they show a slightly above average focus of activity in the north. However, when you look specifically at the Pennine window things change. This has only 4 per cent of the area covered and 1 per cent of the population and yet fully one tenth of the sightings. This is strong evidence that Pennine activity is well beyond the average level.

In fact if you express this as a ratio of the population against sightings recorded then the figures are even more startling. Here the ratio for Britain outside the north is 0.87, for northern England it is 1.46 and for the Pennines it is up to 10! Put simply, in terms of the population living in the Pennines, there are almost twelve times as many sightings than in other parts of Britain. So this clearly *is* a window.

In my survey, cases rated as unexplained in the national total came to 761. This means that approximately 93 per cent of all the reported sightings were explained in some way by the investigators, leaving the other 7 per cent to be regarded as genuinely mysterious. In the Pennines, the unsolved percentage was much higher at 12 per cent. This means that truly interesting cases seem to be reported more often in the Pennines than elsewhere.

You find the same pattern with types of sighting. Just as an illustration (there is not the space to present more), close encounters are where a UFO is alleged to create some sort of effect on the environment or the witness. These feature in 287 of the UK sample (that is 2.8 per cent of the cases). The Pennine cases, however, total 115 – that is 10.1 per cent of the reported cases. So there are four times as many close encounters from the Pennines. Again, if you consider the reported 'close encounters of the third kind' (cases where aliens are allegedly met) the national figure is just 107, that is slightly over 1 per cent. But in the Pennines this increases to 46 out of 1076 – or 4.2 per cent, also more than four times the level of activity elsewhere.

Even more illuminating are the levels of activity within specific parts of the window area. In terms of counties here are the reported totals for the Pennine region:

Cheshire	54	Derbyshire	64
Staffordshire	118	Lancashire	433
North Yorkshire	54	South Yorkshire	109
West Yorkshire	244		

If you look more closely at the locations defined by this book as very active hot spots the results are even more interesting. One in eleven of all reports occurred in the Bacup/Todmorden area – easily the best place to look. Next most active was Ilkley/Wharfedale (one in fifteen), the moors outside Oldham (one in sixteen) and Glossop/Longendale (one in eighteen). Pendle rated 1 in nineteen and Stocksbridge 1 in twenty. No other places logged more than 1 in thirty.

However, in terms of close encounters and alien contacts the two hyperactive zones (Bacup/Todmorden and Ilkley/Wharfedale) clocked nearly one-quarter (for close encounter cases) and one third (for alien contacts) out of all British cases. In fact nearly three-quarters of the Pennine area alien contacts happened within a 10 mile radius of Todmorden! This is surely evidence of where the true centre of the Pennine window lies.

Below are two tables that list the sightings in the Pennines according to the month of the year and to the time of day. (Note that these totals do not add up to 1,076 because dates and times were not always recorded.)

Sightings in the Pennines by Month

Jan	113	Jul	90
Feb	70	Aug	105
Mar	41	Sep	86
Apr	85	Oct	70
May	97	Nov	97
Jun	105	Dec	56

The seasonal totals are: winter (December, January and February) 239; spring (March, April & May) 223; summer (June, July and August) 300; autumn (September, October and November) 253. This does not suggest any major seasonal variation, apart from the summer total which is obviously somewhat dependent upon the influx of hikers to the hills during the better weather. But there is little here to indicate a weather-based factor in the cause of the phenomena. It is far more likely (from a few preliminary studies) that a correlation with seismic activity in the local rocks, or some other variant factor such as levels of atmospheric ionization might provide the serious researcher with interesting patterns.

Sightings in the Pennines by Time of Day

Hrs		Hrs	
00.00 – 01.59	90	12.00 – 13.59	14
02.00 – 03.59	48	14.00 – 15.59	41
04.00 – 05.59	35	16.00 – 17.59	108
06.00 – 07.59	27	18.00 – 19.59	126
08.00 – 09.59	19	20.00 – 21.59	267
10.00 – 11.59	12	22.00 – 23.59	108

The pattern here is obvious. The huge majority of the sightings occur in the evening and late night with a minimum level only during the day. In fact there are over twenty times as many sightings at around 9-10 p.m. as there are at around noon! Naturally, this is partly due to the ease of seeing illuminated phenomena against a darkened sky, not to mention that fact that misperception of mundane things is far more likely in poorer visibility at night. Not clearly shown by this two-hourly breakdown is a small secondary blip in the numbers, which is better illustrated by the following one-hourly split of part of the above table:

20.00 – 20.59: 110 21.00 – 21.59: 157 22.00 – 22.59: 60 23.00 – 23.59: 48
00.00 – 00.59: 51 01.00 – 01.59: 39 02.00 – 02.59: 16 03.00 – 03.59: 32
04.00 – 04.59: 21 05.00 – 05.59: 14

This reveals a small secondary peak around 3 a.m. – something that has appeared in other studies and does therefore seem to be a real factor. In fact close encounters are twice as common during the four hours after midnight as they are in the four hours before that time – another clue to ponder.

Appendix III
High Times in the Pennines

The cyclical nature of activity in the Pennines is illustrated by the flaps and waves that regularly occur. Rather than give a lengthy table of totals reported each year it makes sense to review the highs and lows, since such dates might reveal useful information for the researcher. I will then close with a brief look at two hyperactive periods that help us to trace the close encounters.

Activity in this area was generally steady for the first twenty years of data, at approximately ten sightings reported per year, with just the hint of a flap in late November 1957. In these early years there was no facility to monitor events as there is today, so a good deal that went on was certainly missed. The years 1966 and 1967 showed the first dramatic increase. Fifty-three cases were recorded in that period – about three times the average up until then (or indeed over the next few years). The centre point of what was a widespread wave occurred in the last few days of October and first few days of November 1967 when three-quarters of the sightings occurred, although some of these were misperceptions of the planet Venus. This was very bright in the early morning sky and was witnessed by police officers, and it led to discussions in the House of Commons. One positive result was that the Government tightened up the Ministry of Defence UFO records and made sure that from 1967 a complete archive was kept and released each January (although thirty years late!) to the Public Record Office in Kew.

Totals continued at between ten and fifteen per annum until 1974 when there was a very localized flap in Rossendale in mid- and late November. Then attention switched south in January 1975 when there was a huge flap on the moors between Oldham and Huddersfield involving a fast-moving light dubbed 'the phantom helicopter'. Totals for the year more than doubled (to thirty), and many of these sightings concentrated between 5 and 15 January. Some of them were caused by an unusual astronomical event when a bright star and a planet were close together in the evening sky and were often seen as lights on a dark face-like craft.

By far the biggest explosion of activity in the Pennines, still unsurpassed, came in the years 1976–8. Over 170 sightings were recorded during that period – up to ten times the average. The spring of 1977 was the true focus, with two bursts (the days leading up to 9 March), but there was also a mini-wave between 20 and 27 May when lights in the sky were seen daily.

After 1979 (marked by a dramatic wave in February – see below) totals fell back to the levels of the 1960s. Indeed there was something of a rapid fall-off. By 1982 totals in Britain were massively down – UK figures for 1987, for example, were just one-twentieth of the level for 1977 and one-tenth of that for 1967. Quite what caused this downturn, which continued into the 1990s, is not clear. It may have been partly due to public apathy; the subject had become over reported. Also it was probably down to more sophisticated investigation methods – researchers tending to reject quickly those that appeared likely to be explained.

There was also something of a *Close Encounters of the Third Kind* effect! This Steven Spielberg movie had a royal première in February 1978. It provoked vast amounts of media interest. Whilst it did not generate a 1978 wave as sceptics predicted, it did encourage many people to report older sightings they may otherwise never have mentioned. Perhaps this acted as a fictional appeasing of the appetite for strange things, but only psychologists can answer that.

Even in 2001 reports are running well below the levels before 1980 – although they do seem to have bottomed out.

What is most noteworthy about this trend, however, is that Pennine sightings have shown a far less marked decrease than the rest of the country. Whilst there has been some downturn in reporting, sightings within the window have maintained a more steady flow and still do show the occasional blip of sudden activity. This has been noticeable at the following times: the mid-August 1978 light show in the Wharfedale; electrical phenomena in Calderdale and Rossendale between mid-June and mid-August 1980; a major wave that struck the eastern side of the Pennines between September and November 1980; the Bradford flap in late October 1981; activity tied to an earth tremor in Calderdale on 20 April 1982 (see below); another concentrated wave (not exclusively within the Pennines) between 22 and 25 April 1984; a burst of lights between 14 and 17 August 1987; a small wave in November 1992; flaps of localized activity between 2 and 9 December 1994; activity in Derbyshire in mid-January 1995 and in early 1999; and another south Pennine wave, especially in Derbyshire, centred on October 2000.

Here is how one sixty-hour flap developed. At just after 9 p.m. (21.24 to be precise) on 17 April 1982 reports began of strange lights zipping from the Pennines, seen as far west as north Cheshire, where a pulsing red light was described. In Todmorden at the same time up to a dozen reports were made, suggesting that this was the origin for the lights. A large dark cigar was spotted towards Hebden Bridge, which generated pulses of light that changed colour, being shot westwards as they did so. The lights were seen to divide and repel each other moving across the sky. By the following night, 18 April, many witnesses in Todmorden and Bacup were skywatching for these darting lights. Some mistook the bright star Sirius in their eagerness, but a few more of the splitting lights that seemed to be emerging from the hillsides were observed as well.

Even in daylight the window was active. At 12.50 on 19

April just outside Bradford, for example, three witnesses reported seeing red pulses of light that throbbed white and moved in streaks across the sky westwards. They emitted a 'tingling' sensation onto those below.

The burst of activity ended suddenly at 16.31 when a terrific explosion hit Calderdale. It resembled a jet plane breaking the sound barrier and the MoD were called to investigate that theory as it would be illegal. Police were also investigating the possibility of a plane having crashed near Todmorden. Neither was proved. In fact a modest earthquake had occurred between Todmorden and Hebden Bridge and the sound was the earth audibly flexing its muscles. And the lights seen in the preceding hours in this same part of the Pennine window may well have been produced by the same energy leaking into the atmosphere in visual form.

However, it is worth looking at a second wave of activity in the Pennines for this reveals new answers. We can actually track the progress from the south to the north of the Pennine window. On the night of 22 February 1979 there were three sightings that seem related. At 18.30 above the Staffordshire village of Coven (as in an assembly of magical forces!) a man in his car spotted a series of red and green lights attached to a yellowish glow making a strange noise. At first he assumed it to be a helicopter, but it was over Cannock Chase and this seemed unlikely (investigation later revealed no air traffic locally).

A few minutes later several residents of a housing estate in Lees, a Pennine village just outside Oldham, reported something coming from the south. It seemed to flip upside down and (in familiar style) split into three lights, basically red and green in colour, which shot away over the hills. These people also suspected a helicopter because of the hovering and whining hum. But again there was no airborne traffic. The weather was freezing cold with ice and a layer of snow – not ideal flying weather.

At 18.45 – again a few minutes after the Lees sightings – two 14-year-old girls playing with a sleigh on the snowy slopes at Meanwood, near Leeds, again saw red and green lights heading towards them making a frightening screech or whine. They also assumed it was a helicopter but it slowed to a halt and then began to spiral downwards as if about to crash. Instead it landed on the steep slope and revealed itself to be a small car-sized lens shape with fins. The two girls watched it for about three minutes until it rose vertically, banked sharply and touched down again on an even steeper part of the hill where no helicopter could possibly have landed. It then climbed upwards again and shrieked as it flew away. Investigators on the scene found heavy imprints in the ice and crushed carbonised rock embedded them.

Just over twenty-four hours later, after midnight into 24 February, the fantastic spate of sightings continued. At about 00.05 in Leeds two people inspecting a house spotted a circle of orange and red lights that hovered overhead. Again they thought it must be a helicopter, but as it flew over them heading towards Calderdale it was totally silent. Just before 02.00, Mike Sacks and his wife saw an orange ball of light coming over the Rossendale Valley from the north-east. They were in the bedroom looking after their son, who had tonsillitis. As they watched, the object hovered and descended into the quarry at Stacksteads. The three had a perfect view at close range. Suddenly the red glow, which had lit up the hills below, switched off and a ring of ice blue lights surrounding a dome shape appeared. This thing was now dead still, but in an instant change of direction it headed straight down towards the ground.

Mike phoned me immediately. Meanwhile farmer Alf Kyme, who was helping one of his cows about a mile away, saw the thing descend into the quarry. He saw a ring of orange/red lights, as had just been seen at Leeds. Mike Sacks went to get a camera and walked up the dark moors into the quarry. At about 02.35, he met two police officers who had seen the object from the valley bottom. Unfortunately, when they got to the quarry nothing was visible. And when the policemen were interviewed it was evident that they had seen the orange ball *leaving* the area and heading south-west at about 02.30.

Beyond the Pennine area this story continued.[119] A dozen other witnesses, including a police officer, a fireman, a taxi driver, the residents of a caravan park (whose windows vibrated and woke them up!) as well as a security guard on a Blackpool pier, all saw the object head west across Lancashire at great speed and then cut the coast at about 02.45. They also saw what was clearly a military jet breaking the sound barrier and heading supersonic north-west on an apparent intercept course! The security guard saw both the jet (streaking out over the Irish Sea in its pursuit) and, thirty minutes later, white lights spiralling upwards in a manner eerily like the descent witnessed at Meanwood. These lights climbed from *under* the sea (as if they had been hiding!) recombined and disappeared.

But even this was not the end of the story. For there was one final encounter at the northern edge of this window just before 8 o'clock that morning. This time it occurred in North Yorkshire. The witness was driving his motorbike through Crayke village when he claims he saw a dark teardrop-shaped object landing in the grass. One single round window was visible in the side and behind this a dark-suited figure crouched as if moving something out of sight. The being appeared to look up – perhaps hearing the motorcycle on the otherwise silent road. Stunned, the witness got off his motorbike and stared at this bizarre sight. He could now see two other 'people' in the grass beside the object. They were tall, slim and dressed in all over black wet suits like divers. At this point the witness says he was 'overwhelmed', his mind 'tried to block it out' and 'some form of contact' happened that he cannot put into words. The next thing he knew he was driving away. He says that he arrived at work late, but he was not sure by how much. He kept telling himself that nothing strange had happened, that it was just an ordinary aircraft. This worked for eleven years. But in 1990 nightmares began and from them memories started to intrude from his subconscious –

which is when he realized what had happened and decided to relate this story. Who knows how many other unreported – or unrecalled – encounters happened in the Pennines during that weird weekend in 1979.

Appendix IV
Windows Around the World

About 100 active window areas seem to exist somewhere around the planet. The following list offers just a brief introduction to a handful of these, with pointers to discovering further information.

Most of these areas seem to have far less of an all-embracing and long-standing tradition than you will find in the Pennines, but there is a very obvious overlap in the kind of phenomenon being seen, even if usually less often and with less variety. The pattern is clear enough to suggest that what fuels the Pennine window powers these other areas as well.

What is most remarkable to me is that several of these hot spots have recognized the tourist potential of having such odd things occurring on their doorstep – just as Scotland exploits the Loch Ness monster in amusing ways. These windows in other lands have begun to create cottage industries, built viewing platforms and even have roadway signposts erected by the local councils advising people of what they might see if they stop and watch the hills for a while. Yet the Pennine folk (canny as they can be in many respects) virtually ignore this fantastic phenomenon right in their midst. Why they do so is perhaps an even bigger mystery than the window area itself!

Amazingly, the Pennines is probably in the best position of any window in the world to exploit this opportunity. It is not in the middle of a desert or up a 10,000 foot mountain and thus barely accessible except by strenuous effort.

Although the spots where the Pennine lights are seen are hilly they are rarely all that remote. Literally millions of people live within less than an hour's drive of somewhere alive with activity – indeed more prolific than any of the tourism-exploited regions of Texas or Australia, where at least some effort has been made to take advantage of the fact that these events happen nearby.

The powers that be within the Pennines really should wake up to what they are missing. There should be colourful signs pointing out places to look for the Pennine lights. Enterprising pubs could adopt the name and put on displays and hold lectures. And there should be coach tours attracting visitors to go to see and hear about the places and events. After all the tourists can admire the spectacular Pennine views even if they do not get abducted or have an encounter with a ghostly light! Or have we entirely lost the sense of enterprise that once made Britain proud?

West Wales

During 1904–5 a series of balls of light were seen to emerge from the ground and float around the hills between Barmouth and Harlech. They were associated with miraculous events and a religious revival swept the area. In legend the lights that charged the air with some force were associated with an evangelical preacher, although it is very likely this was much the same thing as occurs today when similar phenomena are associated with aliens. In the 1990s the same area has been the source of humming/buzzing sounds emerging from the rocks, energy fields that cause tingling sensations and, of course, more lights.[120]

USA – Missouri

The Ozark Mountains have stories of strange lights emitting energy fields that date back at least 120 years. Often described as a golden diamond shape they appear in flaps and waves. During one of these in 1973 massive TV interference was created in Piedmont and a transmission tower was knocked out. State University professor Harley Rutledge decided to set up experimental monitor teams which made 152 sightings of strange phenomena and took numerous photographs in a preview of just what universities such as Manchester, Leeds and Sheffield could do if they wanted to make the effort in the Pennines.[121]

USA – Texas

Probably the most famous US window is in southern Texas above a range of hills that runs through Presidio County south-east of El Paso. Focusing on the small town of Marfa (which gives its name to the so-called Marfa Lights) a viewpoint has been created on Highway 90 in one of the most active spots. First reliably recorded in 1883 they are often yellowish/orange glows that emerge from the hills and climb up and down before disappearing in ghostly fashion.[122]

USA – Washington

More recent (and not widely known before 1970) are the orange/yellow lights often seen from the Yakima Indian Reservation east of the volcano- and earthquake-riven Cascades. Often termed 'slow meteors' they create a sense of interaction with witnesses and have affected the engines and lights of police patrols near the Toppenish Ridge. One popular location for events is Goat Rocks.[123]

Norway – Hessdalen

Probably the best-known window in mainland Europe (although not the only one – there is a meteorologically more pleasant one in Provence, France, north of Marseilles) is this frozen valley. Over 70 miles south-east of Trondheim it can become bitterly cold during the long sub-Arctic winter. But the rewards are high for the research teams that have bravely set up camp here since sightings began in 1944. An incredible joint effort between the military, universities and UFOlogists has seen expeditions use sophisticated equipment (including radar, lasers and spectroscopes) to obtain hard evidence of the plasma that powers this window. As elsewhere there are many floating lights but also an assortment of stranger stories, such as are less often associated with windows beyond the Pennines.[124]

Australia – Queensland

Remote in a different sense are these floating balls of light seen in Queensland. Mostly reported in the hinterland that slopes towards the barren Simpson Desert to the east, they have been spotted also in lesser numbers on the coastal strip west of the Atherton Tableland between Cairns and Cooktown. Well promoted in Boulia, one of the most active zones, there is even a Min Min Hotel. The name Min Min lights reflects a long tradition – from at least 1912 (although oral legends date back further to days when stockmen first settled the area). They are believed to be intelligent and to react to those who see them. To the west they have also been linked with a phenomenon akin to crop circles – flattened areas of reeds on coastal swamps – in fact the very ones that in 1966 inspired artists Doug and Dave to fake circles in Britain and start a huge mythology! Aboriginal occupants prefer not to discuss the Min Min lights but are said to consider them 'spirits'. The term 'Min Min' appears to express what the first person who saw them, maybe hundreds or even thousands of years ago, thought upon doing so. It rather neatly sums up the Pennine lights as well. It basically means 'Who? What? Why?'[125]

Appendix V
What are the Windows?

In answer to this question we would have to say, nobody really knows! But it seems appropriate to summarize quickly the main possibilities that have been proposed to explain this phenomenon.

Socio-psychological

The most reasonable sceptical answer to the problem is that there basically is no problem. Window areas are social phenomena created by cultural forces and a heady dose of human psychology. We all love mysteries and the mind does tend to perpetuate them. Mythology has always been a powerful force in human thinking and it may simply be evident in more subtle ways during the twenty-first century, with assorted tales given shape and structure to satisfy our desires as a species. We do know that 95 per cent of what goes on in a window like the Pennines is a misperception of something mundane. Might not everything be? Are more things reported simply because familiarity and support from other witnesses diminishes the ridicule factor? Is it just easier to tell that you have seen a strange light in an area where you know countless others have done so before than some place where any story you may offer is likely to make you seem odd?

The best counter to this suggestion is that there *are* socially created windows, where the influence of the media makes a place seem special and encourages others to speak up. But generally these places are transient and lack the pedigree of reports dating back to times when there was no instant communication. Real windows have that record and seem to have many cases where the phenomenon seen is consistent and consistently odd, involving energy fields and their effects.

Meteorological

Might a window result from a combination of rare and little-understood weather phenomena, including ball lightning (freak balls of energy), vortices that can cause changes in air pressure and have associated electrical energy fields and temperature inversion layers that produce strange moving mirages from assorted mundane lights? All of these things clearly *are* at work within a typical window area, but it is less certain that they are the entire solution, given the diversity of weather in global window areas.

Earth Energies

We do know that strain within rocks generates energy. This is the engine that drives earthquakes. Indeed 'earthquake lights' have long been known to be a rare associated phenomenon observed by some geologists. Several traditions, such as the dragon paths of China and the leys of old England, suggest a familiarity with lines of what today we would recognize as electromagnetic force within the earth. Indeed stone circles or megaliths may have marked these spots as places of reverence aeons ago. The geological fit between window areas and this theory is very strong. Most windows are riven by fault lines and are in areas with tectonic stress. Often the lights around which most window phenomena are built emerge from hills, towers, quarries, masts and other scientifically plausible spots. And, what is more, the theory has been tested scientifically. Rocks put under stress in the laboratory have ejected fast-moving lights that can be filmed by high-speed cameras. There is a gulf between tiny sparks that exist for a fraction of a second and floating energy balls feet across that may endure for several minutes. But in a window area hills and huge physical forces are involved, not samples in a laboratory. Other experiments in Japan reveal that these energies can create plasmas, as recorded at Hessdalen, and many of the physiological and physical effects described by witnesses in this book can be resolved in that way.

Stranger encounters could be visionary experiences involving what seem to be visually creative people. Research by psychologists reveals that this is possible and in Canada brain scientist Dr Michael Persinger has subjected people to the strong energy fields such as earth forces can create. Some have reported altered states of consciousness and visions that resemble alien contacts and out of body states.[126] Together this theory may be leading towards its own resolution.

Time Portals

Certainly in the Pennines there are numerous apparent time-slip encounters. How do these fit into the solutions being proposed? It may be that these are an associated effect – perhaps science will one day reveal that 'emotional energy' can be recorded in a strong electromagnetic field. Rather than literal trips through time (doorways opened up at window areas) the powerful forces at such a place may serve as a recording medium that allows the past to be replayed, rather like a gigantic VCR!

Parallel Universe

The term 'window area' seems to imply that the region acts as a window or portal into another reality. In many myths and legends associated with these areas that has been the belief – dragons sleeping under the earth, knights in a parallel reality waiting to be woken or otherworldly beings such as fairies and boggarts flitting between another world and our own. All these things are the stuff of window areas past. We might wonder if there is some true sense of aware-ness in this fanciful hypothesis. Physicists have, after all, now concluded that multiple realities and dimensions are likely and that we would barely grasp anything beyond our own level. If such realities do exist then any inhabitants may interpenetrate our own world, whereas we are normally restricted to this one abode. These are the rules of a multiple universe.

For instance, we are aware of a two-dimensional world – a flat plane like an ultra-thin sheet of paper. We can put our hand through it and interact with that world. But an inhab-itant of that piece of paper would not be aware of the three-dimensional universe around them, except when it inter-sected their own and magical things happened – and they would (a fist appearing suddenly, growing in size, decreas-ing in size and vanishing, leaving behind physical evidence – a hole! – but no longer existing in the reality of that plane of paper and so dismissed as credulous nonsense by others living in that dimension). Of course, if there are four or five or ten dimensional realities all around us it is we who are in the position of the being on flat paper land. To some the magical nature of the events within the Pennine window and the long belief that other beings can visit us may simply reflect our inevitably limited efforts to comprehend this extraordinary reality during the brief times it interacts with our own.

Alien Bases

Since many of the things seen today are interpreted as alien craft there are suggestions that visitors from another world make their base in window areas. Perhaps they fly in and

238

out of underground caverns and that is why they appear so often in certain locations. Unfortunately the evidence for aliens is, like the evidence for fairies, circumstantial. People *do* see things but that they are real flesh and blood entities rather than some visionary phenomenon is much less evident. Aliens and fairies are probably the same phenomenon – just different terms and cultural reinterpretations of an age-old ineffable experience. UFOs are an unidentified phenomenon, probably not spaceships – but only *probably* not!

Appendix VI
Sources of Information

This list will give a wide range of contacts, information sources and places to go in order to explore the Pennine window.

Organizations

The following regionally based local groups investigate strange phenomena within the Pennines.

Green Dragon
Trees Farm
Ford
Staffordshire Moorlands
ST13 7RW

NARO (Northern Anomalies Research Organization)
6 Silsden Avenue
Lowton
Warrington
WA3 1EN

The next five organizations are primarily UFO investigation groups in the area.

Connect
105 Frizley Gardens
Frizinghall
Bradford
West Yorkshire
BD9 4LY

PRA (Phenomena Research Association)
94 The Circle
Sinfin
Derby
DE24 9HR

SUFOG (Staffordshire UFO Group)
11 Sandy Lane
Rugeley
Staffordshire
WS15 2LB

UFO Network
47 Whincover Grange
Leeds
LS12 5JJ

YUFOS (Yorkshire UFO Society)
224 Bellhouse Road
Sheffield
S5 6HT

The following three organizations are national but have investigated cases in the Pennines. BUFORA (the British UFO Research Association) is the oldest national UFO group, having been in existence for forty years. CONTACT UK has been around for thirty-five years and investigates UFOs as wellas anomalies such as crop circles, and ASSAP, (the Association for the Scientific Study of Anomalous Phenomena) has for twenty years looked into various para-normal activities such as ghosts, poltergeists and time-slips.

ASSAP
20 Paul Street
Frome
BA11 1DX

BUFORA
70 High Street
Wingham
Kent CT3 1BJ

CONTACT UK
PO Box 23
Wheatley
Oxford
OX33 1FL

The following are regional publications that cover Pennine phenomena. (P indicates mainly Pennine based and N northern based. The others cover the Pennines only from time to time.)

Dead of Night (N) (ghosts, monsters, etc)
156 Bolton Road East
New Ferry
Wirral
L62 4RY

Folklore Frontiers (old and modern folk tales)
5 Egton Drive
Seaton Carew
Cleveland
TS25 2AT

Haunted Realm (P)(UFOs and ghosts)
95 Molineaux Road
Sheffield
S5 0JZ

IANDS (near death/out of body experiences)
PO Box 193
London
SW1K 9JZ

Journal of Meteorology (weather anomalies)
54 Frome Road
Bradford-on-Avon
Wilts
BA15 1LD

Northern Earth Mysteries (N)(leys, stone circles etc.)
10 Jubilee Street
Mytholmroyd
HX7 5NP

Northern UFO News (N)(UFOs)
1 Hallsteads Close
Dove Holes
Buxton
Derbyshire
SK17 8BS

Project Red Book(P)(UFOs)
224 Bellhouse Drive
Firth Park
Sheffield
S5 6HT

Strange Times (all anomalies)
Unit 2A
East Cheap
Heaton
Newcastle-upon-Tyne
NE6 5UA

Various groups also produce in-house magazines which are available through their addresses. All three national organizations have publications and long-running Pennine-based magazines are PRA's *OVNI* and the UFO Network's *Newsletter*.

The next two magazines are available widely in newsagents and cover UFOs and anomalies respectively. They are also available on subscription.

Fortean Times
Freepost (SW6096)
Bristol
BS32 0BR
(no stamp needed within the UK)
cihotline@aol.com

UFO Magazine
Lloyds Bank Chambers
West Street
Ilkey
LS29 9DW

As a balance you should also consider the following magazine which is penned by scientists who prefer to take a more rationalist approach to all sorts of anomalies.

The Skeptic
PO Box 475
Manchester
M60 2TH

The final set of addresses are for internet sources of information. However net addresses change, so you may need to do a net search if these prove invalid when you come to try them.

Centre for Fortean Zoology (alien big cats and other animal mysteries)
www.eclipse.co.uk/cfz/

Haunted Valley (a website with skywatch camera, information and links to Glossop Paranormal Investigators, that covers this High Peak hot spot)
www.hauntedvalley.com

UFO Investigators Network (a highly objective invitation only UFO investigation team, several of whom are based in the Pennines and research cases there. Together they have many years experience in the field)
Enquiries@ufoin.org.uk

Finally, if you wish to contact me to report something strange, you are welcome to do so. I will try to offer information (an SAE would be appreciated if you require this) and will otherwise gladly hear your story – in confidence if you prefer. I can be contacted at:

1 Hallsteads Close
Dove Holes
Buxton
Derbyshire
SK17 8BS
email: nufon@currantbun.com

Appendix VII
References

1. Bennett, P., 'The Case of the Missing Pterodactyl' (*UFO Brigantia*, 9, 1985)
2. Barclay, D., 'The Anomalous Aire Valley avian' (*UFO Debate*, 6, 1991)
3. Personal testimony from the witness (see also *Northern UFO News*, December, 1990)
4. Baker, D., 'The Mexborough Footage' (Project Red Book, October & December 2000)
5. Haines, T., *Walking With Dinosaurs* (BBC Books, 1999), p.164
6. Watson, I., *Miracle Visitors* (Gollancz, 1978)
7. Personal communication with the author, 1987
8. Randles, J., *Abduction*, (Hale, 1988 pp.46–9 & 190–4)
9. Clarke, D., 'UFO Abductions and the Celtic Otherworld', (*UFO Brigantia*, 35, 1988)
10. Meaden, G.T., *The Stonehenge Solution*(Souvenir, 1992)
11. Bell, D., *Derbyshire Ghosts and Legends* (Countryside Books, 1993)
12. Clarke, D., *Supernatural Peak District* (Hale, 2001, p.147–60)
13. Randles, J., 'The House on the Moors' (*New UFOlogist*, 1 & 2, 1995)
14. Whitaker, T., *Lancashire Ghosts and Legends* (Hale, 1980)
15. Dillon, J., in *Dead of Night*, 6, 1995
16. Devereux. P., *Earthlights Revelation* (Blandford, 1989)
17. Clarke, D., 'Haunted Hills' (*UFO Brigantia*, 22, 1986)
18. Randles, J. & Grimshawe, T., 'Frightening Car Stop Near Nelson' (*Flying Saucer Review*, Vol 23, No 2, 1977)

19. 'A guided tour of Fairy Land', *Dead of Night*, 14, 1997
20. Cooper, J., *The Case of the Cottingley Fairies* (Hale, 1990)
21. Roberts, A., *Cat Flaps* (Brigantia Books, 1989)
22. *Buxton Advertiser*, 26 October 1999
23. *Daily Telegraph*, 12 May 1997
24. See p.191–7 for various other cases in this same vicinity, some much less readily explicable.
25. UFOIN investigation report by N. Watson
26. Spanish government files translated by V.J. Ballester-Olmos
27. 'The Oz Factor' in Randles, J., *The Little Giant Encyclopedia of UFOs*, pp.166–8 (J. Sterling, 2000)
28. Investigation by Dagless, M., Hart, S., and Mortimer, N., *Northern UFO News*, May 1984
29. See many other examples of this effect in Randles, J., *Time Storms* (Piatkus, 2001)
30. For details of the Alan Godfrey encounter and the aftermath see Randles, J., *The Pennine UFO Mystery* (Grafton, 1983)
31. Randles, J., *Sixth Sense* (Hale, pp.203–5, 1987)
32. Connect investigation by N. Mortimer, in *Northern UFO News*, December 1989
33. 'Bedroom Encounter', *UFO Brigantia*, 8, 1985
34. Randles, J., *The Complete Book of Aliens and Abductions (Piatkus, p.148-50, 1999)*
35. *Hufford, D.*, The Terror that Comes by Night (University of Pennsylvania, 1982)
36. Interview by P. Bennett, in *UFO Brigantia*, 9, 1985
37. Randles, J., *Star Children*, p.41–7 (Hale, 1994)
38. Investigation by M. Clare, 26 May 1985
39. Green, C., and McCreery, C., *Apparitions* (Hamish Hamilton, 1975)
40. Randles, J., and Hough, P., *Death by Supernatural Causes?* (Grafton, 1988)
41. BUFORA case investigation by G. Dixon and P. Ainscough
42. *Time Storms*, op.cit.
43. Devereux, P., *The Illustrated Encylopedia of Ancient Earth Mysteries* (Cassell, 2000)
44. Witness testimony in *UFO Brigantia*, 7, 1985
45. Devereux, P., *Earthlights* (Turnstone, 1982)

References

46. Trollope, P., (with Clarke, D., Randles, J., and Roberts, A.) *The Longendale Lights*, BBC TV North West, November 2000
47. Kozicka, M., *The Mystery of the Min Min Light* (Bolton, Australia 1994)
48. Mortimer, N. in *Fortean Times*, 108, March 1998
49. Strand, E., *Project Hessdalen* (AFU Norway, via Box 11027 600 11 Norrkoping, Sweden, 1986)
50. Letter from witness, via *Ghostwatch*, 13 March 1983
51. *Lancashire Ghosts and Legends*, op.cit., p.106–10
52. *Fact or Fiction?*, BBC Radio (Manchester), September 1986
53. Cranstoun, T., report dated 30 January 1996, 'The House a Knight Built', *Naro Minded*, 6, 1997
54. Carr, P., 'Riddle of the Orbs', *Fortean Times*, March 2001
55. *Doncaster Star*, 16 December 1999
56. Randles, J., and Hough, P., *Life After Death and the World Beyond* (Piatkus, 1996)
57. Randles, J., and Hough, P., in *Scary Stories*, 'After the Wedding', (Futura, 1991)
58. Letter to *Fortean Times*, March 1997
59. Mortimer, N., 'Yorkshire's Water Wolf', *Fortean Times*, Winter 1988
60. Randles, J., 'Poltergeists in *The Paranormal Sourcebook* (Piatkus, 1999)
61. Bradbury, P., 'The Moors of Mossley', *Naro Minded*, 4, 1996
62. Hough, P., 'Wet, Wet, Wet', *Fortean Times*, August 1996
63. Buraj, R., 'Two water poltergeist cases', *SPR Journal*, Vol 61, No. 845, 1996
64. *Time Storms*, op.cit.
65. 'False awakenings', in *The Complete Book of Aliens and Abductions*, op.cit.
66. Letter from Derek Gibson in *Fortean Times*, March 2000
67. Forman, J., *The Mask of Time* (Macdonald & Jane, 1971)
68. Letter to *Fortean Times*, August 1997
69. Miller, J., *States of Mind* (BBC, 1983)
70. Dr Simon Chu, *Daily Mail*, 30 March 2001
71. Randles, J., 'Out of body experiences' in *The Paranormal Sourcebook* (Piatkus, 1999); Ring, K., *Life at Death* (Coward, McCann & Geohegan, New York 1980); Blackmore, S., *Dying*

to Live (Grafton, 1993)

72. Jung, C., and Pauli, W., *Synchronicity* (Routledge & Kegan Paul 1953)
73. Carol Morse in *Naro Minded*, 4, 1996
74. Randles, J., *UFO Crash Landing?* (Cassell, 1997)
75. Hough, P., and Randles, J., *Supernatural Causes* (Unpublished 2001)
76. Warren, L., and Robbins, P., *Left at East Gate* (Michael O'Mara, 1997)
77. Investigation by Iain Johnston, NUFON case 6005
78. Letter to author, 17 October 1986, follow up by Roy Sandbach
79. *Vehicle Interference Catalogue* (BUFORA, 1979)
80. Investigation by D. Chanter and M. Daglass, WYUFORG NUFON case 8531
81. Fort, C., *Lo!* p.213–4 (John Brown, 1997)
82. Frank, L., *The Big Splash* (Avon, 1991)
83. The collected works of Charles Fort are available via *Fortean Times*, John Brown publishing.
84. *Time Storms*, op.cit.
85. Reports direct to author. See also 'Humdinger', J. Billingsley, *Fortean Times*, October 1998
86. Hough, P., and Randles, J., *Spontaneous Human Combustion* (Hale, 1991)
87. Randles, J., *The Truth Behind the MIB*, pp.102–7 (Piatkus, 1997)
88. *Time Storms*, op.cit., pp.59–60
89. Randles, J., and Fuller, P., *Crop Circles: A Mystery Solved?* (Hale, 1995)
90. King, B., 'Soldier's close encounter' *FSR*, Vol 24, No 1, 1978
91. Tributsch, H., *When the Snakes Awake* (MIT Press, 1983)
92. Randles, J., and Hough, P., 'Psychic Detectives' (*Readers Digest*, 2001)
93. Morse, M., *Close to the Light* (Souvenir, 1991)
94. *Star Children*, op.cit.
95. 'Close Encounter in UFO Alley', *International UFO Reporter*, Summer 2001
96. Sutcliffe, H., *The Striding Dales* (Warne, 1893)
97. Hough, P., and Randles, J., 'The NDE' in *The Encylopedia of the Unexplained* (Michael O'Mara, 1995)

References

98. Randles, J., *Aliens: The Real Story* (Hale, 1993)
99. Clarke, D., *Ghosts and Legends of Yorkshire* (Jarrold, 1992), p.46
100. *UFO Debate*, 5, 1990 p.4
101. Hough, P., and Randles, J., *The Complete Book of UFOs*, (Piatkus, 1994), p.307–14
102. Harrison, P., and M., *Life Before Birth* (Futura, 1983)
103. Devereux, P., *The Encyclopedia of Earth Mysteries* (Cassell, 1999)
104. Hough, P., Topliss, I., and Randles, J., NARO case investigation
105. *Supernatural Peak District*, op.cit.
106. Anthony, W., *Haunted Derbyshire* (Breedon Books, 1997)
107. Still, E., BUFORA investigation
108. See *Aliens: The Real Story*, op.cit. p.70–1
109. 'After the Wedding', op.cit.
110. *Sheffield Star*, 25 October and 10 November 1997
111. Randles, J., See paranormal events associated with Alan Garner in *Beyond Explanation*, (Hale, 1985) p.38–9
112. Pickford, D., *Cheshire: Its magic and mystery* (Sigma, 1994)
113. Check out Alan Garner's stories about this haunted area in 'Red Shift' and 'The Weirdstone of Brazingamen'.
114. On-site case study by Roy Sandbach
115. Potter, C., BUFORA investigation
116. *UFO Brigantia*, 39, 1989
117. See physiological effects throughout *Time Storms*, op.cit.
118. *Supernatural Peak District*, op.cit.
119. Randles, J., *UFO Retrievals* (Cassell, 1995)
120. McClure, K., and S., *Stars and Rumours of Stars* (private booklet, 1980)
121. Rutledge, H., *Project Identification* (Prentice-Hall, 1981)
122. *Earthlights Revelation*, op.cit. pp.116–9
123. See articles by Greg Long in various issues of *International UFO Reporter* and *MUFON* 166
124. *Project Hessdalen*, op.cit.
125. *The Mystery of the Min Min Light*, op.cit.
126. Persinger, M., and Lafreniere, G., *Space-Time Transients and Unusual Events* (Prentice-Hall, USA 1977); also interview

with Persinger in *Fortean Times*, 42, 1984; various issues of
Bulletin of Anomalous Experience, available on CD Rom via
D. Gotlib at 79 Hilton Ave., Toronto, Canada, M5R 3E8

Index

Index

Index

Lees, Lancs., 226
Leigh, Alicia, 96–8 ,
leys, 73–4, 176, 198–9, 211
Little Hayward, Staffs., 203–5
Liversedge, West Yorks., 66–8
Lockwood, West Yorks., 137
Longendale lights, 30, 77, 185, 187
Longridge Fell, Lancs., 151–3
Lushman, Rory, 151

Macclesfield, Ches., 86–7, 117–18, 211
Manchester, Lancs., 102–4, 131
Marfa, Texas, window, 78, 233
Markham, Roger, 119, 151
Marple Bridge, Ches., 143
Mayfield, Staffs., 206–7
McCartney, Dr Paul, 77
Meaden, Dr Terence, 26
Meanwood, West Yorks., 227, 228
Menwith Hill, 140, 168, 169, 177, 215
Mera, Stephen, 96
Mexborough, South Yorks., 18–19
Milldale, Derby., 205–6
Mills, Georgina, 81
mine spirits, 165, 187
Min Min lights, 78, 234
Miracle Visitors, 19–21
missing time, 50, 53, 207–8
Mortimer, Nigel, 78–9, 92, 168–9, 176
Mossley, Lancs, 96
Mothman Prophecies, The, 10–11
Mow Cop, Staffs., 199, 214
mythology, 23–7

NARO, 84, 85, 93, 95, 96–100, 120–1, 193, 241
Nazca lines, 74
NDE (near death experience), 160–1, 165
Nelson, Lancs., 35–6, 82, 150
Nether Edge, South Yorks., 196–7
New Mills, Derby, 188–90
NUFON, 218, 244

Oldham, Lancs., 181–3, 213, 224
Oldroyd, Granville, 34
Ollersett Moor, Derby., 43–7, 188
Operation Mainbrace, 141
Oswaldtwistle, Lancs., 149, 150
Otley Chevin, West Yorks., 169
Ozarks, Missouri, window, 232–3

oz factor, 17, 20, 49–51, 55, 57, 59, 62, 104, 111, 122, 125, 143, 144, 145, 160, 167, 204

Pauli, Dr Wolfgang, 112
Pendle Hill, 32–6, 129, 146, 148, 149, 150, 213–14
Persinger, Dr Michael, 17
phantom helicopter, 224
photographic cases, 16, 18 –19, 38–9, 78–9, 86, 140, 170–1, 181–3, 207
Pickford, Doug, 198–9, 202, 208
poltergeists, 93–100, 147–8, 151, 180–1, 186, 200
Potter, Clive, 203, 204
precognition, 100–12
Prestbury, Ches., 199–202, 211
Priestley, Mike, 16
Project Pennine, 80, 162
pterodactyls, 13–21
Pudsey, West Yorks., 15

Quatermass and the Pit, 91

Ravenscliff, West Yorks., 74–5
Rendlesham Forest, 117
reincarnation, 175
Reynolds, David, 204
Ring, Dr Kenneth, 161
Rivelin Valley, South Yorks., 65–6
Roberts, Andy, 18, 42
Rochdale, Lancs., 54–6, 96–100, 184–5, 214
Rose, Bill, 18
Rossendale Valley, Lancs., 42, 119–21, 126–8, 157–63, 224, 227–8

Sacks, Mike, 64, 126–8, 227–8
Scorton, North Yorks., 141–2
Settle, North Yorks., 121–2
Sharneyford, Lancs., 162
SHC (spontaneous human combustion), 136–7
Sheffield, South Yorks., 82
Shipley, West Yorks., 63, 92, 215
Shipley Glen, West Yorks., 13–14
Silkstone Common, South Yorks., 195–6
Singleton, Dr Jim, 171
Size, Nicholas, 166–7

Index